Mastering Visual Studio: A Comprehensive Guide

Kameron Hussain and Frahaan Hussain

Published by Sonar Publishing, 2024.

MASTERING VISUAL STUDIO: A COMPREHENSIVE GUIDE

First edition. January 27, 2024.

ISBN: 979-8224367597

Written by Kameron Hussain and Frahaan Hussain.

Table of Contents

Chapter 1: Introduction to Visual Studio

1.1 Understanding the Visual Studio Interface

1.2 History and Evolution of Visual Studio

Origins and Early Versions

The .NET Era

Continuous Advancements

Embracing Open Source

The Cloud and Beyond

Community and Ecosystem

1.3 Installation and Setup

Installation Options

Workloads and Individual Components

Updates and Maintenance

Licensing and Activation

1.4 Navigating Through Different Versions

Version Numbering

Long-Term Support (LTS) Versions

Compatibility Considerations

Supported Platforms and Technologies

Visual Studio Online Services

Community and Support

1.5 Overview of Key Features and Tools

Integrated Development Environment (IDE)

Solution and Project Management

Debugging and Diagnostics

Version Control Integration

Extensibility and Marketplace

IntelliSense

Code Refactoring

Web and Cloud Development

Mobile App Development

Data Tools

Testing and Quality Assurance

Collaboration and Team Development

Chapter 2: Basics of Project Management

2.1 Creating and Managing Projects

Project Types

Creating a New Project

Solution Files

Solution Explorer

Project Properties

Adding Existing Projects

Project Configuration

Managing Dependencies

Version Control Integration

Templates and Code Generation

2.2 Understanding Solution Explorer

Solution and Project Hierarchy

Project Context Menus

File and Folder Management

Search and Filtering

Renaming and Refactoring

Dependencies and References

Customization

Working with Multiple Solutions

2.3 Configuring Project Properties

Accessing Project Properties

Common Project Properties

Configuring Conditional Compilation Symbols

Platform Targeting

Debugging Options

Applying Configuration Changes

2.4 Version Control Integration

Supported Version Control Systems

Setting Up Version Control

Cloning a Repository

Committing Changes

Branching and Merging

Resolving Conflicts

Pushing and Pulling

History and Annotations

2.5 Debugging and Error Handling Basics

Setting Breakpoints

Starting Debugging

Debugging Features

Error Handling and Exceptions

Debugging Tools

Chapter 3: Coding in Visual Studio

3.1 Writing Code: Tips and Tricks

1. Code Navigation

2. Code Snippets

3. Code Completion and IntelliSense

4. Code Formatting

5. Code Refactoring

6. Snippet Management

7. Debugging Tips

8. Version Control Integration

9. Keyboard Shortcuts

10. Extensions and Add-ons

3.2 Utilizing IntelliSense for Efficient Coding

1. Code Completion

2. Parameter Info

3. Method Overloads

4. Descriptions and Documentation

5. Contextual Suggestions

6. Snippets and Templates

7. Custom Snippets

8. IntelliCode

9. Keyboard Shortcuts

10. Customizing IntelliSense

3.3 Code Refactoring and Formatting

Code Refactoring

Code Formatting

Customizing Code Style

Code Analysis and Inspections

3.4 Implementing Code Snippets

Using Built-In Code Snippets

Common Built-In Snippets

Creating Custom Code Snippets

Modifying Existing Snippets

Snippet Expansion and Editing

Snippet Surround Selection

Snippet Best Practices

3.5 Using the Code Editor Effectively

1. Navigation and Selection

2. Code Formatting

3. Code Indentation

4. Code Snippets

5. IntelliSense

6. Code Folding

7. Multi-Cursor Editing

8. Code Comments

9. Code Outlining

10. Extensions and Customization

Chapter 4: Debugging and Diagnostic Tools

4.1 Introduction to Debugging in Visual Studio

1. Setting Breakpoints

2. Starting Debugging

3. Debugging Controls

4. Debugging Windows

5. Inspecting Variables

6. Conditional Breakpoints

7. Data Tips and Quick Watch

8. Debugging Symbols and Information

9. Exception Handling

10. Debugging Web Applications

4.2 Breakpoints and Step-by-Step Debugging

Setting Breakpoints

Debugging Controls

The Call Stack Window

Data Tips and Watch Window

Stepping Through Code

Conditional Breakpoints

Tips for Effective Debugging

4.3 Using Diagnostic Tools

1. Performance Profiling

2. Debugging Memory Issues

3. IntelliTrace

4. Diagnostic Hub

5. Exception Settings

6. Code Analysis and Code Metrics

4.4 Performance Profiling

Types of Profiling

Starting a Profiling Session

Analyzing Profiling Data

Drill-Down and Analysis

Using Profiling Tools

Optimizing Performance

Iterative Optimization

4.5 Advanced Debugging Techniques

1. Conditional Breakpoints

2. Hit Counts

3. Tracepoints

4. Edit and Continue

5. Remote Debugging

6. IntelliTrace Debugging

7. Time Travel Debugging

8. Performance Profiling

9. Live Unit Testing

Chapter 5: Visual Studio for Web Development

5.1 Setting Up for Web Projects

1. Installation and Project Templates

2. Project Types

3. Integrated Development Environment (IDE)

4. Solution and Project Structure

5. Package Management

6. Debugging Web Applications

7. Web Server Integration

8. Web Deployment

9. Version Control

10. Extensions and Add-ons

5.2 Understanding ASP.NET Framework

1. Introduction to ASP.NET

2. ASP.NET Page Lifecycle

3. ASP.NET Controls

4. State Management

5. ASP.NET Web Forms vs. ASP.NET MVC

6. ASP.NET Web API

7. ASP.NET Routing

8. Data Access

9. Security in ASP.NET

10. Deployment

11. Visual Studio and ASP.NET

5.3 Web Forms vs. MVC: A Comparison

Web Forms

MVC (Model-View-Controller)

Choosing Between Web Forms and MVC

5.4 Developing with JavaScript and TypeScript

JavaScript in Web Development

TypeScript in Web Development

Visual Studio and JavaScript/TypeScript

5.5 Web Debugging Tools

Browser Developer Tools Integration

Remote Debugging

Browser Compatibility Testing

Page Inspector

Profiling and Performance Analysis

Browser Extensions and Add-Ons

Continuous Integration and Testing

Advanced Debugging Techniques

Chapter 6: Visual Studio for Desktop Application Development

6.1 Building Windows Forms Applications

6.2 Working with WPF

Creating a WPF Project

XAML and Declarative UI

Data Binding in WPF

Styles and Templates

Animation and Visual Effects

Debugging and Testing

Deployment

6.3 Understanding XAML

Declarative UI Design

Hierarchical Structure

Property Elements and Attributes

Data Binding in XAML

Resources and Styles

XAML in Visual Studio

6.4 Leveraging User Controls and Components

What are User Controls?

Creating User Controls

Example of a User Control

Using the User Control

Advantages of User Controls

What are Custom Components?

When to Use User Controls vs. Custom Components

6.5 Packaging and Deployment

Packaging Your Application

Distributing Your Application

Versioning and Updates

Digital Signing

Installation Prerequisites

Testing and Compatibility

Documentation and Support

7.1 Integrating Databases

Database Types

Connecting to Databases

Data Access

Database Projects

Data Tools

Database Debugging

Conclusion

7.2 SQL Server and Entity Framework

Introduction to Entity Framework

Setting Up Entity Framework with SQL Server

Code-First vs. Database-First

Migrations

Conclusion

7.3 Managing Database Connections

Connection Pooling

Connection Strings

Connection State Management

Connection Resilience

Conclusion

7.4 Using LINQ for Data Queries

Introduction to LINQ

LINQ to SQL

LINQ to Entity Framework

Benefits of LINQ

Conclusion

7.5 Database Project Management

Creating a Database Project

Schema Design and Development

Deploying Database Changes

Data Scripting and Seeding

Continuous Integration and Deployment

Conclusion

Chapter 8: Working with Mobile Applications

8.1 Setting Up for Mobile Development

Choosing a Mobile Development Approach

Setting Up Visual Studio for Mobile Development

Creating a Mobile App Project

Conclusion

8.2 Xamarin: Cross-Platform Development

Understanding Xamarin Basics

Creating a Xamarin Project

Debugging and Testing

Building and Deployment

Xamarin.Forms vs. Xamarin.Native

Conclusion

8.3 Debugging Mobile Applications

Debugging Basics

Debugging Xamarin.Android

Debugging Xamarin.iOS

Common Debugging Scenarios

Debugging Best Practices

8.4 Mobile UI Design Principles

1. User-Centered Design

2. Consistency

3. Simplicity

4. Navigation

5. Responsive Design

6. Touch-Friendly Interfaces

7. Typography and Readability

8. Visual Hierarchy

9. Feedback and Confirmation

10. Accessibility

11. Performance

12. Testing and Iteration

13. Platform Guidelines

14. Prototyping

15. User Onboarding

16. A/B Testing

8.5 Deploying to App Stores

1. App Store Registration

2. App Store Guidelines

3. App Icons and Screenshots

4. App Store Optimization (ASO)

5. Testing and Debugging

6. Privacy Policy

7. App Store Submission

8. App Store Optimization (ASO)

9. Launch Plan

10. User Support and Feedback

11. App Updates

12. Marketing and Promotion

13. Analytics and Monitoring

14. App Monetization

15. Legal Considerations

16. Internationalization

Chapter 9: Visual Studio Extensions and Customization

9.1 Exploring the Visual Studio Marketplace

Navigating the Marketplace

Search and Discover Extensions

Installing Extensions

Managing Installed Extensions

Popular Extension Categories

Creating Your Own Extensions

Community Contributions and Collaboration

9.2 Installing and Managing Extensions

Installing Extensions

Managing Installed Extensions

Handling Extension Conflicts

Practices for Extension Management

9.3 Customizing the IDE

Customizing Visual Studio Appearance

Customizing Keyboard Shortcuts

Extensions and Add-ons

Code Editor Customization

Customizing Tool Windows

Customizing Debugging

Workspace Customization

Version Control Customization

Customizing Project Templates

Customizing Work Item Tracking

9.4 Creating Your Own Extensions

Types of Extensions

Creating Code Snippets

Creating Item Templates

Creating Visual Studio Extensions

9.5 Community Contributions and Resources

1. Online Forums and Communities

2. Visual Studio Extensions

3. Blogs and Tutorials

4. GitHub Repositories

5. User Groups and Meetups

6. Documentation and Official Resources

7. GitHub Discussions

8. Social Media

9. Contributing to Open Source

Chapter 10: Testing and Quality Assurance

10.1 Introduction to Automated Testing in Visual Studio

What Is Automated Testing?

Benefits of Automated Testing

Testing Frameworks in Visual Studio

Writing Your First Automated Test

Test-Driven Development (TDD)

10.2 Unit Testing Frameworks

MSTest

NUnit

xUnit

10.3 Integration and Functional Testing

Integration Testing

Functional Testing

10.4 Code Coverage and Analysis

Understanding Code Coverage

Using Visual Studio for Code Coverage

Benefits of Code Coverage

10.5 Continuous Integration and Deployment

Understanding Continuous Integration (CI)

Setting Up CI in Visual Studio

Continuous Deployment (CD)

Implementing CD in Visual Studio

Best Practices for CI/CD

Chapter 11: Collaborating with Teams in Visual Studio

Section 11.1: Using Team Foundation Server (TFS)

Understanding Team Foundation Server (TFS)

Setting Up Team Foundation Server

Creating and Managing Team Projects

Version Control with TFS

Work Item Tracking and Agile Planning

Continuous Integration and Build Automation

Collaborative Coding with Visual Studio Live Share

Conclusion

Section 11.2: Collaborative Coding with Live Share

What is Visual Studio Live Share?

Getting Started with Live Share

Collaborative Coding Features

Advanced Features

Security and Privacy

Conclusion

Section 11.3: Version Control with Git and Visual Studio

Git Basics

Git in Visual Studio

Common Git Workflows

Conclusion

Section 11.4: Managing Work Items and Tracking Progress

Work Items and Agile Methodologies

Work Item Tracking in Visual Studio

Agile Planning and Execution

Integration with Version Control

Conclusion

Section 11.5: Best Practices for Team Development

1. Version Control

2. Code Reviews

3. Continuous Integration (CI)

4. Continuous Deployment (CD)

5. Coding Standards

6. Documentation

7. Agile Methodologies

8. Testing

9. Task Tracking

10. Communication

11. Security

12. Performance Optimization

13. Backup and Disaster Recovery

Chapter 12: Visual Studio and Cloud Integration

Section 12.1: Connecting to Azure Services

Azure Dev Tools for Visual Studio

Creating Azure Resources

Publishing to Azure

Azure SDKs and Libraries

Section 12.2: Developing Cloud Applications

Choosing the Right Cloud Service Model

Developing with Azure App Service

Azure Functions for Serverless Applications

Containerized Applications

Monitoring and Scaling

Section 12.3: Managing Cloud Resources

Azure Resource Groups

Azure Resource Manager (ARM) Templates

Azure DevTest Labs

Resource Tagging

Resource Locks

Section 12.4: Cloud Deployment and Monitoring

Cloud Deployment Strategies

Azure DevOps Integration

Azure Application Insights

Azure Monitor

Third-party Monitoring Solutions

Section 12.5: Security Considerations in Cloud Development

Data Encryption

Identity and Access Management

Security Patching and Updates

Threat Detection and Monitoring

Compliance and Auditing

Secure Coding Practices

Secure DevOps

Security Awareness and Training

Incident Response Plan

Chapter 13: Advanced Programming Techniques

Section 13.1: Understanding Design Patterns

Section 13.2: Asynchronous Programming and Threading

Understanding Asynchronous Programming

Threading and Parallelism

Choosing Between Asynchronous Programming and Threading

Section 13.3: Advanced Data Structures

1. Hash Tables

2. Linked Lists

3. Trees

4. Graphs

5. Heaps

Section 13.4: Implementing Security in Applications

1. Authentication and Authorization

2. Data Encryption

3. Secure Coding Practices

4. Authentication Protocols

5. Identity and Access Management (IAM)

Section 13.5: Memory Management and Optimization

1. Understanding Memory Management in .NET

2. Memory Profiling and Analysis

3. Managing Large Data Sets

4. Disposing of Resources

5. Optimizing Data Structures

6. Finalizers and Resource Cleanup

7. Memory Pressure and Monitoring

8. Memory Optimization Techniques

9. Testing and Profiling

Chapter 14: Working with Graphics and Game Development

Section 14.1: Introduction to Graphics Programming

1. Understanding Graphics Programming

2. Graphics Libraries and APIs

3. Coordinate Systems

4. Drawing Primitives

5. Color and Shading

6. Transformations

7. Rasterization

8. Rendering Pipeline

9. Graphics Hardware

10. Game Development and Graphics

11. Graphics Programming Languages

12. Getting Started

Section 14.2: Using DirectX and Unity in Visual Studio

1. DirectX with Visual Studio

2. Unity with Visual Studio

3. Choosing the Right Tool

Section 14.3: Developing 2D and 3D Games

1. Choosing a Game Engine

2. Game Development with Visual Studio

3. Graphics and Game Design

4. Testing and Debugging

5. Deployment and Distribution

Section 14.4: Graphics Debugging and Performance

1. Graphics Debugging Tools

2. Performance Profiling

3. Debugging Graphics-Related Issues

4. Optimizing Graphics Performance

5. Cross-Platform Considerations

Section 14.5: Publishing and Monetizing Games

1. Choosing a Distribution Platform

2. Game Monetization Models

3. Game Marketing and Promotion

4. Game Localization

5. User Support and Updates

6. Protecting Your Intellectual Property (IP)

7. Monitoring and Analytics

8. Revenue Sharing and Payment Processing

9. Game Reviews and Ratings

10. Community Building

11. Adaptation and Long-Term Planning

Chapter 15: Scripting and Automation in Visual Studio

Section 15.1: Automating Tasks with MSBuild

Section 15.2: Customizing Build Processes

1. MSBuild Properties and Targets

2. Using Visual Studio Macros

3. Visual Studio Extensibility

4. Third-Party Build Tools

5. CI/CD Pipelines

Section 15.3: Scripting with PowerShell

1. Understanding PowerShell

2. Running PowerShell Scripts

3. Automating Tasks

4. Integration with Visual Studio

5. PowerShell Modules and Libraries

6. Error Handling and Logging

Section 15.4: Using the Command Line Interface

1. Understanding the Visual Studio CLI

2. Accessing the Visual Studio CLI

3. Common CLI Commands

4. Customizing CLI Commands

5. Batch Processing and Automation

6. Error Handling and Logging

Section 15.5: Continuous Integration Automation

1. Setting Up CI Pipelines

2. Automated Testing

3. Continuous Deployment

4. Monitoring and Notifications

5. Branch Policies and Pull Requests

6. Conclusion

Chapter 16: Visual Studio and the Internet of Things (IoT)

16.1 Setting Up for IoT Projects

16.1.1 Choosing the Right IoT Platform

16.1.2 Installing Visual Studio Extensions

16.1.3 Configuring IoT Devices

16.1.4 Creating an IoT Project

16.1.5 Writing Code for IoT

16.1.6 Debugging IoT Applications

16.1.7 Deploying IoT Solutions

16.1.8 Testing and Monitoring

16.1.9 IoT Security Considerations

16.2 Developing for Windows IoT Core

16.2.1 Windows IoT Core Overview

16.2.2 Setting Up Windows IoT Core

16.2.3 Installing the Windows IoT Core Extension

16.2.4 Creating a Windows IoT Core Project

16.2.5 Writing Code for Windows IoT Core

16.2.6 Building User Interfaces

16.2.7 Debugging and Deploying

16.2.8 IoT Connectivity

16.2.9 Security and Updates

16.3 Working with Raspberry Pi and Arduino

16.3.1 Raspberry Pi and Windows IoT Core

16.3.2 Arduino and Windows IoT Core

16.4 IoT Prototyping and Testing

16.4.1 IoT Prototyping

16.4.2 IoT Testing

16.5 Deploying IoT Solutions

16.5.1 Preparing for Deployment

16.5.2 Choosing the Deployment Model

16.5.3 Deploying with Visual Studio

16.5.4 Post-Deployment Considerations

17.1 Integrating AI and ML Tools

AI and ML in Modern Software

17.1.1 AI and ML Tools in Visual Studio

17.1.2 Getting Started with AI and ML in Visual Studio

17.2 Using ML.NET for Machine Learning

Introduction to ML.NET

Getting Started with ML.NET

ML.NET and Visual Studio Integration

17.3 Building AI-powered Applications

AI Frameworks and Libraries

AI-Powered Application Scenarios

Building AI-Powered Applications in Visual Studio

17.4 Data Analysis and Visualization

Data Analysis Tools in Visual Studio

Data Visualization with Visual Studio

Data Analysis Workflow

Example Data Visualization (Matplotlib)

17.5 Ethical Considerations in AI Development

Ethical Challenges in AI

Ethical AI Development Practices

Ethical AI Checklist

18.1 Enhancing Productivity in Visual Studio

Keyboard Shortcuts

IntelliSense

Code Snippets

Templates and Project Wizards

Extensions and Add-ons

Task Automation

Debugging Tools

Code Navigation

Version Control Integration

Live Share

18.2 Keyboard Shortcuts and Productivity Tools

Customizing Keyboard Shortcuts

Keyboard Shortcut Reference

Productivity Tools

Third-party Productivity Extensions

18.3 Code Management Best Practices

1. Modularization and Separation of Concerns

2. Version Control

3. Code Documentation

4. Code Reviews

5. Refactoring

6. Unit Testing

7. Continuous Integration and Continuous Deployment (CI/CD)

8. Code Analysis

9. Code Reviews and Pull Requests

10. Code Metrics

11. Code Templates and Snippets

12. Code Navigation

13. Code Analysis Rules

14. Continuous Learning

18.4 Troubleshooting Common Issues

1. Compilation Errors

2. Runtime Exceptions

3. Debugging Tools

4. IntelliSense and Code Completion

5. Version Control Conflicts

6. Performance Bottlenecks

7. Third-party Library Compatibility

8. Browser Compatibility (Web Development)

9. Data Connectivity Issues

10. Documentation and Online Resources

18.5 Staying Updated with Visual Studio

1. Security Updates

2. Bug Fixes and Stability

3. New Features and Productivity Enhancements

4. Language and Platform Support

5. Compatibility with Third-party Tools

6. Performance Improvements

7. Access to Online Services

8. How to Stay Updated

19.1 Emerging Trends in Software Development

1. Artificial Intelligence and Machine Learning (AI/ML)

2. Low-Code and No-Code Development

3. Serverless Computing

4. DevOps and Continuous Integration/Continuous Deployment (CI/CD)

5. Blockchain and Cryptocurrency

6. Edge Computing

7. Quantum Computing

8. Cybersecurity and Privacy

9. Sustainable and Green Computing

10. Remote Work and Collaboration

19.2 Future Updates and Roadmap of Visual Studio

1. Visual Studio Release Cadence

2. Improved Performance

3. Enhanced Collaboration Tools

4. AI-Powered Code Assistance

5. Cross-Platform Development

6. Cloud Integration

7. Focus on Accessibility and Inclusivity

8. Community Feedback and Input

19.3 Visual Studio and Open Source Development

1. Open Source Language Support

2. Visual Studio Code (VS Code)

3. GitHub Integration

4. Open Source Extensions

5. Collaboration with Open Source Communities

6. Licensing and Usage

19.4 Integrating Emerging Technologies

1. Machine Learning and AI Integration

2. IoT Development

3. Cloud Integration

4. Containerization

5. Mixed Reality Development

6. Quantum Computing

19.5 The Evolving Role of Developers

1. Full-Stack Developers

2. DevOps Engineers

3. Cloud-Native Developers

4. AI and Machine Learning Specialists

5. Security Champions

6. Continuous Learners

20.1 Analyzing Successful Visual Studio Projects

Understanding the Importance of Case Studies

The Structure of a Case Study

Case Study Examples

E-commerce Platform Migration

Mobile App Development for Healthcare

IoT Solution for Agriculture

AI-Powered Chatbot for Customer Support

Industry Insights and Expert Interviews

Interview with a Software Development Manager

Insights from a DevOps Engineer

A Conversation with a Visual Studio Extension Developer

Lessons from Failed Projects

Lack of Clear Project Scope

Inadequate Testing and Quality Assurance

Poor Version Control Practices

Insufficient Documentation

Inadequate Communication and Collaboration

Project Showcase: From Concept to Code

1. Project Initiation

2. Planning and Design

3. Development

4. Testing and Quality Assurance

5. Deployment and Release

6. Maintenance and Updates

7. Project Completion and Evaluation

Building a Comprehensive Portfolio with Visual Studio

1. Selecting Projects for Your Portfolio

2. Cleaning and Organizing Code

3. Creating Project Documentation

4. Showcasing UI/UX Design

5. Version Control and Collaboration

6. Highlighting Specializations

7. Continuous Learning and Certifications

8. Hosting Your Portfolio

Chapter 1: Introduction to Visual Studio

1.1 Understanding the Visual Studio Interface

Visual Studio is a powerful integrated development environment (IDE) created by Microsoft, designed to facilitate software development across a wide range of platforms and technologies. In this section, we will delve into the fundamental aspects of the Visual Studio interface, helping you get comfortable with the IDE.

When you first open Visual Studio, you are greeted with a versatile workspace that can be customized to suit your preferences. The primary components of the interface include:

1. **Menu Bar:** Located at the top, the menu bar provides access to various commands and options organized into menus, such as File, Edit, View, etc.
2. **Toolbar:** Below the menu bar, you'll find the toolbar, which offers quick access to frequently used tools and actions. It often includes buttons for tasks like building, debugging, and running your projects.
3. **Solution Explorer:** On the right-hand side of the screen, the Solution Explorer is a critical tool for managing your projects and their files. It displays a hierarchical view of your solution and its components.
4. **Code Editor:** The central area of the IDE is occupied by the code editor. This is where you write, edit, and view your source code files. Visual Studio provides robust code editing features, including syntax highlighting, code completion, and error checking.

5. **Tool Windows:** These are additional windows that can be docked or undocked to the IDE's interface. Examples include the Output window for displaying build and debug messages, the Properties window for configuring properties of selected items, and the Error List window for managing code errors.
6. **Solution and Project Tabs:** Above the code editor, tabs represent the open solutions and projects. You can switch between different solutions or projects by clicking on their respective tabs.
7. **Status Bar:** At the very bottom of the IDE, the status bar provides essential information, such as the current line and column number, and also includes various buttons for toggling features like line endings and code page.

Visual Studio allows for extensive customization of the interface. You can rearrange and resize windows, create custom layouts, and even install extensions that enhance your workflow.

Whether you're a beginner or an experienced developer, understanding the Visual Studio interface is crucial for efficient and productive software development. As you explore this IDE further, you'll discover many features and tools that streamline your coding experience.

In the next sections of this chapter, we will delve into the history and evolution of Visual Studio, discuss the installation and setup process, explore how to navigate through different versions, and provide an overview of key features and tools that make Visual Studio an indispensable tool for developers.

1.2 History and Evolution of Visual Studio

The history of Visual Studio is a fascinating journey that has seen it evolve into one of the most widely used integrated development environments in the world. Understanding its history provides valuable insights into the IDE's growth and the technology landscape it has influenced.

Origins and Early Versions

Visual Studio's story begins in the early 1990s when Microsoft introduced its first development environment, Visual Basic. This marked the inception of a new era in software development, as Visual Basic simplified Windows application development through its visual design tools and rapid application development capabilities.

In 1997, Microsoft released Visual Studio 97, a suite that integrated Visual Basic, Visual C++, and Visual FoxPro. This marked the birth of the Visual Studio brand. With the introduction of Visual Studio 6.0, the IDE gained popularity and was adopted by developers worldwide.

The .NET Era

The release of Visual Studio .NET in 2002 brought significant changes. It was closely tied to the launch of the Microsoft .NET Framework, which introduced a new way of building and deploying applications. Visual Studio .NET supported multiple programming languages, including C#, VB.NET, and C++. This shift towards managed code and a unified development platform set the stage for modern application development.

Continuous Advancements

Visual Studio has seen a pattern of continuous enhancements and version updates. With each new iteration, Microsoft introduced features aimed at improving developer productivity and expanding platform support. Notable versions include Visual Studio 2005, which introduced support for web development with ASP.NET, and Visual Studio 2010, which brought a revamped user interface and enhanced debugging tools.

Embracing Open Source

In recent years, Microsoft has made significant strides in embracing open source development. Visual Studio has integrated with Git, a popular version control system, making it easier for developers to work on open source projects. Microsoft's acquisition of GitHub in 2018 further solidified its commitment to the open source community.

The Cloud and Beyond

Visual Studio has evolved to meet the demands of cloud computing and modern software development practices. Integration with Microsoft Azure, cloud services, and containerization tools has become a key focus. Visual Studio 2019, the latest version at the time of my knowledge cutoff, introduced enhanced support for cloud-native development and AI integration.

Community and Ecosystem

Visual Studio's success can also be attributed to its vibrant community and ecosystem. The Visual Studio Marketplace allows developers to discover and install extensions that enhance the IDE's functionality. It's a hub for extensions, templates, and tools created by both Microsoft and the community.

In conclusion, Visual Studio's history is a testament to its adaptability and commitment to staying at the forefront of software development. Its evolution from a Windows-centric IDE to a versatile tool supporting a wide array of technologies reflects the ever-changing landscape of software development. As you explore Visual Studio, you'll find a rich history that has shaped the way we build and create software today.

1.3 Installation and Setup

Installing and setting up Visual Studio is the crucial first step in your journey to becoming an efficient developer. In this section, we will explore the process of installing Visual Studio and configuring it to meet your development needs.

Installation Options

Microsoft offers various editions of Visual Studio, each tailored to specific development scenarios. The most common editions include:

- **Visual Studio Community:** This edition is free and suitable for individual developers, open source contributors, and small teams. It provides a comprehensive set of tools for building a wide range of applications.

- **Visual Studio Professional:** Geared towards professional developers and small teams, this edition offers advanced features for building high-quality applications. It includes tools for web, mobile, desktop, cloud, and more.

- **Visual Studio Enterprise:** Designed for larger teams and enterprise-level development, this edition provides advanced debugging, testing, and collaboration tools. It supports complex projects and offers additional services such as DevOps integration.

You can download the edition that best suits your needs from the Visual Studio website. The installation process typically involves running the installer, selecting your preferred edition, and customizing the components you want to install.

Workloads and Individual Components

Visual Studio provides a flexible installation process through the concept of "workloads" and individual components. Workloads are predefined sets of tools and features tailored to specific types of development. Examples of workloads include "Desktop development with C++," "ASP.NET and web development," and "Mobile development with .NET."

While selecting a workload, you can further fine-tune your installation by choosing individual components within that workload. This allows you to install only the tools and libraries you need, minimizing the disk space and resources required.

Updates and Maintenance

After installing Visual Studio, it's essential to keep it up to date. Microsoft regularly releases updates, bug fixes, and feature enhancements. Visual Studio's integrated update mechanism makes it easy to stay current. You can configure it to automatically download and install updates or manually control the update process.

Visual Studio also supports extensions and add-ons, which can further enhance your development experience. The Visual Studio Marketplace is the go-to place for discovering and installing these extensions, ranging from code analysis tools to project templates and themes.

Licensing and Activation

Depending on the edition you choose, Visual Studio may require activation. Visual Studio Community and Visual Studio Professional usually require sign-in with a Microsoft account for activation. Visual Studio Enterprise, which is typically used in enterprise settings, may involve volume licensing agreements.

It's crucial to understand the licensing terms associated with your edition to ensure compliance and access to the features you require. Microsoft provides detailed documentation on licensing and activation procedures for each edition.

In summary, the installation and setup of Visual Studio are pivotal to your development journey. By selecting the right edition, workloads, and components, you can tailor the IDE to your specific needs. Regularly updating Visual Studio and exploring the vibrant ecosystem of extensions will help you maximize its capabilities and productivity.

1.4 Navigating Through Different Versions

Navigating through the various versions of Visual Studio is essential for developers, as each version brings new features, enhancements, and compatibility changes. In this section, we'll explore how to understand and work with different versions of Visual Studio.

Version Numbering

Visual Studio versions are typically identified by their year of release. For example, Visual Studio 2019 was released in 2019, and Visual Studio 2022 was released in 2022. This version numbering system makes it easy to track when a specific version was introduced.

Long-Term Support (LTS) Versions

Microsoft occasionally releases Long-Term Support (LTS) versions of Visual Studio. LTS versions are designed to receive updates and security patches for an extended period, making them suitable for stable and long-term projects. These versions provide a predictable support cycle, typically spanning several years, ensuring that you can maintain your projects without frequent migrations.

Compatibility Considerations

When working with different versions of Visual Studio, it's essential to consider compatibility. Newer versions may introduce language features, frameworks, or tools that are not available in older versions. Conversely, older projects may require specific older versions of Visual Studio to ensure compatibility.

Visual Studio often provides tools and migration guides to help you upgrade projects to newer versions. It's advisable to thoroughly test your code and dependencies when migrating to a different version to identify any compatibility issues.

Supported Platforms and Technologies

Visual Studio evolves to support the latest platforms and technologies. For instance, as new versions of Windows are released, Visual Studio is updated to provide development tools and templates for these platforms. Similarly, support for web technologies, mobile platforms, and cloud services may vary between versions.

When choosing a Visual Studio version, consider the platforms and technologies you intend to work with. Ensure that the version you select aligns with your project's requirements and targets the desired platforms.

Visual Studio Online Services

Microsoft offers various online services and integrations that can enhance your development workflow. These services may evolve and change with different Visual Studio versions. Examples include Azure DevOps (formerly known as Visual Studio Team Services) for collaboration and DevOps, as well as Azure cloud services for deployment and hosting.

Check the documentation and release notes for your specific version to understand which online services are integrated and how they can benefit your projects.

Community and Support

The Visual Studio community is active and provides valuable resources, including forums, blogs, and tutorials. Keep in mind that the availability of community support and resources may vary depending on the popularity and adoption of specific Visual Studio versions.

Staying connected with the Visual Studio community can help you overcome challenges, discover best practices, and learn about tips and tricks specific to your version of Visual Studio.

In conclusion, navigating through different versions of Visual Studio is essential for developers who want to stay current and leverage the latest features and technologies. Understanding version numbering, considering compatibility, and staying informed about supported platforms and services are crucial steps in choosing the right version for your projects. Whether you're working with an LTS version for long-term stability or adopting the latest release for cutting-edge development, Visual Studio offers a range of options to suit your needs.

1.5 Overview of Key Features and Tools

Visual Studio is renowned for its rich set of features and tools that streamline the software development process. In this section, we'll provide an overview of some key features and tools that make Visual Studio an indispensable tool for developers.

Integrated Development Environment (IDE)

At its core, Visual Studio is a comprehensive integrated development environment. It offers a robust code editor with features like syntax highlighting, code completion, and error checking. The code editor supports a wide range of programming languages, making it versatile for various development tasks.

Solution and Project Management

Visual Studio introduces the concept of solutions and projects, which help organize your code and resources efficiently. A solution can contain multiple projects, making it easy to manage complex applications. The Solution Explorer provides a hierarchical view of your solution and allows you to navigate and manipulate project files effortlessly.

Debugging and Diagnostics

Debugging is a critical part of software development, and Visual Studio excels in this area. It offers a powerful debugger with features like breakpoints, watch windows, and call stacks. Visual Studio's diagnostic tools enable you to analyze application performance, memory usage, and code profiling to identify and resolve issues effectively.

Version Control Integration

Visual Studio seamlessly integrates with popular version control systems like Git, Team Foundation Version Control (TFVC), and others. This integration allows for collaborative development, efficient code sharing, and easy tracking of changes. You can commit, branch, merge, and resolve conflicts directly from within the IDE.

Extensibility and Marketplace

Visual Studio's extensibility is a standout feature. You can enhance the IDE's functionality by installing extensions and add-ons from the Visual Studio Marketplace. These extensions range from productivity tools to code analysis and project templates. The marketplace is a hub for both Microsoft and community-created extensions.

IntelliSense

IntelliSense is a code completion and suggestion feature that significantly boosts productivity. It provides context-aware suggestions as you type, reducing the need to remember method names, variable names, and API details. IntelliSense supports multiple programming languages and frameworks.

Code Refactoring

Visual Studio includes a set of code refactoring tools that help improve code quality and maintainability. You can easily rename variables, extract methods, encapsulate fields, and perform other refactorings with just a few clicks. Refactoring tools assist in writing clean and efficient code.

Web and Cloud Development

Visual Studio offers robust support for web and cloud development. Whether you're building web applications using ASP.NET or developing cloud-native solutions with Azure, Visual Studio provides templates, debugging tools, and integration with Azure services to streamline your development process.

Mobile App Development

For mobile app development, Visual Studio supports cross-platform development using technologies like Xamarin. You can create native mobile apps for iOS, Android, and Windows using a shared codebase. Visual Studio also offers mobile emulators for testing your apps on various devices.

Data Tools

Data-related development is simplified with Visual Studio's data tools. You can integrate databases into your projects, manage database connections, and use tools like Entity Framework and LINQ for data querying. Visual Studio also supports database project management for version control and schema updates.

Testing and Quality Assurance

Visual Studio provides comprehensive testing tools, including unit testing frameworks, integration testing, and code coverage analysis. You can create and run test cases, automate testing processes, and ensure the quality of your software through continuous integration and deployment.

Collaboration and Team Development

Visual Studio supports collaboration among team members through tools like Team Foundation Server (TFS) and Git integration. You can manage work items, track progress, and implement best practices for team development. Live Share, a collaborative coding feature, enables real-time code sharing and debugging with teammates.

In conclusion, Visual Studio's feature set is extensive and designed to cater to a wide range of development scenarios. Whether you're working on desktop applications, web development, mobile apps, or cloud solutions, Visual Studio offers a comprehensive set of tools to enhance your productivity and streamline your development workflow. As you explore Visual Studio further, you'll discover how these features can be leveraged to create high-quality software efficiently.

Chapter 2: Basics of Project Management

2.1 Creating and Managing Projects

In the realm of software development, projects are the core entities that encompass your code, resources, and configurations. Visual Studio provides a robust environment for creating, organizing, and managing projects efficiently.

Project Types

Visual Studio supports a wide range of project types, each tailored to specific development scenarios. When creating a new project, you'll have the option to choose from project templates that correspond to your development goals. Some common project types include:

- **Console Application:** Used for command-line applications.
- **Windows Forms Application:** For developing desktop applications with a Windows user interface.
- **ASP.NET Web Application:** Ideal for building web applications using the ASP.NET framework.
- **Class Library:** To create reusable class libraries that can be shared across multiple projects.
- **Xamarin.Forms App:** For cross-platform mobile app development using Xamarin.Forms.

- **Azure Functions:** Used for creating serverless functions in the Azure cloud.

- **SQL Server Database Project:** For managing database schemas and scripts.

- **Unit Test Project:** To create unit tests for your code.

Creating a New Project

To create a new project in Visual Studio, follow these steps:

1. Open Visual Studio.
2. Click on the "File" menu.
3. Select "New" and then "Project."
4. In the "Create a new project" dialog, you can search for and select the desired project template based on your requirements.
5. Configure the project settings such as the name, location, and solution name.
6. Click the "Create" button to generate the project structure and initial files.

Solution Files

A solution in Visual Studio is a container that can hold one or more projects. Solutions are used to group related projects together and manage dependencies between them. When you create a new project, Visual Studio will typically create a solution to hold that project.

Solution Explorer

The Solution Explorer is a crucial tool for managing projects and their files within a solution. You can access it from the View menu or by pressing "Ctrl + Alt + L." In the Solution Explorer, you can:

- View the hierarchy of your solution and projects.
- Add, remove, and organize files.
- Set project dependencies.
- Configure project properties.

Project Properties

Each project in Visual Studio has a set of properties that define its behavior and settings. You can access these properties by right-clicking on the project in the Solution Explorer and selecting "Properties." Here, you can configure settings related to build, debugging, and deployment.

Adding Existing Projects

Visual Studio also allows you to add existing projects to a solution. This is useful when you want to work on multiple projects within the same solution. You can do this by right-clicking on the solution in the Solution Explorer, selecting "Add," and then choosing "Existing Project."

Project Configuration

Projects in Visual Studio support multiple configurations, such as Debug and Release. Each configuration can have its own settings, including compiler optimizations and debugging information. You can switch between different configurations using the “Configuration Manager” in Visual Studio.

Managing Dependencies

Projects often depend on external libraries and components. Visual Studio provides tools for managing these dependencies. You can use NuGet, a package manager for .NET projects, to easily add and update packages. Additionally, Visual Studio can automatically restore missing packages when you open a project.

Version Control Integration

Visual Studio has built-in support for version control systems like Git and Team Foundation Version Control (TFVC). You can initialize a Git repository for your project, commit changes, and manage branches directly from the IDE. This integration simplifies collaboration and code sharing among team members.

Templates and Code Generation

Visual Studio includes project templates that simplify the creation of common project types. These templates generate initial code, configuration files, and folder structures, saving you time and effort. You can also create custom project templates to standardize your development process within your organization.

In summary, creating and managing projects is a fundamental aspect of software development in Visual Studio. By understanding project types, using solution files, and utilizing tools like Solution Explorer, project properties, and version control integration, you can efficiently organize and develop your software projects. Whether you’re building desktop applications, web services, or mobile apps,

Visual Studio provides the necessary tools to streamline your project management tasks.

2.2 Understanding Solution Explorer

The Solution Explorer is a central component of Visual Studio's user interface, providing developers with a hierarchical view of the solution's structure. In this section, we'll explore the key features and functionalities of the Solution Explorer, which is an essential tool for managing projects and their associated files.

Solution and Project Hierarchy

When you open a solution in Visual Studio, you'll see the solution and project hierarchy displayed in the Solution Explorer. At the top level, you have the solution itself, which can contain one or more projects. Projects, in turn, contain files and folders related to your development work.

The hierarchy allows you to organize your code, resources, and other assets efficiently. You can expand and collapse nodes in the Solution Explorer to navigate through the structure and locate specific files or components.

Project Context Menus

Right-clicking on a project in the Solution Explorer opens a context menu that provides various options for managing the project. Some common actions available in the context menu include:

- **Build:** Compiles the project, checking for syntax errors and generating the output.

- **Rebuild:** Cleans and rebuilds the project, ensuring a clean build without any artifacts from previous builds.

- **Set as Startup Project:** Specifies which project should be executed when you run your solution. In multi-project solutions, you can set one project as the entry point.

- **Properties:** Opens the project's properties window, allowing you to configure various settings, including build configurations, debugging, and references.

- **Add:** Provides options to add new items to the project, such as classes, forms, or resource files.

- **Open Folder in File Explorer:** Opens the project's directory in Windows File Explorer for direct access to project files.

File and Folder Management

The Solution Explorer displays all the files and folders within a project. You can create new folders, organize files into specific directories, and even add existing files to the project. To do this, right-click on the project or folder where you want to add a file, choose "Add," and then select the type of file or item you want to add.

Search and Filtering

The Solution Explorer includes search functionality that allows you to quickly find specific files or items within your solution. You can use the search box at the top of the Solution Explorer to enter keywords and filter the displayed items based on your search criteria.

Renaming and Refactoring

Renaming files, folders, or items in the Solution Explorer is straightforward. Right-click on the item you want to rename, choose "Rename," and then enter the new name. Visual Studio will automatically update references to the renamed item within your codebase, ensuring consistency.

Dependencies and References

The Solution Explorer also provides visibility into project dependencies and references. When you expand a project node, you can see references to external libraries, assemblies, and other projects within your solution. This view helps you understand the relationships and dependencies between different parts of your project.

Customization

Visual Studio allows you to customize the appearance and behavior of the Solution Explorer to suit your preferences. You can choose to show or hide specific files or folders, group items by type, and arrange them alphabetically or hierarchically.

Working with Multiple Solutions

If you work with multiple solutions simultaneously, Visual Studio provides the ability to have multiple Solution Explorer instances open. This feature is handy for comparing and referencing code across different solutions or projects.

In summary, the Solution Explorer is a powerful tool within Visual Studio that aids in project and file management. By understanding its features, context menus, search capabilities, and customization options, you can efficiently navigate, organize, and work with the various components of your software projects. Whether you're developing a small application or a complex solution with multiple projects, the Solution Explorer simplifies the management of your code and resources.

2.3 Configuring Project Properties

Configuring project properties in Visual Studio is a fundamental aspect of software development. It allows you to tailor the behavior and settings of your projects to meet specific requirements. In this section, we'll explore how to access and modify project properties within the Visual Studio IDE.

Accessing Project Properties

To access the properties of a project in Visual Studio, follow these steps:

1. In the Solution Explorer, right-click on the project for which you want to configure properties.
2. Select "Properties" from the context menu. This opens the project properties window, where you can view and modify various settings.

Common Project Properties

The project properties window is organized into several categories, each containing specific settings and configurations. Some of the common project properties you may encounter include:

- **Application:** In this category, you can configure settings related to the application's entry point, output type (e.g., console application or Windows application), and target framework.

• **Build:** The build properties allow you to customize the build process, including compiler options, output directory, and conditional compilation symbols. You can specify whether to build for specific configurations (e.g., Debug or Release) and platforms (e.g., x86 or x64).

• **Debug:** Debug properties are crucial for setting up debugging options. You can define the startup action (e.g., starting an external program or attaching to a process), enable debugging information, and specify command-line arguments.

• **Application Package:** For projects targeting specific platforms or deployment scenarios, this category provides options to configure packaging, signing, and manifest settings.

• **References:** The references section allows you to manage project references and assembly references. You can add, remove, and update references to external libraries and components.

• **Code Analysis:** If you're using code analysis tools like Code Analysis for .NET or Roslyn analyzers, this category lets you enable or disable code analysis and specify additional rule sets.

• **Code Style:** Visual Studio also provides code style configurations, allowing you to define coding conventions and formatting rules for your project.

Configuring Conditional Compilation Symbols

Conditional compilation symbols are identifiers that control whether certain sections of code are included during compilation. These symbols are often used to create different builds for specific scenarios, such as debugging or release versions of an application.

To configure conditional compilation symbols for your project, navigate to the "Build" category in the project properties window. In the "Conditional compilation symbols" field, you can specify the symbols you want to define or remove. For example, you might use the symbol "DEBUG" in your code and define it for the Debug configuration. This way, you can conditionally include debugging-related code when building in Debug mode.

Platform Targeting

In the "Build" category, you can also configure the target platform for your project. Depending on your project type, you can choose between different platform options, such as x86, x64, AnyCPU, or specific mobile platforms. The choice of platform can affect the compatibility and performance of your application.

Debugging Options

The "Debug" category in project properties allows you to set up various debugging options, such as specifying the startup action and defining command-line arguments for debugging. Debugging configurations are essential for identifying and resolving issues in your code during development.

Applying Configuration Changes

After making changes to project properties, remember to save your modifications by clicking the "Apply" or "OK" button in the project properties window. This ensures that your changes take effect and are applied to the project's build and debugging configurations.

In conclusion, configuring project properties in Visual Studio is a crucial part of software development. By accessing and modifying project properties, you can customize various aspects of your projects, including build settings, debugging options, platform targeting, and conditional compilation symbols. These configurations allow you to tailor your projects to meet specific requirements and ensure smooth development and debugging processes.

2.4 Version Control Integration

Version control is a critical aspect of modern software development, enabling collaborative work, tracking changes, and ensuring code integrity. Visual Studio offers seamless integration with popular version control systems, making it easier for developers to manage and collaborate on projects. In this section, we'll explore version control integration within Visual Studio.

Supported Version Control Systems

Visual Studio supports various version control systems, with Git and Team Foundation Version Control (TFVC) being the most widely used options.

- **Git:** Git is a distributed version control system known for its speed and flexibility. Visual Studio provides robust Git integration, allowing you to clone, create, and manage Git repositories directly from the IDE. You can commit changes, create branches, and perform merges with ease.

- **Team Foundation Version Control (TFVC):** TFVC is a centralized version control system designed for enterprise-level development. Visual Studio offers comprehensive support for TFVC, enabling check-in, check-out, branching, and merging of code. It also provides features like shelvesets for code review and gated check-ins for quality control.

Setting Up Version Control

To use version control in Visual Studio, you'll need to connect your project to a version control system. Here's how you can set up version control within Visual Studio:

1. Open your project or solution in Visual Studio.
2. Go to the "View" menu and select "Team Explorer." This opens the Team Explorer pane on the right side of the IDE.
3. In Team Explorer, click on the "Manage Connections" button, which looks like a plug icon. This allows you to connect to a version control system.
4. Choose the version control system you want to use (e.g., Git or TFVC).
5. Follow the prompts to authenticate and connect to your version control system.

Cloning a Repository

If you're using Git, one of the common tasks is cloning an existing Git repository. Cloning creates a copy of a remote repository on your local machine, allowing you to work on the codebase. To clone a Git repository within Visual Studio:

1. Open Team Explorer as described earlier.
2. Click on the "Clone" button, which resembles a folder

icon with an arrow pointing down.
3. Provide the URL of the Git repository you want to clone.
4. Specify the local directory where you want to store the cloned repository.
5. Click the "Clone" button to initiate the cloning process.

Committing Changes

Once your project is connected to a version control system, you can start making changes to your code. Visual Studio provides a "Changes" view in Team Explorer that shows all the modified, added, or deleted files in your project. To commit your changes:

1. Open Team Explorer.
2. Click on the "Changes" button, which displays the list of pending changes.
3. Enter a commit message that describes the purpose of your changes.
4. Click the "Commit All" button to commit your changes to the version control system.

Branching and Merging

Branching and merging are essential concepts in version control, enabling parallel development and collaboration. Visual Studio makes it easy to create branches, switch between them, and merge changes. In Team Explorer, you can access the "Branches" view to manage your branches.

Resolving Conflicts

In collaborative development, conflicts may arise when two or more developers modify the same file concurrently. Visual Studio provides conflict resolution tools that help you review and merge conflicting changes. You can use the "Conflicts" view in Team Explorer to address conflicts and ensure a smooth merging process.

Pushing and Pulling

To synchronize your local changes with the remote repository, you can use the "Push" and "Pull" operations. Pushing sends your local commits to the remote repository, while pulling retrieves changes from the remote repository to your local copy. These operations ensure that your code is up-to-date and in sync with the central codebase.

History and Annotations

Visual Studio allows you to explore the history of your code using tools like "History" and "Annotations" (also known as "Blame" or "Annotate"). The "History" view in Team Explorer shows the commit history of a file or folder, enabling you to review changes over time. Annotations provide line-by-line attribution of changes, helping you identify who made each modification and when.

In conclusion, version control integration within Visual Studio streamlines the process of managing code changes, collaborating with team members, and ensuring code quality. Whether you're using Git for distributed version control or TFVC for centralized version control, Visual Studio offers a unified interface and a range of features to support your version control workflows. By mastering version control integration, you can enhance your productivity and effectively manage software development projects of any scale.

2.5 Debugging and Error Handling Basics

Debugging is an essential skill for developers, and Visual Studio offers a comprehensive set of tools to help you identify and resolve issues in your code. In this section, we'll explore the basics of debugging and error handling within Visual Studio.

Setting Breakpoints

Breakpoints are markers that you can place in your code to pause the program's execution at a specific point. This allows you to inspect variables, step through code, and diagnose issues step by step. To set a breakpoint in Visual Studio:

1. Open the source code file where you want to set the breakpoint.
2. Click in the margin to the left of the line of code where you want to pause execution. A red dot will appear, indicating a breakpoint.
3. Alternatively, you can press F9 while the cursor is on the desired line to toggle a breakpoint.

Starting Debugging

To start debugging your application in Visual Studio, you can use one of the following methods:

- Press F5 to start debugging with the application's default startup configuration.

- Press Ctrl + F5 to start debugging without attaching the debugger. This is useful for running your application without stopping at breakpoints, allowing you to observe its behavior in a more natural context.

- Use the Debug menu and select "Start Debugging."

• Click the green "Start Debugging" button in the toolbar.

Debugging Features

Once your application is running in debug mode, Visual Studio provides several debugging features to help you analyze and troubleshoot issues:

1. Breakpoints and Stepping

• **Step Into (F11):** This action allows you to step into a method or function call, taking you to the first line of code within that method.

• **Step Over (F10):** Use this to execute a method or function call without stepping into it. The debugger will move to the next line in the current method.

• **Step Out (Shift + F11):** If you've stepped into a method and want to return to the caller method, use this action.

• **Run to Cursor (Ctrl + F10):** Place the cursor on a line of code, and this command will continue program execution until it reaches that line.

2. Watches and Locals

• **Watches:** You can add variables or expressions to the Watches window to monitor their values as you step through code.

- **Locals:** The Locals window displays information about local variables within the current scope.

3. Immediate Window

The Immediate Window allows you to execute arbitrary code and inspect variables during debugging. It's particularly useful for testing expressions and quickly evaluating code snippets.

4. Call Stack

The Call Stack window shows the call hierarchy of methods and functions that led to the current point in your code. You can navigate through the call stack to understand the flow of execution.

5. Debugging Windows

Visual Studio provides various debugging windows, such as the Output window, Debug Output window, and Immediate window. These windows display additional information, logs, and output that can assist in debugging.

Error Handling and Exceptions

Error handling is an important aspect of software development to gracefully handle unexpected issues that may arise during runtime. Visual Studio allows you to catch and handle exceptions efficiently. To add exception handling to your code:

1. Surround the code that may throw an exception with a try block.
2. Use a catch block to specify how to handle the exception if it occurs.

3. Optionally, include a finally block to execute code regardless of whether an exception occurred.

Here's an example of a simple try-catch block in C#:

```
try
{
// Code that may throw an exception
int result = 10 / 0; // This will throw a DivideByZeroException
}
catch (DivideByZeroException ex)
{
// Handle the exception
Console.WriteLine("An error occurred: " + ex.Message);
}
finally
{
// Cleanup or other actions (optional)
}
```

Debugging Tools

Visual Studio also offers specialized debugging tools to diagnose issues in specific scenarios, such as:

- **Diagnostic Tools:** These tools provide insights into memory usage, CPU usage, and application performance.

- **Performance Profiling:** Visual Studio includes profiling tools to analyze application performance and identify bottlenecks.

- **IntelliTrace:** IntelliTrace records program execution history, allowing you to debug issues that occurred in the past.

- **Code Analysis:** You can use static code analysis tools to identify potential issues and code quality improvements.

In conclusion, debugging and error handling are crucial skills for developers, and Visual Studio provides a robust set of tools to make the process efficient and effective. By setting breakpoints, using debugging features like stepping and watches, and handling exceptions gracefully, you can identify and resolve issues in your code more efficiently. Debugging tools and specialized diagnostics further enhance your ability to maintain and improve the quality of your software projects.

Chapter 3: Coding in Visual Studio

3.1 Writing Code: Tips and Tricks

Writing code is at the heart of software development, and Visual Studio offers a rich set of features and productivity tools to help you write code efficiently. In this section, we'll explore some tips and tricks to streamline your coding experience within Visual Studio.

1. Code Navigation

Go to Definition (F12)

Use the "Go to Definition" feature by placing your cursor on a method, class, or variable and pressing F12. This action takes you to the definition of the selected item, allowing you to explore its implementation.

Navigate Backward (Ctrl + -)

After using "Go to Definition," you can quickly return to your previous location in the code by pressing Ctrl + -. This is useful for jumping back and forth between different parts of your codebase.

Find All References (Shift + F12)

To see where a particular method, class, or variable is used throughout your project, use the "Find All References" feature by selecting the item and pressing Shift + F12. Visual Studio will display a list of references, helping you understand its usage context.

2. Code Snippets

Visual Studio provides code snippets that allow you to insert predefined code templates quickly. For example, you can type "for" and press Tab twice to generate a for loop template. You can also create custom code snippets to save time on repetitive tasks.

3. Code Completion and IntelliSense

Visual Studio's IntelliSense feature provides code completion suggestions as you type. Press Ctrl + Space to trigger IntelliSense, and you'll get a list of suggested methods, properties, and variable names. Use arrow keys to navigate the list and press Tab to select a suggestion.

4. Code Formatting

Consistent code formatting enhances code readability. Visual Studio allows you to format your code automatically or manually using the "Format Document" (Ctrl + K, Ctrl + D) and "Format Selection" (Ctrl + K, Ctrl + F) commands.

5. Code Refactoring

Visual Studio supports code refactoring to improve code quality and maintainability. You can refactor code by right-clicking on a variable, method, or class name and selecting options like "Rename," "Extract Method," or "Change Signature."

6. Snippet Management

You can manage your code snippets and create custom ones through the "Code Snippet Manager" (Ctrl + K, Ctrl + B). This tool allows you to import, export, and organize your code snippets effectively.

7. Debugging Tips

Immediate Window

The Immediate Window (Ctrl + Alt + I) is a powerful debugging tool that lets you execute code during debugging sessions. It's helpful for evaluating expressions, testing functions, and manipulating variables on the fly.

Conditional Breakpoints

Instead of breaking execution at every occurrence of a breakpoint, you can set conditional breakpoints. Right-click on a breakpoint and select "Condition." Enter a condition that must be met for the breakpoint to trigger.

Data Tips and Quick Watch

Hover over a variable while debugging to see its current value in a Data Tip. You can also use the "Quick Watch" feature (Shift + F9) to inspect variables and expressions in a dedicated window.

8. Version Control Integration

Visual Studio's version control integration is essential for code collaboration. Use the Team Explorer to commit changes, create branches, and manage your source control operations directly from the IDE.

9. Keyboard Shortcuts

Learning keyboard shortcuts can significantly boost your productivity. Visual Studio offers a vast array of keyboard shortcuts for various tasks. You can customize shortcuts and even export/import settings to maintain consistency across environments.

10. Extensions and Add-ons

Visual Studio's extensibility allows you to enhance your development environment by installing extensions and add-ons from the Visual Studio Marketplace. These extensions can add new features, tools, and language support to your IDE.

In conclusion, writing code efficiently is a critical skill for developers, and Visual Studio provides a plethora of tools and features to help you streamline the coding process. By mastering code navigation, using code snippets, leveraging code completion and IntelliSense, formatting code consistently, and utilizing debugging tips, you can become a more productive and effective coder within the Visual Studio IDE. Additionally, exploring version control integration, keyboard shortcuts, and extensions can further enhance your coding experience and make you a more proficient developer.

3.2 Utilizing IntelliSense for Efficient Coding

IntelliSense is a powerful feature in Visual Studio that enhances your coding experience by providing context-aware suggestions and completions while you write code. It offers a range of capabilities, from auto-completing code to displaying function signatures and descriptions. In this section, we'll explore how to utilize IntelliSense effectively to boost your coding productivity.

1. Code Completion

IntelliSense's code completion feature suggests keywords, variables, methods, and other code elements as you type. To trigger code completion, press Ctrl + Space or simply continue typing. Visual

Studio will present a dropdown list of suggestions based on the context.

For example, if you're writing C# code and start typing "Cons," IntelliSense might suggest "Console" as a completion, and you can press Tab or Enter to accept the suggestion.

2. Parameter Info

When you're calling a method or function, IntelliSense provides parameter information, making it easier to understand what each parameter expects. After opening the parentheses, IntelliSense will display a tooltip that describes the parameter and its data type. You can press Tab to move to the next parameter or Shift + Tab to go back to the previous one.

3. Method Overloads

If a method or function has multiple overloads (different sets of parameters), IntelliSense will display all available overloads in a dropdown. You can select the one that matches your requirements, and IntelliSense will automatically generate the code with the correct parameter list.

4. Descriptions and Documentation

IntelliSense also provides descriptions and documentation for code elements. When you hover over a class, method, or variable, a tooltip with a summary and additional information will appear. This can be especially helpful when working with libraries or APIs that you're not familiar with.

5. Contextual Suggestions

IntelliSense adapts to the programming language you're using and the context of your code. For example, if you're writing JavaScript, it will offer suggestions for JavaScript-specific functions and objects. If you're working with HTML, it will provide HTML tag suggestions.

6. Snippets and Templates

Visual Studio includes code snippets and templates that you can access through IntelliSense. For instance, you can type "for" and press Tab twice to generate a for loop structure automatically. Similarly, you can use snippets for common code patterns like try-catch blocks, switch statements, or property getters and setters.

7. Custom Snippets

You can create custom code snippets to speed up your coding tasks further. To create a custom snippet, go to the "Tools" menu, select "Code Snippets Manager," and import your snippet or create a new one. This can be particularly useful for frequently used code patterns specific to your project or coding style.

8. IntelliCode

IntelliCode is an AI-assisted extension of IntelliSense that provides intelligent code completion suggestions based on patterns in your own codebase and popular coding practices. It can help you make more informed coding choices by suggesting relevant code elements.

9. Keyboard Shortcuts

While working with IntelliSense, knowing some keyboard shortcuts can save you time:

- Ctrl + Space: Trigger code completion.
- Tab or Enter: Accept the selected suggestion or complete the code.
- Ctrl + Shift + Space: Show parameter info for the current method call.
- Ctrl + J: Display a list of available IntelliSense options when multiple suggestions are present.

10. Customizing IntelliSense

Visual Studio allows you to customize IntelliSense behavior and appearance to match your preferences. You can adjust settings related to font size, completion behavior, and code suggestions in the options menu.

In conclusion, IntelliSense is a powerful tool in Visual Studio that significantly enhances your coding efficiency and accuracy. By mastering its features, including code completion, parameter info, method overloads, descriptions, and contextual suggestions, you can write code more quickly and with fewer errors. Additionally, exploring code snippets, creating custom snippets, and leveraging IntelliCode can further boost your productivity and streamline your coding tasks within the Visual Studio IDE.

3.3 Code Refactoring and Formatting

Code refactoring and formatting are essential practices in software development that help improve code readability, maintainability, and quality. Visual Studio provides a range of tools and features to assist you in these tasks. In this section, we'll explore code refactoring and formatting techniques within Visual Studio.

Code Refactoring

Refactoring is the process of restructuring existing code to make it more efficient, maintainable, and readable without changing its external behavior. Visual Studio offers several code refactoring tools to assist in this process:

1. **Rename:** You can rename variables, methods, classes, or other code elements easily by placing the cursor on the identifier and pressing F2. Visual Studio will automatically update all references to that identifier throughout your codebase.
2. **Extract Method:** To simplify code and promote reusability, you can extract a block of code into a separate method. Select the code, right-click, and choose "Quick Actions and Refactorings" to access the "Extract Method" option.
3. **Change Signature:** If you need to modify the parameters of a method, Visual Studio allows you to change the method signature while automatically updating all call sites.
4. **Inline Variable or Method:** Conversely, you can inline a variable or method when it no longer serves a meaningful purpose or adds unnecessary complexity to your code.
5. **Encapsulate Field:** This refactoring action helps you encapsulate a public field into a property, allowing better control over access and providing an opportunity for validation or computed properties.
6. **Move Type to Another Namespace:** When organizing your code, you can move a class or type to a different namespace while ensuring that all references are updated accordingly.

Code Formatting

Code formatting ensures that your code adheres to a consistent style and structure, making it more readable and maintainable. Visual Studio provides robust code formatting options and customization capabilities:

1. **Automatic Formatting:** Visual Studio can automatically format your code as you type or when you save a file. To enable automatic formatting, go to "Tools" > "Options" > "Text Editor" > "Your Programming Language" > "Formatting" and configure the desired formatting rules.
2. **Indentation and Spacing:** You can specify your preferred indentation style (e.g., tabs or spaces) and set the number of spaces or tabs per indent level. Visual Studio will enforce these rules during formatting.
3. **Code Style Preferences:** Visual Studio allows you to define code style preferences for various aspects of your code, such as naming conventions, code layout, and code quality. You can customize these preferences to match your coding standards.
4. **Format Document and Format Selection:** You can manually format your code using the "Format Document" (Ctrl + K, Ctrl + D) and "Format Selection" (Ctrl + K, Ctrl + F) commands. These options apply formatting rules to the entire document or the selected code block, respectively.
5. **EditorConfig Support:** Visual Studio seamlessly integrates with EditorConfig, an open-standard file format that defines coding style rules. You can create an .editorconfig file in your project to enforce coding style conventions consistently.

Customizing Code Style

Visual Studio allows you to customize code style rules at both the project and solution levels. You can define specific formatting preferences for your team and ensure that everyone follows the same coding standards. This consistency improves code maintainability and collaboration.

Code Analysis and Inspections

Visual Studio includes built-in code analysis and inspection tools that help identify code issues, adherence to coding standards, and potential improvements. By running code analysis, you can catch errors and enforce best practices in your codebase.

In conclusion, code refactoring and formatting are essential practices that contribute to code quality and maintainability. Visual Studio provides a range of tools and features to assist in these tasks, making it easier for developers to refactor code, enforce coding standards, and maintain a consistent code style. By utilizing these capabilities, you can improve the readability and maintainability of your code, collaborate more effectively with your team, and ensure that your software projects adhere to best practices.

3.4 Implementing Code Snippets

Code snippets are predefined code templates that can be quickly inserted into your code to perform common tasks, structure code blocks, or reduce repetitive typing. Visual Studio offers a range of built-in code snippets and allows you to create custom snippets tailored to your specific development needs. In this section, we'll explore how to implement and utilize code snippets effectively within Visual Studio.

Using Built-In Code Snippets

Visual Studio provides a collection of built-in code snippets for various programming languages and scenarios. To insert a built-in code snippet:

1. Open the source code file where you want to insert the snippet.
2. Position the cursor at the location where you want to insert the code.
3. Type the snippet shortcut, which is usually a shorthand keyword followed by pressing Tab. For example, to insert a for loop in C#, type "for" and press Tab. Visual Studio will automatically expand the snippet.
4. Tab through the placeholders within the snippet to replace them with your specific code.
5. Press Enter to accept the changes and move to the next location.
6. Continue editing or modifying the code as needed.

Common Built-In Snippets

Here are some examples of commonly used built-in code snippets in Visual Studio:

- **for:** Inserts a for loop structure with placeholders for the loop variable, condition, and increment.

- **if:** Inserts an if statement with a condition placeholder.

- **try:** Inserts a try-catch block with placeholders for catching exceptions.

- **prop:** Inserts a property declaration with placeholders for property type and name.

- **foreach:** Inserts a foreach loop structure with placeholders for the collection and iteration variable.

Creating Custom Code Snippets

In addition to built-in snippets, you can create custom code snippets tailored to your specific coding patterns or project requirements. Here's how to create a custom code snippet:

1. Go to "Tools" > "Code Snippets Manager" in Visual Studio.
2. Select the language for which you want to create the snippet (e.g., C# or VB.NET).
3. Click the "Add" button and provide a title, shortcut, and description for your snippet.
4. In the "Snippet" box, define the code template using placeholders enclosed in $ symbols. For example:

```
public void LogError(string message)

{

// TODO: Log the error message

}
```

1. Save the snippet, and it will be available for use in your code files.
2. To insert your custom snippet, type the shortcut you defined and press Tab.
3. Customize the placeholders as needed to fit your specific code.

Modifying Existing Snippets

Visual Studio allows you to modify existing code snippets or create custom variations of built-in snippets. You can access and edit snippet files from the "Code Snippets Manager." This flexibility enables you to tailor snippets to your team's coding conventions or project requirements.

Snippet Expansion and Editing

After inserting a code snippet, you can navigate through its placeholders by pressing Tab. Visual Studio will highlight the current placeholder, allowing you to replace it with your code. You can also use Shift + Tab to navigate backward through placeholders.

If you want to edit an inserted snippet or make changes to a custom snippet, simply navigate to the desired location within the snippet and modify the code as needed.

Snippet Surround Selection

You can select a block of code and then surround it with a snippet. To do this, highlight the code block, right-click, and choose "Surround With" from the context menu. You can then select a snippet from the available options to wrap around your selected code.

Snippet Best Practices

When creating or using code snippets, consider the following best practices:

- Keep snippets concise and focused on specific tasks.

- Use descriptive shortcut names to make snippets easy to remember.

- Document custom snippets with clear descriptions and examples.

- Share commonly used custom snippets with your team to boost productivity.

In conclusion, code snippets are a valuable tool in Visual Studio that can significantly enhance your coding efficiency. Whether you're using built-in snippets or creating custom ones, they help you reduce repetitive typing, adhere to coding conventions, and streamline common coding tasks. By effectively implementing and utilizing code snippets, you can save time, reduce errors, and improve the consistency of your codebase.

3.5 Using the Code Editor Effectively

The code editor is where developers spend a significant amount of their time writing, editing, and maintaining code. Visual Studio provides a robust code editor with a wide range of features to enhance your productivity and code quality. In this section, we'll explore tips and techniques for using the code editor effectively in Visual Studio.

1. Navigation and Selection

Go to Line (Ctrl + G)

You can quickly navigate to a specific line number by pressing Ctrl + G and entering the line number you want to jump to. This is handy when you need to find and edit code in a large file.

Find and Replace (Ctrl + F and Ctrl + H)

The Find (Ctrl + F) and Replace (Ctrl + H) features allow you to search for specific text within the code and replace it with another text. You can use regular expressions and various search options to refine your search.

Navigate to (Ctrl + ,)

The "Navigate to" feature (Ctrl + ,) is a powerful search tool that helps you find files, types, methods, and symbols in your project quickly. Just start typing and let Visual Studio suggest matches as you go.

Select All Occurrences (Ctrl + Shift + L)

Selecting all occurrences of a word or symbol in your code can be helpful when you want to make consistent changes. Select a word, press Ctrl + Shift + L, and Visual Studio will highlight all occurrences for simultaneous editing.

2. Code Formatting

Consistent code formatting enhances readability and maintains a professional coding style. Visual Studio offers automatic code formatting options:

- **Format Document (Ctrl + K, Ctrl + D):** This command will format the entire document according to your code style preferences, ensuring that your code follows the specified formatting rules.

- **Format Selection (Ctrl + K, Ctrl + F):** If you have a specific code block selected, this command will format only the selected portion of code.

3. Code Indentation

Proper code indentation is crucial for code readability. Visual Studio allows you to adjust and customize your code's indentation style:

- **Tab or Space Indentation:** You can configure Visual Studio to use tabs or spaces for indentation. To set your preference, go to "Tools" > "Options" > "Text Editor" > "Your Programming Language" > "Tabs."

- **Indentation Size:** Customize the number of spaces or tabs for each level of indentation in the same "Tabs" options.

4. Code Snippets

As mentioned in earlier sections, Visual Studio provides built-in code snippets and supports custom code snippets. These are invaluable for quickly generating common code patterns and reducing repetitive typing.

5. IntelliSense

IntelliSense is a key feature that helps you write code faster and with fewer errors. It provides auto-completion suggestions, parameter info, and method signatures as you type.

6. Code Folding

Code folding allows you to collapse and expand sections of code to focus on relevant portions. Visual Studio supports code folding for methods, regions, and comment blocks. You can fold code by clicking the small arrows in the margin or by using keyboard shortcuts (Ctrl + M, Ctrl + M to toggle folding).

7. Multi-Cursor Editing

Visual Studio supports multi-cursor editing, allowing you to edit multiple instances of a selected text simultaneously. To add additional cursors, hold down the Alt key and click in the locations where you want to insert cursors.

8. Code Comments

Proper code commenting is essential for documentation and understanding code. Visual Studio supports commenting and uncommenting code blocks with keyboard shortcuts (Ctrl + K, Ctrl + C for commenting, Ctrl + K, Ctrl + U for uncommenting).

9. Code Outlining

Code outlining helps you collapse and expand sections of code to improve code readability. You can use the outlining feature to hide or show parts of your code, making it easier to navigate and understand complex files.

10. Extensions and Customization

Visual Studio's extensibility allows you to enhance the code editor further by installing extensions and customizing the editor's behavior to match your coding preferences.

In conclusion, the code editor is the developer's primary workspace, and mastering its features can significantly boost productivity and code quality. Visual Studio offers a plethora of tools and capabilities for code navigation, selection, formatting, indentation, and editing.

By utilizing these features effectively, you can write, edit, and maintain code more efficiently, ensuring that your software projects are well-organized, readable, and maintainable.

Chapter 4: Debugging and Diagnostic Tools

4.1 Introduction to Debugging in Visual Studio

Debugging is an essential part of software development, allowing developers to identify and resolve issues in their code. Visual Studio provides a powerful set of debugging tools and features to help you locate and fix bugs efficiently. In this section, we'll introduce you to the fundamentals of debugging in Visual Studio.

1. Setting Breakpoints

A breakpoint is a designated point in your code where the debugger will pause execution, allowing you to inspect variables, evaluate expressions, and step through code step by step. To set a breakpoint:

- Click in the margin to the left of the line of code where you want to break. A red circle will appear, indicating the breakpoint.

- You can also set breakpoints by clicking on a line of code and pressing F9.

2. Starting Debugging

To start debugging your application, you can either press F5 or select "Start Debugging" from the "Debug" menu. Visual Studio will launch your application and pause execution at the first breakpoint encountered.

3. Debugging Controls

Once in debug mode, you can use the following debugging controls in the Visual Studio IDE:

- **Continue (F5):** Resumes code execution until the next breakpoint or until the program exits.
- **Pause (Ctrl + Break):** Interrupts code execution, allowing you to pause and inspect the current state of the application.
- **Step Into (F11):** Steps into a method call, allowing you to debug the called method.
- **Step Over (F10):** Steps over a method call, executing it without diving into the method's code.
- **Step Out (Shift + F11):** Steps out of the current method, returning to the calling method.
- **Stop Debugging (Shift + F5):** Terminates the debugging session and returns to normal editing mode.

4. Debugging Windows

Visual Studio provides various debugging windows that display information about your application's state and help you diagnose issues. Some commonly used debugging windows include:

- **Watch Window:** Allows you to monitor the values of specific variables or expressions while debugging.
- **Locals Window:** Displays information about local variables in the current scope.

- **Call Stack Window:** Shows the call stack, helping you understand the execution flow.

- **Immediate Window:** Enables you to execute code and evaluate expressions interactively while debugging.

- **Breakpoints Window:** Lists all active breakpoints, allowing you to enable, disable, or delete them.

5. Inspecting Variables

During debugging, you can inspect the values of variables by hovering your mouse over them in the code editor, or by adding them to the Watch Window. You can also add expressions to the Watch Window to monitor specific calculations or conditions.

6. Conditional Breakpoints

Visual Studio allows you to set conditional breakpoints that trigger only when a specified condition is met. Right-click on a breakpoint and select "Condition" to define the condition.

7. Data Tips and Quick Watch

While debugging, you can hover over a variable to see its current value in a Data Tip. Additionally, you can use the "Quick Watch" feature (Shift + F9) to inspect variables and expressions in a dedicated window.

8. Debugging Symbols and Information

For effective debugging, make sure your code includes debugging symbols (PDB files) and that you have access to the source code. Without symbols, debugging becomes limited, and you won't be able to step into or set breakpoints within certain parts of your code.

9. Exception Handling

Visual Studio provides robust exception handling tools. You can configure how Visual Studio responds to exceptions, whether by breaking execution when an exception is thrown or ignoring specific exceptions during debugging.

10. Debugging Web Applications

When debugging web applications, Visual Studio offers specific tools for web development debugging, including the ability to attach the debugger to a running web process, inspect HTTP requests and responses, and debug client-side JavaScript code.

In conclusion, debugging is a critical skill for software developers, and Visual Studio's debugging tools and features greatly simplify the process of identifying and resolving issues in your code. By setting breakpoints, using debugging controls, and leveraging debugging windows, you can effectively diagnose and fix bugs in your applications. Additionally, Visual Studio offers various advanced debugging capabilities, such as conditional breakpoints, data inspection, and exception handling, to streamline your debugging workflow and enhance your productivity as a developer.

4.2 Breakpoints and Step-by-Step Debugging

Breakpoints and step-by-step debugging are fundamental techniques for locating and diagnosing issues in your code during debugging sessions in Visual Studio. In this section, we'll delve into the details of setting breakpoints and using step-by-step debugging effectively.

Setting Breakpoints

Breakpoints are markers in your code that pause program execution when reached, allowing you to inspect variables, evaluate expressions, and analyze the program's state at specific points. Setting breakpoints is a key part of debugging. Here's how to set breakpoints in Visual Studio:

1. **Click in the Margin:** You can set a breakpoint by clicking in the margin to the left of the line of code where you want the program to pause. A red circle will appear, indicating the breakpoint.
2. **Keyboard Shortcut:** Place the cursor on the line of code where you want the breakpoint and press F9. This will toggle the breakpoint on or off.
3. **Context Menu:** Right-click on the line of code and select "Toggle Breakpoint" from the context menu.
4. **Conditional Breakpoints:** You can set breakpoints with conditions. Right-click on a breakpoint, choose "Condition," and define a condition that must be met for the breakpoint to trigger.

Debugging Controls

Once you've set breakpoints, you can control program execution using the debugging controls:

- **Start Debugging (F5):** Initiates debugging and runs the program until a breakpoint is encountered or the program exits.

- **Step Into (F11):** Allows you to step into a method call, exploring its code during debugging.

- **Step Over (F10):** Executes the current line of code and advances to the next line, without diving into method calls.

- **Step Out (Shift + F11):** Steps out of the current method, returning to the calling method.

- **Stop Debugging (Shift + F5):** Terminates the debugging session and returns to normal editing mode.

The Call Stack Window

The Call Stack window is a valuable tool for understanding the flow of execution in your code. It shows the hierarchy of method calls that led to the current point in your code. You can open the Call Stack window during debugging sessions to navigate through the call stack and examine the state of each method in the stack.

Data Tips and Watch Window

While debugging, you can hover over a variable or expression in your code to see its current value in a Data Tip. Additionally, you can use the Watch Window to monitor the values of specific variables and expressions as you step through your code. To add variables or expressions to the Watch Window, right-click on them in the code editor and choose "Add Watch" or directly type them into the Watch Window.

Stepping Through Code

Step-by-step debugging is a powerful technique that helps you understand how your code behaves. When you step through code, you can see the impact of each line of code on variables and program state. Here's how to use step-by-step debugging:

1. **Start Debugging:** Launch your application in debug mode (F5).
2. **Set Breakpoints:** Set breakpoints at the locations you want to start debugging from.
3. **Step Into (F11):** Use this command to step into method calls. It allows you to explore the inner workings of methods.
4. **Step Over (F10):** Use this command to execute the current line of code and move to the next line. It's helpful for skipping over methods when you're not interested in their internal details.
5. **Step Out (Shift + F11):** Use this command to exit the current method and return to the calling method.
6. **Continue (F5):** Resume program execution until the next breakpoint or until the program exits.

Conditional Breakpoints

In addition to standard breakpoints, Visual Studio supports conditional breakpoints. These breakpoints only trigger when specific conditions are met. To set a conditional breakpoint:

1. Right-click on an existing breakpoint.
2. Choose "Condition."
3. Define the condition that must be true for the breakpoint to pause execution.

Conditional breakpoints are useful for debugging scenarios where you want to focus on specific situations or values.

Tips for Effective Debugging

Here are some tips for effective debugging with breakpoints and step-by-step debugging:

• Set breakpoints strategically at key points in your code to focus on relevant areas.

• Use conditional breakpoints to narrow down debugging to specific scenarios or conditions.

• Pay attention to the Call Stack window to understand the sequence of method calls.

• Utilize the Watch Window and Data Tips to monitor variable values and expressions.

• Practice stepping through code to gain a deeper understanding of program flow.

• Don't forget to use the Stop Debugging command when you're finished with your debugging session.

Debugging with breakpoints and step-by-step debugging is a vital skill for developers, enabling them to identify and fix issues in their code efficiently. Visual Studio provides a range of tools and controls to facilitate this process, helping developers gain insights into their code's behavior and ultimately deliver more robust software.

4.3 Using Diagnostic Tools

Diagnostic tools in Visual Studio are indispensable for identifying and resolving issues in your code by providing insights into runtime behavior, performance bottlenecks, and memory usage. In this section, we'll explore the diagnostic tools available in Visual Studio and how to use them effectively.

1. Performance Profiling

Performance profiling is essential for optimizing your code and identifying performance bottlenecks. Visual Studio offers a range of profiling tools to help you pinpoint areas of your application that can be optimized. Here's how to use performance profiling:

- **Start Profiling:** To begin profiling your application, go to "Debug" > "Performance Profiler" and select the profiling type you need, such as CPU Usage, Memory Usage, or .NET Object Allocation. Click the "Start" button to launch the profiler.

- **Analyze Profiling Data:** Once profiling is complete, Visual Studio generates detailed reports and graphs that show which parts of your code consume the most CPU time or memory. You can analyze this data to identify performance bottlenecks and memory leaks.

- **Use Profiling Tools:** Visual Studio provides various profiling tools, such as the CPU Usage tool, Memory Usage tool, and more. These tools help you understand your application's performance characteristics and guide optimization efforts.

2. Debugging Memory Issues

Memory-related issues, such as memory leaks and excessive memory consumption, can severely impact application performance. Visual Studio includes tools for diagnosing and fixing memory problems:

- **Memory Usage Tool:** This tool helps you track memory usage during application execution. It provides insights into memory allocation, deallocation, and potential memory leaks.

- **Object Allocation Tracking:** Visual Studio can track object allocations and show you where memory is being allocated and deallocated. This is especially useful for managing memory in managed languages like C#.

- **Memory Dump Analysis:** Visual Studio allows you to analyze memory dumps, which are snapshots of an application's memory state at a particular moment. You can use memory dumps to diagnose memory-related issues in production environments.

3. IntelliTrace

IntelliTrace is a powerful debugging tool in Visual Studio that captures historical debugging information during application execution. It enables you to step back in time to examine the state of your application at different points in its execution. Here's how to use IntelliTrace:

- **Enable IntelliTrace:** You can enable IntelliTrace by going to "Debug" > "Options" > "IntelliTrace" and configuring the settings. Once enabled, IntelliTrace collects data about function calls, exceptions, and more.

- **Review Historical Debugging Data:** After a debugging session, you can review the captured data in the IntelliTrace window. This allows you to investigate issues that occurred earlier in the execution process.

- **Step Back in Time:** With IntelliTrace, you can step back in time during debugging to see the state of your application at specific points. This is incredibly useful for understanding the root causes of issues.

4. Diagnostic Hub

The Diagnostic Hub is a central location in Visual Studio for collecting and analyzing diagnostic data. It integrates various diagnostic tools, including the Performance Profiler, IntelliTrace, and Memory Usage tools. Here's how to use the Diagnostic Hub:

- **Open Diagnostic Hub:** You can access the Diagnostic Hub by going to "Debug" > "Start Diagnostic Tools Without Debugging."

- **Choose Diagnostic Tools:** In the Diagnostic Hub, you can select the diagnostic tools you want to use for your debugging session. Each tool provides specific insights into different aspects of your application's behavior.

- **Collect and Analyze Data:** Start the data collection and analysis process by clicking the "Start" button. Visual Studio will gather diagnostic information as your application runs.

- **Review Results:** After data collection, you can review the results in the Diagnostic Hub, allowing you to diagnose issues and optimize your code.

5. Exception Settings

Exception settings in Visual Studio allow you to control how the debugger handles exceptions during debugging sessions. You can specify whether to break on all exceptions, unhandled exceptions, or specific exceptions. Exception settings are useful for diagnosing and handling exceptions in your code.

6. Code Analysis and Code Metrics

Visual Studio provides built-in static code analysis tools that help you identify potential issues in your code, such as code smells, performance bottlenecks, and security vulnerabilities. Additionally, you can use code metrics to evaluate code quality and complexity.

In conclusion, diagnostic tools in Visual Studio are invaluable for identifying and resolving issues in your code, optimizing performance, and managing memory effectively. By leveraging profiling tools, memory analysis, IntelliTrace, and the Diagnostic Hub, you can gain deep insights into your application's behavior and diagnose complex problems. Additionally, exception settings, code analysis, and code metrics assist in maintaining code quality and addressing potential issues early in the development process. These tools empower developers to create more reliable and efficient software applications.

4.4 Performance Profiling

Performance profiling is a critical aspect of software development that allows developers to analyze and optimize the performance of their applications. Visual Studio provides a comprehensive set of performance profiling tools that help identify bottlenecks, memory leaks, and other performance-related issues. In this section, we will delve into the details of performance profiling in Visual Studio.

Types of Profiling

Visual Studio offers several types of profiling, each designed to address different aspects of an application's performance:

• **CPU Usage Profiling:** This type of profiling helps identify CPU-bound bottlenecks in your code. It provides information on which methods consume the most CPU time, allowing you to optimize those areas.

• **Memory Usage Profiling:** Memory profiling is crucial for identifying memory leaks and excessive memory usage. It provides insights into object allocation, deallocation, and memory consumption patterns.

• **.NET Object Allocation Profiling:** Specifically designed for managed .NET applications, this profiling type tracks object allocations and helps you understand memory allocation patterns.

• **Concurrency Profiling:** Concurrency profiling is used to identify synchronization and thread-related performance issues in multi-threaded applications.

Starting a Profiling Session

To start a profiling session in Visual Studio, follow these steps:

1. Go to the "Debug" menu.
2. Select "Performance Profiler."
3. Choose the type of profiling you want to perform (e.g., CPU Usage, Memory Usage).
4. Click the "Start" button to launch the profiling session.

Analyzing Profiling Data

Once a profiling session is complete, Visual Studio provides detailed reports and graphical representations of the collected data. These reports are invaluable for identifying performance issues and bottlenecks. Here are some key aspects of analyzing profiling data:

- **CPU Usage Report:** The CPU Usage report shows a breakdown of CPU time consumed by different methods in your code. It helps you identify which methods are CPU-intensive and may require optimization.

- **Memory Usage Report:** The Memory Usage report provides insights into memory allocation, deallocation, and memory consumption patterns. It helps you detect memory leaks and excessive memory usage.

- **.NET Object Allocation Report:** This report is specific to managed .NET applications and focuses on object allocations. It shows which types of objects are frequently allocated and can help optimize memory usage.

- **Concurrency Profiling Report:** Concurrency profiling reports help identify synchronization and threading issues. They provide information on thread contention and thread interactions.

Drill-Down and Analysis

In addition to high-level reports, Visual Studio allows you to drill down into the details of profiling data. You can explore individual methods, call stacks, and memory allocations to understand the root causes of performance issues.

Using Profiling Tools

Visual Studio's profiling tools provide various features for in-depth analysis:

- **Performance Markers:** You can add custom performance markers to your code using the System.Diagnostics.Stopwatch class. These markers help you measure the execution time of specific code sections.

- **Function Timing:** Profiling tools display the execution time of individual functions, making it easy to identify which functions are consuming the most time.

- **Memory Snapshots:** Memory profiling tools allow you to take memory snapshots during a profiling session. You can compare snapshots to detect memory leaks and track memory usage changes over time.

- **Concurrency Visualizer:** The Concurrency Visualizer provides a timeline view of thread activity, helping you understand how threads interact and where contention occurs.

Optimizing Performance

Once you have identified performance issues using profiling, you can work on optimizing your code. Some common optimization strategies include:

- **Algorithmic Improvements:** Review and optimize algorithms and data structures to reduce computational complexity.

- **Caching:** Implement caching mechanisms to reduce the need for repetitive calculations or data retrieval.

- **Resource Management:** Properly manage resources such as database connections, file handles, and network connections to avoid resource leaks.

- **Parallelization:** Utilize parallel programming techniques to leverage multi-core processors and improve execution speed.

- **Memory Management:** Address memory leaks and excessive memory usage by optimizing object lifetimes and memory allocation patterns.

Iterative Optimization

Performance optimization is often an iterative process. After making changes to address identified issues, it's essential to re-run profiling sessions to verify improvements and identify new bottlenecks. The goal is to achieve a balance between functionality and performance, ensuring that your application meets both requirements effectively.

In conclusion, performance profiling is a crucial step in the software development process, enabling developers to identify and address performance bottlenecks, memory leaks, and concurrency issues. Visual Studio's profiling tools provide valuable insights into an application's behavior, allowing developers to optimize code for better performance. By leveraging profiling reports, function timing data, and memory snapshots, developers can systematically improve their applications' performance and deliver high-quality software.

4.5 Advanced Debugging Techniques

In addition to basic debugging with breakpoints and step-by-step debugging, Visual Studio offers a range of advanced debugging techniques and tools to help developers diagnose complex issues and streamline the debugging process. In this section, we'll explore some of these advanced debugging techniques.

1. Conditional Breakpoints

Conditional breakpoints allow you to specify conditions under which a breakpoint should trigger. This is particularly useful when you want to break execution only when specific conditions are met, such as when a variable reaches a certain value. To set a conditional breakpoint, right-click on a breakpoint and choose "Condition." You can then define the condition that must be true for the breakpoint to pause execution.

Conditional breakpoints can significantly reduce the noise in your debugging sessions and help you focus on the critical moments in your code.

2. Hit Counts

Hit counts are another way to control when breakpoints trigger. With hit counts, you can specify that a breakpoint should only activate after it has been hit a certain number of times. This is valuable for debugging code that is executed multiple times, such as loops or recursive functions.

To set a hit count breakpoint, right-click on a breakpoint and choose "Hit Count." You can then specify the desired hit count, and the breakpoint will pause execution when that count is reached.

3. Tracepoints

Tracepoints allow you to log custom messages to the Output window or a file during debugging, without the need to break execution. You can use tracepoints to record information about the state of your application or the values of specific variables at certain points in your code.

To create a tracepoint, right-click on a line of code, choose "Insert Tracepoint," and enter the message you want to log. When the tracepoint is reached during debugging, the message will be displayed in the Output window or written to a file.

4. Edit and Continue

Edit and Continue is a powerful feature in Visual Studio that allows you to make code changes while debugging and apply those changes without restarting the debugging session. This feature can significantly speed up the debugging process when you need to make quick code adjustments.

To use Edit and Continue, simply edit your code while in a debugging session, and Visual Studio will automatically apply the changes without requiring you to stop and restart debugging.

5. Remote Debugging

Sometimes, you may need to debug an application running on a remote machine or device, such as a server or a mobile device. Visual Studio provides remote debugging tools that allow you to attach the debugger to a remote process and debug it as if it were running locally.

Remote debugging can be invaluable for troubleshooting issues in production environments or testing applications on different platforms.

6. IntelliTrace Debugging

IntelliTrace is a historical debugging tool that captures a detailed history of your application's execution, including function calls, variable values, and exceptions. With IntelliTrace, you can step backward in time to review the application's state at different points during execution.

IntelliTrace is particularly useful for diagnosing intermittent or hard-to-reproduce issues, as it provides a complete record of what happened in your application.

7. Time Travel Debugging

Time Travel Debugging (TTD) is an advanced debugging feature that allows you to record the execution of your application and replay it later for debugging purposes. With TTD, you can step forward and backward through the recorded execution, making it easier to pinpoint the root causes of complex issues.

TTD is particularly beneficial for debugging issues that occur over extended periods or in scenarios where reproducing the problem is difficult.

8. Performance Profiling

While performance profiling is not a debugging technique per se, it is an essential tool for diagnosing and optimizing performance-related issues in your code. Visual Studio's performance profiling tools, as discussed in previous sections, provide valuable insights into CPU usage, memory usage, and other performance metrics.

By using performance profiling alongside debugging, you can identify and address performance bottlenecks in your application effectively.

9. Live Unit Testing

Visual Studio's Live Unit Testing feature allows you to continuously run unit tests in the background as you write and modify your code. Live Unit Testing provides immediate feedback on the status of your unit tests, highlighting failed tests and code coverage in real-time.

By incorporating unit testing into your debugging workflow, you can catch and fix issues early in the development process, ensuring code quality and reliability.

In conclusion, Visual Studio offers a wide range of advanced debugging techniques and tools to help developers tackle complex issues, improve productivity, and optimize their code effectively. From conditional breakpoints and hit counts to tracepoints and Edit and Continue, these features empower developers to streamline the debugging process and gain deeper insights into their code's behavior. Additionally, remote debugging, IntelliTrace, and Time Travel Debugging enable developers to troubleshoot issues in various scenarios, including remote environments and hard-to-reproduce problems. By mastering these advanced debugging techniques, developers can become more proficient at identifying and resolving software issues efficiently.

Chapter 5: Visual Studio for Web Development

5.1 Setting Up for Web Projects

Web development is a fundamental part of modern software development, and Visual Studio provides robust tools and features for building web applications. In this section, we'll explore the initial setup and configuration required to start working on web projects in Visual Studio.

1. Installation and Project Templates

Before you can begin web development in Visual Studio, you need to ensure that you have the necessary components and tools installed. Visual Studio offers different editions, including Visual Studio Community, Visual Studio Professional, and Visual Studio Enterprise. Make sure you have the edition that supports web development.

During installation, you can select the workload "ASP.NET and web development" to install the required components and project templates for web development.

2. Project Types

Visual Studio supports various project types for web development, including:

- **ASP.NET Web Forms:** This project type is suitable for building web applications with a visual drag-and-drop interface for designing web pages.

- **ASP.NET MVC (Model-View-Controller):** MVC is a design pattern for building web applications that separates the application into three main components: Models (data), Views (UI), and Controllers (logic).

- **ASP.NET Core:** ASP.NET Core is a cross-platform framework for building modern, scalable web applications. It's highly suitable for cloud-based and containerized applications.

- **Node.js:** Visual Studio also provides tools for Node.js development, allowing you to build server-side applications using JavaScript or TypeScript.

3. Integrated Development Environment (IDE)

Once you've installed the necessary components and project templates, you can start working in the Visual Studio integrated development environment (IDE). The IDE provides features like code editing, debugging, project management, and a rich set of tools for web development.

4. Solution and Project Structure

In Visual Studio, web projects are organized within solutions, which can contain one or more projects. A solution typically represents the entire application, while projects within the solution may include web applications, class libraries, or other components.

The project structure may vary depending on the project type, but common elements in web projects include:

- **wwwroot:** This folder contains static web assets like HTML, CSS, JavaScript files, and images.

- **Controllers:** In ASP.NET MVC and ASP.NET Core projects, this folder contains controller classes that handle HTTP requests and responses.

- **Views:** This folder contains the UI templates and views that are rendered in response to user requests.

- **Models:** Models represent the data structures and business logic of the application.

- **Startup.cs:** In ASP.NET Core projects, this file contains configuration and startup logic for the application.

5. Package Management

Web development often involves using third-party libraries and packages. Visual Studio provides tools for managing these packages conveniently. NuGet is a package manager that integrates seamlessly with Visual Studio, allowing you to search for, install, and update packages directly from the IDE.

6. Debugging Web Applications

Debugging web applications in Visual Studio is similar to debugging other types of applications. You can set breakpoints in your code, inspect variables, and step through the execution flow. Additionally, Visual Studio includes features for debugging JavaScript and client-side code when building web applications.

7. Web Server Integration

Visual Studio includes an integrated development web server that can host your web applications during development. This server is suitable for testing and debugging your applications locally. For production deployment, you would typically use a production-grade web server like IIS (Internet Information Services) or host your application in the cloud.

8. Web Deployment

When it's time to deploy your web application, Visual Studio offers various options for web deployment. You can publish your application to a web server, a cloud platform like Azure, or package it as a container for deployment in container orchestration platforms like Docker and Kubernetes.

9. Version Control

Version control is essential for collaborative web development projects. Visual Studio provides built-in integration with popular version control systems like Git and Team Foundation Server (TFS). You can manage your source code, track changes, and collaborate with team members seamlessly.

10. Extensions and Add-ons

Visual Studio's extensibility allows you to enhance your web development workflow by adding extensions and add-ons from the Visual Studio Marketplace. These extensions can provide additional features, templates, and tools to streamline your web development tasks.

In summary, setting up for web projects in Visual Studio involves ensuring you have the right edition and components installed, selecting the appropriate project type, and familiarizing yourself with the IDE, project structure, and web development tools. Visual Studio provides a comprehensive environment for web development, making it a versatile choice for building web applications of varying complexity.

5.2 Understanding ASP.NET Framework

ASP.NET is a powerful web development framework provided by Microsoft for building dynamic and robust web applications. In this section, we will delve into the key concepts and components of ASP.NET Framework to help you understand how it works and how to leverage its features for web development in Visual Studio.

1. Introduction to ASP.NET

ASP.NET is a part of the broader .NET framework and is designed for building web applications and services. It provides a robust platform for creating web pages and web services using a variety of programming languages, including C# and VB.NET. ASP.NET applications can run on Windows servers and are known for their scalability and performance.

2. ASP.NET Page Lifecycle

Understanding the ASP.NET page lifecycle is crucial for web developers. Each web page in an ASP.NET application goes through a series of stages during its lifecycle, including initialization, loading, rendering, and unloading. Developers can hook into various events in this lifecycle to add custom logic, handle user input, and perform other tasks.

3. ASP.NET Controls

ASP.NET controls are reusable components that provide a rich and interactive user interface for web applications. They can be categorized into server controls and HTML controls. Server controls are ASP.NET-specific controls that run on the server and are rendered as HTML on the client side. HTML controls, on the other hand, are standard HTML elements that can be enhanced with server-side functionality.

4. State Management

ASP.NET offers several mechanisms for managing state in web applications. These include ViewState, Session State, Application State, and Cookies. ViewState allows you to maintain the state of controls on a page across postbacks. Session State and Application State store data on the server that can be accessed by multiple users. Cookies are small pieces of data stored on the client's browser.

5. ASP.NET Web Forms vs. ASP.NET MVC

ASP.NET offers two primary frameworks for building web applications: ASP.NET Web Forms and ASP.NET MVC (Model-View-Controller). Web Forms is a more traditional approach, where web pages are built with server controls and event-driven programming. MVC, on the other hand, follows the Model-View-Controller architectural pattern, providing greater control over the application's structure and behavior.

6. ASP.NET Web API

ASP.NET Web API is a framework for building HTTP services that can be consumed by various clients, including web browsers, mobile devices, and desktop applications. It is commonly used to create RESTful APIs that expose data and functionality over HTTP.

7. ASP.NET Routing

Routing is a critical aspect of modern web applications. ASP.NET provides a powerful routing engine that allows you to define URL patterns and map them to specific controllers and actions. This enables clean and user-friendly URLs and enhances the overall structure of your web application.

8. Data Access

Data access is a fundamental part of web development. ASP.NET offers various data access technologies, including ADO.NET, Entity Framework, and LINQ. These technologies allow you to connect to databases, retrieve and manipulate data, and interact with data models seamlessly.

9. Security in ASP.NET

Security is paramount in web development. ASP.NET provides robust security features, including authentication and authorization mechanisms, cross-site scripting (XSS) protection, input validation, and protection against common web vulnerabilities such as SQL injection and CSRF (Cross-Site Request Forgery).

10. Deployment

Once you have developed your ASP.NET web application, you need to deploy it to a web server for public access. Visual Studio simplifies the deployment process by providing various deployment options, including FTP, Web Deploy, and publishing to cloud platforms like Azure. You can also package your application as a Docker container for containerized deployment.

11. Visual Studio and ASP.NET

Visual Studio offers extensive support for ASP.NET development. It provides project templates, code scaffolding, debugging tools, and a rich set of extensions to enhance your ASP.NET development experience. Visual Studio's integrated development environment (IDE) streamlines the creation, testing, and deployment of ASP.NET web applications.

In conclusion, understanding ASP.NET Framework is essential for web developers using Visual Studio. ASP.NET provides a powerful and flexible platform for building web applications and services, offering features for state management, controls, data access, security, and more. Whether you choose ASP.NET Web Forms or ASP.NET MVC, Visual Studio's integration with ASP.NET simplifies the development process and accelerates the creation of dynamic and responsive web applications.

5.3 Web Forms vs. MVC: A Comparison

When developing web applications with Visual Studio and ASP.NET, you have two primary architectural choices: Web Forms and MVC (Model-View-Controller). Both approaches have their advantages and are suitable for different scenarios. In this section, we'll compare Web Forms and MVC to help you understand their differences and decide which one is the right fit for your project.

Web Forms

Web Forms is a mature and event-driven framework for building web applications in ASP.NET. It follows a component-based model, allowing developers to create web pages with a rich set of server controls, such as buttons, textboxes, and data grids. Here are some key characteristics of Web Forms:

1. **Stateful and Event-Driven:** Web Forms are stateful by default, meaning they automatically handle the maintenance of control values and their states across postbacks. Event-driven programming is a central concept, with server controls triggering server-side events for processing user interactions.
2. **Rapid Development:** Web Forms provide a rapid development experience, enabling developers to create web applications quickly. The visual designer in Visual Studio allows for drag-and-drop UI design.
3. **View State:** Web Forms rely on ViewState to maintain control state across postbacks. While ViewState simplifies development, it can lead to larger page sizes and increased bandwidth usage.
4. **Page Lifecycle:** Web Forms pages follow a specific lifecycle with events like Page_Load, Page_Init, and Page_PreRender, allowing developers to handle various aspects of page initialization, data binding, and rendering.
5. **Complex Event Handling:** Handling complex UI interactions and server events is straightforward in Web Forms, making it suitable for applications with rich, interactive user interfaces.
6. **Component Reusability:** Web Forms promote component reusability through user controls, custom controls, and third-party control libraries.

MVC (Model-View-Controller)

MVC is an architectural pattern that separates an application into three main components: Models (data and logic), Views (presentation layer), and Controllers (request processing and interaction between Model and View). ASP.NET MVC is an implementation of this pattern for web development. Here are some key characteristics of ASP.NET MVC:

1. **Stateless and Controller-Centric:** MVC follows a stateless and controller-centric approach, where controllers are responsible for processing requests and returning views. The framework doesn't automatically maintain control state across requests.
2. **Full Control Over HTML:** Developers have full control over HTML and markup in MVC, allowing for clean and customizable front-end code.
3. **URL Routing:** MVC uses URL routing, enabling developers to define custom URL patterns and map them to controller actions. This results in clean and SEO-friendly URLs.
4. **Testability:** MVC promotes testability by separating concerns and providing clear separation between the Model, View, and Controller. This makes unit testing easier and encourages good software design practices.
5. **Lightweight:** MVC is known for its lightweight and minimalistic approach, making it suitable for applications where performance and scalability are critical.
6. **RESTful Services:** ASP.NET MVC is well-suited for building RESTful services and APIs, allowing developers to expose data and functionality over HTTP.

Choosing Between Web Forms and MVC

The choice between Web Forms and MVC depends on your project requirements and development preferences:

- **Web Forms** is a suitable choice when you need to develop applications rapidly, especially when you have a complex, event-driven UI. It simplifies many aspects of web development and provides a visual design experience. Web Forms is often preferred for line-of-business applications and projects with tight deadlines.

- **MVC** is a better fit when you prioritize clean, maintainable code and want full control over the HTML markup. It is an excellent choice for applications where testability, scalability, and separation of concerns are critical. MVC is commonly used for public-facing websites, content-driven sites, and APIs.

In some cases, a hybrid approach is also possible, where you can use Web Forms for certain parts of your application and MVC for others, leveraging the strengths of both frameworks within the same project.

Ultimately, the choice between Web Forms and MVC should align with your project's goals, team expertise, and development philosophy. Each approach has its strengths, and Visual Studio provides robust support for both, allowing you to choose the one that best suits your needs.

5.4 Developing with JavaScript and TypeScript

When building web applications in Visual Studio, the integration of JavaScript and TypeScript plays a crucial role in enhancing the functionality and interactivity of your web pages. In this section, we'll explore the importance of JavaScript and TypeScript in web development and how Visual Studio supports these languages.

JavaScript in Web Development

JavaScript is a widely used scripting language for front-end web development. It allows developers to create dynamic and interactive web pages by manipulating HTML and CSS, handling user events, and communicating with back-end services. Here are some key aspects of using JavaScript in web development:

1. **Client-Side Interactivity:** JavaScript is primarily executed in the web browser, enabling client-side interactivity and real-time updates without requiring server round-trips.
2. **DOM Manipulation:** JavaScript can interact with the Document Object Model (DOM) to dynamically change the content, structure, and behavior of web pages. This makes it essential for creating responsive user interfaces.
3. **Event Handling:** JavaScript enables event-driven programming, allowing developers to respond to user actions, such as clicks, keypresses, and mouse movements, by executing custom code.
4. **Asynchronous Operations:** JavaScript supports asynchronous programming through features like callbacks, promises, and async/await. This is crucial for handling asynchronous tasks like fetching data from APIs.
5. **Third-Party Libraries:** JavaScript has a vast ecosystem of third-party libraries and frameworks, such as jQuery, React, Angular, and Vue.js, which simplify development tasks and enhance functionality.
6. **Cross-Browser Compatibility:** Visual Studio provides tools to ensure cross-browser compatibility by identifying and addressing issues that may arise due to differences in browser implementations of JavaScript.

TypeScript in Web Development

TypeScript is a superset of JavaScript that adds static typing and additional features to the language. It provides benefits such as improved code quality, better tooling support, and enhanced maintainability. Here's why TypeScript is valuable in web development:

1. **Static Typing:** TypeScript introduces static typing, allowing developers to declare variable types and catch type-related errors during development, reducing runtime errors.
2. **Enhanced Tooling:** Visual Studio offers excellent TypeScript integration, including code intelligence, type checking, and auto-completion, making development more productive.
3. **Strong IDE Support:** TypeScript benefits from Visual Studio's rich IDE features, including refactoring, navigation, and debugging, making it easier to work with large codebases.
4. **Modern JavaScript Features:** TypeScript supports modern JavaScript features and ECMAScript standards, ensuring compatibility with the latest web technologies.
5. **Type Definitions:** TypeScript uses type definitions (.d.ts files) to provide type information for third-party libraries, enabling better code validation and IntelliSense support.
6. **Transpilation:** TypeScript code is transpiled into JavaScript, making it compatible with all browsers and ensuring that your web applications run smoothly in various environments.

Visual Studio and JavaScript/TypeScript

Visual Studio provides robust support for JavaScript and TypeScript development, offering features like:

- **Syntax Highlighting:** Visual Studio's code editor provides syntax highlighting for JavaScript and TypeScript, making code more readable.

- **IntelliSense:** IntelliSense provides context-aware code suggestions, method signatures, and documentation tooltips, improving code productivity.

- **Debugging:** Visual Studio allows for interactive debugging of JavaScript and TypeScript code, with features like breakpoints, watch windows, and call stack navigation.

- **NPM Integration:** Visual Studio integrates with the Node Package Manager (NPM) for managing JavaScript and TypeScript packages, making it easy to install and update libraries.

- **Task Runners:** Visual Studio supports task runners like Grunt and Gulp, which are commonly used in front-end development for automating tasks such as minification and bundling of scripts and styles.

- **TypeScript Support:** Visual Studio offers dedicated support for TypeScript, including project templates, compilation settings, and TypeScript-specific tools.

In conclusion, JavaScript and TypeScript are indispensable languages in modern web development, enabling interactive and feature-rich web applications. Visual Studio provides a comprehensive development environment for working with these languages, offering code editing, debugging, tooling, and integration with third-party libraries. Whether you choose JavaScript for its flexibility or TypeScript for its type safety, Visual Studio enhances your web development workflow and helps you create responsive and high-quality web applications.

5.5 Web Debugging Tools

Effective debugging is a crucial aspect of web development in Visual Studio. Web applications often involve complex client-side code, asynchronous operations, and various browser-specific issues. In this section, we'll explore the web debugging tools provided by Visual Studio to help you identify and resolve issues in your web projects.

Browser Developer Tools Integration

Visual Studio offers seamless integration with popular web browsers' developer tools, such as Google Chrome, Mozilla Firefox, Microsoft Edge, and Internet Explorer. This integration allows you to debug and inspect client-side code directly from within Visual Studio. Here are some key features of this integration:

- **Debugging JavaScript:** You can set breakpoints, step through JavaScript code, and inspect variables and objects in your client-side scripts. Visual Studio's debugger is closely integrated with browser developer tools, providing a consistent debugging experience.

- **DOM Inspection:** You can inspect the Document Object Model (DOM) of your web page, view and manipulate HTML elements, and check CSS styles, making it easier to diagnose layout and rendering issues.

- **Network Monitoring:** Browser developer tools integrated into Visual Studio allow you to monitor network requests, view response data, and check for errors in AJAX requests and API calls.

- **Console Output:** You can access the browser's console output directly in Visual Studio, which is helpful for capturing and analyzing log messages and debugging JavaScript errors.

Remote Debugging

In addition to local debugging, Visual Studio supports remote debugging of web applications. This feature is particularly useful when you need to debug web applications deployed to remote servers or devices. Visual Studio provides tools to set up remote debugging sessions and attach to running processes, enabling you to diagnose issues in production environments.

Browser Compatibility Testing

Browser compatibility is a significant concern in web development. Visual Studio includes tools for testing web applications across multiple browsers and versions. You can use the browser debugging integration to switch between different browsers and simulate various browser environments, ensuring your web application works correctly for all users.

Page Inspector

Visual Studio's Page Inspector is a tool that helps you inspect and debug web pages directly in the development environment. It provides a live view of your web page, including HTML, CSS, and JavaScript, while allowing you to navigate through the page's structure and styles. Page Inspector simplifies the identification of layout and rendering issues and streamlines the debugging process.

Profiling and Performance Analysis

Web debugging isn't limited to identifying issues; it also includes optimizing and improving the performance of your web applications. Visual Studio offers profiling and performance analysis tools that help you identify bottlenecks, memory leaks, and performance problems in your code. You can use these tools to enhance the overall user experience of your web applications.

Browser Extensions and Add-Ons

Visual Studio supports browser extensions and add-ons that enhance web debugging capabilities. These extensions, often available from the Visual Studio Marketplace, provide additional tools for analyzing and troubleshooting web applications. Some extensions offer features like automated testing, code validation, and performance monitoring.

Continuous Integration and Testing

Web debugging doesn't end with development; it extends to continuous integration and testing. Visual Studio supports integrating web debugging into your continuous integration (CI) and continuous deployment (CD) pipelines, allowing you to automate testing and debugging as part of your development workflow.

Advanced Debugging Techniques

Advanced debugging techniques, such as conditional breakpoints, watch windows, and memory profiling, are available in Visual Studio. These techniques help you pinpoint issues in your web applications more effectively and efficiently. You can set conditions for breakpoints, monitor specific variables, and analyze memory usage to identify and resolve complex problems.

In summary, Visual Studio provides a comprehensive set of web debugging tools and features that streamline the process of identifying and resolving issues in web applications. The integration with browser developer tools, remote debugging capabilities, compatibility testing, and performance analysis tools make Visual Studio a robust choice for web developers who need to ensure the quality, reliability, and performance of their web projects. By leveraging these tools, you can optimize your web applications and provide an exceptional user experience.

Chapter 6: Visual Studio for Desktop Application Development

6.1 Building Windows Forms Applications

In this section, we will delve into the world of building Windows Forms applications using Visual Studio. Windows Forms, also known as WinForms, is a graphical user interface (GUI) framework provided by Microsoft for creating Windows desktop applications. It allows developers to design and build rich, interactive desktop applications with a wide range of controls and components.

Creating a Windows Forms Project

To get started with Windows Forms development in Visual Studio, follow these steps:

1. **Open Visual Studio:** Launch Visual Studio and select "Create a new project."
2. **Choose Project Template:** In the "Create a new project" dialog, search for "Windows Forms App (.NET Core)" in the template search box. Select this template as the basis for your project.
3. **Configure Project:** Specify the project name, location, and solution name. You can also choose the target framework and authentication type if applicable. Click "Create" to generate the project.
4. **Design the User Interface:** Visual Studio will create a default Windows Form for you. You can now design your application's user interface by dragging and dropping controls from the toolbox onto the form. Customize the properties of these controls using the Properties window.
5. **Write Code:** To add functionality to your Windows Forms application, double-click on a control to generate an event handler and write code in C# or VB.NET. For example, you can write code to handle button clicks, text input, and more.

Working with Controls

Windows Forms provides a wide variety of controls that you can use to build your application's user interface. Some common controls include buttons, textboxes, labels, checkboxes, radio buttons, list boxes, and more. These controls can be customized in terms of appearance and behavior to meet your application's requirements.

For instance, you can set the properties of a button control to change its text, size, and color. You can also wire up event handlers to respond to user interactions with the control. Here's an example of handling a button click event in C#:

```
private void button1_Click(object sender, EventArgs e)

{

MessageBox.Show("Button clicked!");

}
```

Layout and Design

Visual Studio provides a drag-and-drop interface for designing the layout of your Windows Forms. You can use layout panels such as FlowLayoutPanel, TableLayoutPanel, and SplitContainer to arrange controls neatly on your form. These panels help create responsive and organized UIs.

Data Binding

Windows Forms applications often work with data from various sources, such as databases or APIs. Visual Studio offers data-binding features that simplify the process of connecting controls to data sources. You can bind controls like DataGridViews and ComboBoxes to data tables or collections, making it easy to display and manipulate data in your application.

Debugging and Testing

Visual Studio provides robust debugging capabilities for Windows Forms applications. You can set breakpoints, inspect variables, and step through your code to identify and fix issues. Additionally, you can use the integrated Test Explorer to run unit tests and ensure the reliability of your application.

Deployment

Once you've developed your Windows Forms application, Visual Studio assists with deployment. You can create installation packages (MSI files) to distribute your application to end-users. Visual Studio simplifies the process of creating installer packages, ensuring a smooth deployment experience.

In conclusion, Visual Studio offers a powerful environment for building Windows Forms applications. With its integrated design tools, extensive control library, and debugging support, you can create feature-rich desktop applications for Windows with ease. Whether you're developing small utilities or complex business applications, Windows Forms in Visual Studio provides the tools you need to succeed.

6.2 Working with WPF

In this section, we will explore working with Windows Presentation Foundation (WPF) in Visual Studio. WPF is a modern and powerful UI framework for building Windows desktop applications. It offers a rich set of features, including flexible layout, data binding, styles, templates, and animations, allowing developers to create visually appealing and responsive applications.

Creating a WPF Project

To start working with WPF in Visual Studio, follow these steps:

1. **Open Visual Studio:** Launch Visual Studio and select "Create a new project."
2. **Choose Project Template:** In the "Create a new project" dialog, search for "WPF App (.NET Core)" in the template search box. Select this template as the basis for your project.
3. **Configure Project:** Specify the project name, location, and solution name. You can also choose the target framework and authentication type if applicable. Click "Create" to generate the project.
4. **Design the User Interface:** Visual Studio will create a default WPF window for you. You can design your application's user interface using XAML (Extensible Application Markup Language). XAML allows you to define the layout and appearance of controls in a declarative way. You can also use the Design view in Visual Studio to visually design your UI.

XAML and Declarative UI

XAML is the language used to define the user interface in WPF applications. It separates the UI definition from the application logic, promoting a clean and maintainable code structure. Here's an example of a simple XAML layout:

```
<Window x:Class="MyWpfApp.MainWindow"

xmlns="http://schemas.microsoft.com/winfx/2006/xaml/presentation"

xmlns:x="http://schemas.microsoft.com/winfx/2006/xaml"
```

```
Title="My WPF App" Height="350" Width="525">

<Grid>

<TextBlock Text="Hello, WPF!" HorizontalAlignment="Center" VerticalAlignment="Center"/>

</Grid>

</Window>
```

In this example, we define a window containing a Grid layout with a TextBlock control that displays “Hello, WPF!” in the center of the window.

Data Binding in WPF

WPF provides robust data-binding capabilities, allowing you to connect UI elements to data sources. You can bind controls to properties, collections, or data contexts, making it easy to display and update data dynamically. Data binding simplifies the synchronization of UI and data, reducing the need for manual updates.

```
<TextBlock Text="{Binding Username}" />
```

In this example, the TextBlock's Text property is bound to a property called Username in the data context. When the Username property changes, the TextBlock automatically updates its text.

Styles and Templates

WPF supports the creation of styles and templates for controls, enabling consistent and customizable UI designs. You can define styles for various controls, specifying properties like fonts, colors, and margins. Templates allow you to completely redefine the visual structure of controls.

<**Style** TargetType="Button">

<**Setter** Property="Background" Value="Blue"/>

<**Setter** Property="Foreground" Value="White"/>

</**Style**>

This style sets the background of all buttons to blue and the text color to white.

Animation and Visual Effects

WPF provides a powerful animation framework for adding dynamic behavior to your UI. You can create animations for properties like size, position, opacity, and more. Additionally, WPF supports visual effects such as drop shadows, gradients, and transparency to enhance the visual appeal of your application.

Debugging and Testing

Visual Studio offers comprehensive debugging and testing tools for WPF applications. You can set breakpoints, inspect XAML, and debug data binding issues. Additionally, you can use the integrated Test Explorer to run unit tests and ensure the reliability of your application.

Deployment

Deploying a WPF application is made easier with Visual Studio's publishing capabilities. You can create installer packages (MSI files) to distribute your application to end-users. Visual Studio assists in creating deployment packages that include all required dependencies, ensuring a smooth installation process.

In summary, Windows Presentation Foundation (WPF) in Visual Studio empowers developers to create modern and visually appealing desktop applications. With XAML for declarative UI, data binding, styles, animations, and a robust set of debugging tools, WPF provides a powerful framework for building Windows desktop applications that meet the demands of today's users. Whether you're designing business applications or consumer-facing software, WPF offers the flexibility and features you need to succeed.

6.3 Understanding XAML

In this section, we will dive into Extensible Application Markup Language (XAML), a crucial aspect of Windows Presentation Foundation (WPF) development in Visual Studio. XAML is a markup language used to define the user interface (UI) and structure of WPF applications. It provides a declarative way to design and layout controls, making it easier to separate the presentation layer from the application's logic.

Declarative UI Design

XAML stands out for its declarative nature, allowing developers and designers to describe the UI elements and their properties in a structured manner. This approach promotes a clear separation of concerns, with the UI design residing in XAML files while application logic is typically written in code-behind files (e.g., C# or VB.NET).

Here's a simple XAML example that defines a WPF window with a button:

```
<Window x:Class="MyWpfApp.MainWindow"

xmlns="http://schemas.microsoft.com/winfx/2006/xaml/presentation"

xmlns:x="http://schemas.microsoft.com/winfx/2006/xaml"

Title="My WPF App" Height="350" Width="525">

<Grid>

<Button Content="Click Me" HorizontalAlignment="Center" VerticalAlignment="Center"/>

</Grid>

</Window>
```

In this snippet, we declare a Window containing a Grid layout with a Button control. We specify properties such as the window's title, size, and button content in a clear and readable manner.

Hierarchical Structure

XAML documents have a hierarchical structure that mirrors the layout of UI elements. Elements are nested inside other elements, creating a tree-like structure that represents the UI's composition. This hierarchy is crucial for organizing the visual components of an application.

```
<Window>

<Grid>

<Button/>

<TextBox/>
```

</Grid>

</Window>

In this example, the Window contains a Grid, which, in turn, contains a Button and a TextBox. This structure helps define the relationship between UI elements and their placement on the screen.

Property Elements and Attributes

In XAML, you can set properties for elements using either property elements or attributes. Property elements allow you to set a property's value within the element's opening and closing tags. Attributes, on the other hand, set property values directly within an element's opening tag.

<Button>

<Button.Content>

Click Me

</Button.Content>

</Button>

In this example, we set the Button's Content property using a property element. Alternatively, you can set it as an attribute:

<Button Content="Click Me"/>

Both approaches are valid and serve the same purpose.

Data Binding in XAML

XAML provides robust support for data binding, allowing you to connect UI elements to data sources. You can bind controls to properties, collections, and data contexts, making it easy to display and update data dynamically in your application's UI.

```
<TextBlock Text="{Binding UserName}" />
```

In this example, the TextBlock's Text property is bound to the UserName property in the data context. When the UserName property changes, the TextBlock automatically updates its text.

Resources and Styles

XAML allows you to define resources, such as colors, brushes, and templates, which can be reused throughout your application. This approach promotes consistency and maintainability in UI design.

```
<Window.Resources>

<Style TargetType="Button">

<Setter Property="Background" Value="Blue"/>

<Setter Property="Foreground" Value="White"/>

</Style>

</Window.Resources>
```

In this snippet, we define a style for all Button controls in the Window's resources. This style sets the background color to blue and the text color to white for all buttons, ensuring a consistent look and feel.

XAML in Visual Studio

Visual Studio provides a user-friendly XAML editor that offers features like code completion, syntax highlighting, and a visual designer. This editor simplifies the process of creating and editing

XAML files, making it accessible to both experienced developers and designers.

In conclusion, XAML is a fundamental aspect of WPF development in Visual Studio, offering a declarative way to define the UI structure and design. Its hierarchical structure, support for data binding, resources, and styles make it a powerful tool for building modern Windows desktop applications. Whether you're creating a simple user interface or a complex application, understanding XAML is essential for WPF development in Visual Studio.

6.4 Leveraging User Controls and Components

In this section, we will explore the concept of user controls and components in Windows Presentation Foundation (WPF) development using Visual Studio. User controls and components are essential building blocks for creating modular and reusable parts of your WPF applications. They enable you to encapsulate functionality, promote code reusability, and maintain a structured and organized codebase.

What are User Controls?

A user control is a custom, reusable UI element that you create by combining existing WPF controls and defining their behavior and appearance. User controls are an excellent way to encapsulate a specific piece of functionality or a UI element that you want to reuse across multiple parts of your application.

Creating a user control typically involves defining the layout and behavior of the control using XAML and code-behind. Once created, you can easily reuse the user control in different windows or pages of your application.

Creating User Controls

To create a user control in Visual Studio, follow these steps:

1. **Right-click on your project** in the Solution Explorer and select "Add" > "New Item."
2. In the "Add New Item" dialog, **select "User Control (WPF)"** from the list of item templates.
3. **Specify a name** for your user control, and Visual Studio will generate two files: a XAML file for defining the control's layout and a code-behind file for implementing its behavior.
4. Customize the XAML and code-behind files to create the desired functionality and appearance for your user control.

Example of a User Control

Let's create a simple user control that displays a customizable message using XAML and C#. Here's the XAML code for the user control:

```
<UserControl x:Class="MyWpfApp.MessageControl"

xmlns="http://schemas.microsoft.com/winfx/2006/xaml/presentation"

xmlns:x="http://schemas.microsoft.com/winfx/2006/xaml">

<Grid>

<TextBlock x:Name="messageText" HorizontalAlignment="Center" VerticalAlignment="Center" FontSize="16"/>

</Grid>
```

```
</UserControl>
```

In this XAML, we define a TextBlock element to display the message, and we give it the name "messageText" for later reference.

Next, let's add code-behind to customize the behavior of the user control:

```
using System.Windows;

using System.Windows.Controls;

namespace MyWpfApp

{

public partial class MessageControl : UserControl

{

public MessageControl()

{

InitializeComponent();

}

public string Message

{

get { return messageText.Text; }

set { messageText.Text = value; }

}

}
```

```
}
```

In the code-behind, we create a property called “Message” that allows us to set and get the message displayed by the user control.

Using the User Control

Now that we have created the MessageControl user control, we can easily use it in our main window or any other XAML file by including it as follows:

```
<Window x:Class="MyWpfApp.MainWindow"

xmlns="http://schemas.microsoft.com/winfx/2006/xaml/presentation"

xmlns:x="http://schemas.microsoft.com/winfx/2006/xaml"

xmlns:local="clr-namespace:MyWpfApp"

Title="Main Window" Height="350" Width="525">

<Grid>

<local:MessageControl Message="Hello, User Control!" HorizontalAlignment="Center" VerticalAlignment="Center"/>

</Grid>

</Window>
```

In this example, we reference the MessageControl user control using the “local” namespace and set its “Message” property to display the message “Hello, User Control!”

Advantages of User Controls

User controls offer several advantages in WPF development:

- **Reusability:** You can reuse user controls across multiple parts of your application, promoting code reusability and maintainability.

- **Encapsulation:** User controls encapsulate functionality, making it easier to manage and understand complex UI elements.

- **Separation of Concerns:** By dividing your UI into user controls, you can separate the presentation layer (XAML) from the logic (code-behind), improving code organization.

- **Customization:** User controls allow you to create custom, self-contained components with customizable properties and behaviors.

What are Custom Components?

Custom components, also known as custom controls, are a more advanced form of encapsulation in WPF. Unlike user controls, which are typically composed of existing WPF controls, custom components are created from scratch and provide a higher level of customization.

Custom components are defined entirely in code, and they can have a more complex API and behavior. Creating custom components is more involved than user controls and often requires a deeper understanding of WPF's control template system.

When to Use User Controls vs. Custom Components

In practice, the choice between user controls and custom components depends on your application's requirements:

- Use **user controls** when you want to encapsulate and reuse a specific piece of UI functionality and you are comfortable with using XAML and code-behind.

- Use **custom components** when you need complete control over the control's appearance and behavior and are willing to invest the effort in creating them from scratch.

In conclusion, user controls and custom components are valuable tools in WPF development in Visual Studio. They allow you to encapsulate, reuse, and organize UI functionality effectively. By choosing the appropriate approach for your needs, you can create modular and maintainable WPF applications.

6.5 Packaging and Deployment

Packaging and deployment are crucial aspects of Visual Studio application development, especially when it comes to distributing your Windows desktop applications to end-users. In this section, we will explore the steps and best practices for packaging and deploying your applications effectively.

Packaging Your Application

Before deploying your application, you need to package it into a format that can be easily distributed. Visual Studio provides tools and options for creating installation packages and distributing your application.

ClickOnce Deployment

ClickOnce is a deployment technology that allows you to publish your Windows application to a web server or network file share. Users can then install and update the application with a single click. ClickOnce deployments can be configured to automatically check for updates and apply them as needed.

To create a ClickOnce deployment:

1. Right-click on your project in Solution Explorer and select "Properties."
2. Navigate to the "Publish" tab and configure your deployment settings, including the publishing location, updates, and prerequisites.
3. Click "Publish Now" to generate the deployment files.

Windows Installer (MSI)

Another common method for packaging Windows applications is to create a Windows Installer package (MSI). Visual Studio allows you to create MSI installers using tools like WiX (Windows Installer XML) or third-party installer creators.

To create an MSI installer with WiX:

1. Install WiX Toolset, which provides the necessary tools for creating MSI installers.
2. Create a WiX project in your Visual Studio solution.
3. Define the components, features, and installation behavior in the WiX project.
4. Build the WiX project to generate the MSI installer.

Distributing Your Application

Once you have packaged your application, you need to distribute it to end-users. Here are some common distribution methods:

Web Deployment

You can distribute your application through a website or a web server. This is particularly convenient for ClickOnce deployments. Users can simply navigate to a web page, click a link, and install the application directly from the web.

Network Share

If your organization has a network share or file server, you can place the deployment files there. Users can access the share and install the application by running the setup executable.

Physical Media

For distributing applications to users who may not have internet access, you can use physical media like DVDs or USB drives. Create an installer package and copy it to the physical media for distribution.

App Stores

If your application is intended for a broader audience, consider publishing it on app stores like the Microsoft Store. App stores provide a centralized platform for users to discover and install applications.

Versioning and Updates

When distributing your application, it's essential to consider versioning and updates. You should have a versioning strategy in place to track different releases of your application. This helps users and administrators identify the version they are using and facilitates updates.

ClickOnce Updates

For ClickOnce deployments, you can configure automatic update checks. When users launch the application, ClickOnce can check for updates on the server and apply them if available. This ensures that users are always running the latest version.

Version Numbering

Use a consistent version numbering scheme (e.g., Semantic Versioning) for your application. Update the version number in the deployment manifest or MSI installer with each release.

Digital Signing

To ensure the integrity and authenticity of your application, consider digitally signing it with a code signing certificate. Digital signatures assure users that the application hasn't been tampered with and that it comes from a trusted source.

Installation Prerequisites

When creating your installer package, consider the prerequisites for your application. Ensure that users have the required software components and dependencies installed on their systems. You can include these prerequisites in your installer package or provide links for users to download them.

Testing and Compatibility

Before deploying your application to a wide audience, thoroughly test it on different Windows versions and configurations. Ensure that it runs smoothly and doesn't encounter compatibility issues.

Documentation and Support

Finally, provide clear documentation and support channels for your users. Include instructions for installation, troubleshooting common issues, and contact information for support. User-friendly documentation can enhance the user experience and reduce support requests.

In conclusion, packaging and deploying your Windows desktop application in Visual Studio require careful planning and attention to detail. By following best practices, you can ensure a smooth and reliable distribution process, allowing users to access and enjoy your application with ease.

7.1 Integrating Databases

In this section, we will delve into the essential topic of integrating databases into your Visual Studio projects. Databases are a fundamental component of many software applications, and Visual Studio provides robust tools and features for working with databases seamlessly.

Database Types

Visual Studio supports various types of databases, including:

- **SQL Server**: Microsoft SQL Server is a popular relational database management system (RDBMS) that integrates seamlessly with Visual Studio. You can create and manage SQL Server databases, write SQL queries, and develop database-driven applications within Visual Studio.

- **SQLite**: SQLite is a lightweight, file-based database engine that is often used in mobile and desktop applications. Visual Studio includes tools for working with SQLite databases, making it easy to create and manage them.

- **Entity Framework**: Entity Framework is an Object-Relational Mapping (ORM) framework that simplifies database access in .NET applications. Visual Studio provides extensive support for Entity Framework, enabling you to model your database schema using code and interact with it using C# or VB.NET.

- **Other Databases**: Visual Studio also offers tools and extensions for working with other databases like MySQL, PostgreSQL, and Oracle, allowing you to integrate these databases into your projects.

Connecting to Databases

To integrate a database into your Visual Studio project, you need to establish a connection to the database server. Here are the general steps:

1. **Create a Database Connection**: Visual Studio provides wizards and dialogs to create database connections. You can specify the database server, authentication method,

and credentials.

2. **Database Explorer**: Once connected, you can access the Database Explorer in Visual Studio. It provides a graphical interface to explore the database schema, tables, views, and stored procedures.
3. **Data Connections**: In the Server Explorer or Solution Explorer, you can view and manage your database connections. You can also add new connections or modify existing ones as needed.

Data Access

Visual Studio offers several methods for accessing and manipulating data in databases:

- **SQL Server Data Tools (SSDT)**: SSDT is an integrated toolset for database development. You can use it to create, modify, and deploy SQL Server databases and their objects. It also supports schema comparisons and data comparisons.

- **Entity Framework**: Entity Framework simplifies data access by providing an object-oriented interface to databases. You can create data models using Entity Framework and perform CRUD (Create, Read, Update, Delete) operations using C# or VB.NET code.

- **LINQ to SQL**: LINQ to SQL is another ORM framework that integrates with Visual Studio. It allows you to use LINQ (Language-Integrated Query) to query and manipulate database data directly from your code.

Database Projects

Visual Studio allows you to create Database Projects, which are specialized project types for managing database schema and objects. With Database Projects, you can:

- Define the structure of your database using SQL scripts and schemas.
- Version-control your database schema, enabling collaboration and change tracking.
- Generate deployment scripts to update databases in various environments (development, staging, production).

Data Tools

Visual Studio includes a set of Data Tools that enhance your database development experience. These tools provide features such as:

- Database schema comparison and synchronization to keep database structures in sync across environments.
- Data comparisons to identify and synchronize differences in data between databases.
- SQL Server Object Explorer for managing SQL Server databases and objects.

Database Debugging

Visual Studio also supports database debugging, allowing you to set breakpoints in stored procedures, functions, and triggers. You can step through your database code to diagnose and fix issues.

Conclusion

Integrating databases into your Visual Studio projects is essential for building data-driven applications. Visual Studio provides a rich set of tools and features that simplify database development, data access, and database project management. Whether you are working with SQL Server, SQLite, or other databases, Visual Studio offers the tools you need to streamline your database-related tasks.

7.2 SQL Server and Entity Framework

SQL Server and Entity Framework are powerful tools for database management and data access in Visual Studio. In this section, we'll explore how to work with SQL Server databases using Entity Framework, a popular Object-Relational Mapping (ORM) framework that simplifies database interactions in .NET applications.

Introduction to Entity Framework

Entity Framework (EF) is an ORM framework that allows developers to work with databases using object-oriented code. Instead of writing raw SQL queries, you can interact with the database using C# or VB.NET classes and LINQ queries.

Here are the key components of Entity Framework:

- **Entity Data Model (EDM)**: EDM represents the conceptual model of your database. It includes entities (objects that correspond to database tables) and their relationships.

- **Entity Framework Provider**: EF uses a provider to connect to a specific database. For SQL Server, you'll use the SQL Server provider.

- **DbContext**: DbContext is a class that represents the database session. It is responsible for querying and saving data to the database.

Setting Up Entity Framework with SQL Server

To work with Entity Framework and SQL Server, follow these steps:

1. **Install Entity Framework**: If Entity Framework is not already installed in your project, you can add it using NuGet Package Manager. Open the Package Manager Console and run the following command:

```
Install-Package EntityFramework
```

1. **Create a DbContext**: Create a class that inherits from DbContext. This class represents your database context and includes properties that correspond to your database tables.

```
public class MyDbContext : DbContext
{
public DbSet<Customer> Customers { get; set; }
public DbSet<Order> Orders { get; set; }
}
```

1. **Connection String**: In your project's configuration file

(usually app.config or web.config), define a connection string that specifies the SQL Server database server and credentials:

```
<connectionStrings>

<add name="MyDbContext"

connectionString="Server=YourServer;Database=YourDatabase;Us
Id=YourUsername;Password=YourPassword;"

providerName="System.Data.SqlClient" />

</connectionStrings>
```

1. **Querying Data**: You can use LINQ queries to retrieve data from the database:

```
using (var context = new MyDbContext())

{

var customers = context.Customers.Where(c => c.City
== "New York").ToList();

}
```

1. **Saving Data**: Entity Framework makes it easy to insert, update, and delete records in the database:

```
using (var context = new MyDbContext())

{
```

```
var newCustomer = new Customer { Name = "John Smith", City = "Los Angeles" };

context.Customers.Add(newCustomer);

context.SaveChanges();

}
```

Code-First vs. Database-First

Entity Framework supports two main development approaches: Code-First and Database-First.

- **Code-First**: In Code-First development, you define your data model in code, and Entity Framework generates the database schema based on your model.
- **Database-First**: In Database-First development, you start with an existing database, and Entity Framework generates the data model and classes that represent database tables.

You can choose the approach that best suits your project requirements.

Migrations

Entity Framework Migrations allow you to evolve your database schema over time without losing data. You can create and apply migrations to update the database schema as your application evolves.

Conclusion

Integrating SQL Server databases with Entity Framework in Visual Studio offers a convenient and efficient way to work with databases in .NET applications. By defining your data model using C# classes and utilizing LINQ queries, you can streamline data access and database management tasks. Whether you prefer Code-First or Database-First development, Entity Framework provides the flexibility and tools you need to work seamlessly with SQL Server databases.

7.3 Managing Database Connections

In this section, we will explore how to effectively manage database connections in Visual Studio when working with databases. Managing database connections is crucial for ensuring the stability and performance of your applications.

Connection Pooling

Visual Studio, in combination with ADO.NET, implements a feature called connection pooling. Connection pooling is a mechanism that manages and recycles database connections to optimize performance. Instead of opening and closing a new database connection for each database operation, connection pooling allows you to reuse existing connections from a pool.

Here's how connection pooling works:

1. When your application requests a database connection, ADO.NET checks if there is an available connection in the pool.
2. If an idle connection is available, it is retrieved from the pool and assigned to your application.

3. After your application finishes using the connection, it is not immediately closed. Instead, it is returned to the pool for future use.
4. If the pool reaches its maximum size or if a connection becomes invalid, new connections are created and added to the pool.

This pooling mechanism reduces the overhead of opening and closing connections, improving database access performance.

Connection Strings

A critical aspect of managing database connections is configuring connection strings. A connection string is a string that specifies how to connect to a database server. It includes information such as the server's address, authentication credentials, and database name.

Here is an example of a SQL Server connection string:

Server=myServerAddress;Database=myDatabase;User Id=myUsername;Password=myPassword;

In Visual Studio, connection strings are typically stored in configuration files like app.config or web.config for easy maintenance. You can use different connection strings for development, testing, and production environments, allowing flexibility in managing database connections.

Connection State Management

When working with database connections in Visual Studio, it's essential to manage the connection state properly. A connection can be in one of the following states:

- **Open**: The connection is open and can be used to execute commands against the database.
- **Closed**: The connection is closed and cannot be used to execute commands. It needs to be explicitly opened before use.
- **Broken**: The connection is no longer valid and cannot be used. It may become broken due to various reasons, such as a network issue.

To manage connection state, you should follow these best practices:

- Open the connection just before executing a database command and close it as soon as you are done.
- Use the using statement to ensure that the connection is properly disposed of, even if an exception occurs.
- Implement error handling to handle situations where the connection becomes broken.

Connection Resilience

In real-world applications, database servers may experience occasional downtime or network issues. To make your applications more resilient to such situations, consider implementing features like retry policies and connection timeouts.

A retry policy automatically attempts to reconnect to the database if a connection attempt fails. You can configure the number of retries and the delay between retries to suit your application's requirements.

Additionally, setting a connection timeout ensures that your application doesn't hang indefinitely if it cannot establish a connection to the database. It specifies the maximum time your application will wait for a connection before giving up and raising an error.

Conclusion

Managing database connections in Visual Studio is a critical aspect of building robust and performant database-driven applications. By understanding connection pooling, configuring connection strings, and implementing proper connection state management, you can ensure that your applications work seamlessly with databases. Additionally, considering connection resilience techniques enhances the reliability of your applications in the face of database server issues.

7.4 Using LINQ for Data Queries

LINQ (Language-Integrated Query) is a powerful feature in Visual Studio that allows you to query data from various data sources using a unified syntax. LINQ can be used with databases, collections, XML, and more. In this section, we'll focus on using LINQ for data queries with databases, particularly SQL Server, in Visual Studio.

Introduction to LINQ

LINQ is a set of language extensions that provide a more readable and concise way to query data. It allows you to express queries directly in C# or VB.NET code, making it easier to work with data in your applications.

The key components of LINQ include:

- **Data Source**: The source of data you want to query, such as a database, collection, or XML document.

- **LINQ Query**: The query expression that defines the data you want to retrieve or manipulate.

- **Query Execution**: The execution of the LINQ query to retrieve or manipulate data from the data source.

LINQ to SQL

LINQ to SQL is a specific implementation of LINQ that enables you to work with SQL Server databases seamlessly. It provides a mapping between your C# or VB.NET classes and database tables, allowing you to write LINQ queries using strongly-typed objects.

Here's how you can use LINQ to SQL in Visual Studio:

1. **Data Context Class**: Create a data context class that represents the database. This class inherits from DataContext and contains properties that represent database tables.

```
public class MyDataContext : DataContext

{

public Table<Customer> Customers;

public Table<Order> Orders;

public MyDataContext(string connectionString) : base(connectionString) { }

}
```

1. **Querying Data**: You can use LINQ queries to retrieve data from the database using your data context class.

```
using (var context = new MyDataContext(connectionString))
{
var query = from c in context.Customers
where c.City == "New York"
select c;
var results = query.ToList();
}
```

1. **Updating Data**: LINQ to SQL also allows you to update data in the database using your strongly-typed objects.

```
using (var context = new MyDataContext(connectionString))
{
var customer = context.Customers.Single(c => c.CustomerID == 1);
customer.City = "Los Angeles";
context.SubmitChanges();
}
```

LINQ to Entity Framework

In addition to LINQ to SQL, you can use LINQ with Entity Framework, as mentioned in previous sections. Entity Framework offers even more flexibility in working with databases and allows you to work with different database providers, including SQL Server, MySQL, and SQLite.

Benefits of LINQ

The benefits of using LINQ for data queries in Visual Studio include:

- Readable and expressive code: LINQ queries are more human-readable and maintainable compared to traditional SQL queries.

- Strongly-typed queries: LINQ allows you to use strongly-typed objects, reducing the risk of runtime errors.

- Integration with Visual Studio: Visual Studio provides tools and IntelliSense support for writing and debugging LINQ queries.

- Portability: LINQ queries can be easily adapted to work with different data sources, reducing development effort when switching databases.

Conclusion

Using LINQ for data queries in Visual Studio provides a powerful and efficient way to work with data, especially when interacting with SQL Server databases. Whether you choose LINQ to SQL or LINQ to Entity Framework, you can write queries that are easy to read, maintain, and debug. LINQ's integration with Visual Studio enhances your development experience and helps you build robust database-driven applications.

7.5 Database Project Management

In Visual Studio, database project management is an essential aspect of database development. A database project is a specialized project type that allows you to design, develop, and maintain your database schema, including tables, views, stored procedures, and other database objects. This section covers key aspects of managing database projects in Visual Studio.

Creating a Database Project

To start managing your database in Visual Studio, you can create a new database project:

1. **Create Project**: Open Visual Studio, go to File > New > Project, and select the "SQL Server Database Project" template.
2. **Configure Connection**: In the project properties, configure the database connection to your target SQL Server instance. This connection is used for schema comparisons and deployment.
3. **Import Existing Database**: If you already have an existing database, you can import its schema into the project by using the "Import Database" feature.

Schema Design and Development

Once you have a database project, you can design and develop your database schema using Visual Studio's powerful tools:

- **Table Design**: Create tables, define columns, primary keys, foreign keys, and constraints using a visual designer.

• **Views and Stored Procedures**: Design and manage views and stored procedures with SQL scripts.

• **Schema Comparison**: Visual Studio allows you to compare your database project with a target database, identify differences, and generate update scripts.

• **Version Control**: You can use version control systems like Git to manage changes to your database project, enabling collaboration and tracking changes over time.

Deploying Database Changes

Deploying database changes is a crucial part of database project management. Visual Studio provides tools to generate deployment scripts and publish changes to your target database:

1. **Generate Scripts**: You can generate deployment scripts for your database project to review and execute manually or include in your deployment pipeline.
2. **Publish Profile**: Create a publish profile to specify deployment settings, including the target database, authentication, and deployment options.
3. **Publish Database**: Use the publish profile to deploy changes to the target database. Visual Studio will generate and execute the necessary SQL scripts to bring the target database in sync with your project's schema.
4. **Database Lifecycle**: Visual Studio supports various stages of the database development lifecycle, such as development, testing, staging, and production, allowing you to manage database changes at each stage.

Data Scripting and Seeding

In addition to schema management, you can use Visual Studio to script and seed data in your database:

- **Data Scripts**: Write SQL scripts to populate tables with initial data or update existing data.
- **Data Generation Plans**: Visual Studio provides data generation plans to generate large volumes of test data for your database during development and testing.

Continuous Integration and Deployment

Database project management in Visual Studio can be integrated into your continuous integration (CI) and continuous deployment (CD) pipelines. By automating the deployment process, you can ensure that changes are tested and deployed consistently across different environments.

Conclusion

Effective database project management in Visual Studio streamlines the development and maintenance of database schemas. Whether you're designing new databases or working with existing ones, Visual Studio provides a comprehensive set of tools for schema design, version control, deployment, and data management. By incorporating database projects into your development workflow, you can ensure that your databases are well-maintained and evolve alongside your applications.

Chapter 8: Working with Mobile Applications

8.1 Setting Up for Mobile Development

Mobile application development is a thriving field, and Visual Studio offers a robust environment for building mobile apps for various platforms, including iOS, Android, and Windows. This section focuses on setting up your development environment and tools for mobile app development in Visual Studio.

Choosing a Mobile Development Approach

Before you begin, it's important to decide on the mobile development approach you want to pursue:

1. **Native Development**: This approach involves writing platform-specific code for each target platform (e.g., Swift for iOS, Java/Kotlin for Android, C# for Windows). Native apps offer the best performance and access to platform-specific features but require separate codebases for each platform.
2. **Cross-Platform Development**: Cross-platform development tools, like Xamarin (now part of .NET MAUI), Flutter, or React Native, allow you to write code in a single language (e.g., C#, Dart, JavaScript) and compile it for multiple platforms. This approach reduces development time and code duplication but may have some performance trade-offs.

Setting Up Visual Studio for Mobile Development

Here are the steps to set up Visual Studio for mobile app development:

1. **Install Visual Studio**: If you haven't already, download and install Visual Studio. Ensure you select the workload for mobile development during installation.
2. **Install Platform-Specific SDKs**: Depending on your target platforms, you'll need to install the relevant SDKs. For iOS development, you'll need Xcode on macOS. For Android development, you'll need Android Studio and the Android SDK.
3. **Install Mobile Development Tools**: If you're developing with Xamarin, .NET MAUI, or another cross-platform framework, install the necessary extensions or components within Visual Studio. These tools provide templates, emulators, and debugging support for mobile development.

Creating a Mobile App Project

Once your development environment is set up, you can create a new mobile app project:

1. **File > New > Project**: In Visual Studio, go to the File menu and select "New" > "Project."
2. **Choose Project Template**: Select a mobile app project template that matches your chosen development approach. For example, you can choose "Blank App (Xamarin.Forms)" for cross-platform development.
3. **Configure Project**: Configure the project settings, including the target platforms, app name, and project location.

4. **Coding and Design**: Visual Studio provides a rich environment for coding, designing user interfaces, and debugging your mobile app. You can use XAML (for Xamarin.Forms) or platform-specific UI frameworks to design your app's user interface.
5. **Testing and Debugging**: Visual Studio includes emulators and simulators for testing your app on different devices and platforms. You can also connect physical devices for debugging.
6. **Build and Deploy**: Build your app for your target platforms and deploy it to simulators, emulators, or physical devices. Visual Studio provides tools to generate app packages for distribution through app stores.

Conclusion

Setting up Visual Studio for mobile app development is the first step toward creating mobile applications for a wide range of platforms. Whether you choose native or cross-platform development, Visual Studio provides a comprehensive set of tools and resources to streamline the development process. With the right setup, you can leverage Visual Studio's features to build, test, and deploy mobile apps that meet the needs of your target audience.

8.2 Xamarin: Cross-Platform Development

Xamarin is a popular cross-platform development framework that allows you to create mobile apps for iOS, Android, and Windows using a single codebase. Xamarin leverages the C# programming language and the .NET ecosystem, making it a powerful choice for developers who want to maximize code reuse and efficiency. In this section, we'll delve into Xamarin and how to get started with cross-platform mobile app development in Visual Studio.

Understanding Xamarin Basics

Xamarin enables you to write native user interfaces and access platform-specific features while sharing business logic across platforms. Here's an overview of Xamarin's key components:

- **Xamarin.Forms**: Xamarin.Forms is a UI framework that allows you to define your app's user interface using XAML, a declarative markup language. You create a single UI definition that renders natively on each platform.

- **Xamarin.Android and Xamarin.iOS**: For more platform-specific control or advanced scenarios, you can use Xamarin.Android and Xamarin.iOS projects to write platform-specific code.

- **Xamarin.Essentials**: Xamarin.Essentials is a library that provides a consistent API for accessing device features such as sensors, file system, and connectivity across iOS, Android, and Windows.

Creating a Xamarin Project

To create a Xamarin project in Visual Studio, follow these steps:

1. **File > New > Project**: Open Visual Studio, go to the File menu, and select "New" > "Project."
2. **Select Xamarin Project Template**: Choose a Xamarin project template based on your target platforms and preferred UI framework. For example, you can choose "Blank App (Xamarin.Forms)".
3. **Configure Project Settings**: Specify project details, including the app name, target platforms (iOS, Android,

Windows), and code-sharing strategy.

4. **Design the User Interface**: Xamarin.Forms projects use XAML for defining the user interface. You can design your app's pages, layout, and controls using XAML markup.
5. **Write Shared Code**: Implement the app's business logic and functionality in shared code files written in C#. These files will be shared across all target platforms.
6. **Platform-Specific Code**: When necessary, you can include platform-specific code in separate files within Xamarin.Android and Xamarin.iOS projects.

Debugging and Testing

Xamarin provides debugging and testing tools to ensure your app works correctly on each platform:

- **Emulators and Simulators**: Visual Studio includes emulators and simulators for iOS and Android, allowing you to test your app on different device configurations.

- **Device Debugging**: You can connect physical devices for debugging. Xamarin offers robust tools for debugging and inspecting code while your app runs on a device.

Building and Deployment

To build and deploy your Xamarin app, follow these steps:

1. **Build Configuration**: Configure build settings for each platform, such as release or debug mode.
2. **Build Solution**: Build your solution to generate platform-specific app packages or APKs.
3. **Deployment**: Deploy your app to emulators, simulators, or physical devices for testing and debugging.

4. **App Store Distribution**: Generate app packages suitable for submission to app stores like Apple App Store, Google Play, or Microsoft Store.

Xamarin.Forms vs. Xamarin.Native

Xamarin.Forms simplifies cross-platform development by providing a single UI definition, making it suitable for many apps. However, for apps with highly customized user interfaces or complex platform-specific requirements, you may choose Xamarin.Native to write separate UI code for each platform.

Conclusion

Xamarin is a versatile framework that empowers developers to create cross-platform mobile apps with shared code and native performance. By leveraging Xamarin's capabilities and Visual Studio's development environment, you can efficiently build and maintain mobile applications for iOS, Android, and Windows while reducing development time and effort.

8.3 Debugging Mobile Applications

Debugging is a critical part of the mobile app development process. It helps identify and fix issues, ensuring that your app functions correctly and delivers a great user experience. In this section, we'll explore how to debug mobile applications developed using Xamarin in Visual Studio.

Debugging Basics

Debugging in Xamarin with Visual Studio is similar to debugging other .NET applications. Here are some fundamental debugging techniques:

- **Setting Breakpoints**: You can set breakpoints in your code by clicking on the left margin of the code editor or pressing F9. Breakpoints pause the execution of your app at specific lines, allowing you to inspect variables and step through code.

- **Stepping Through Code**: While debugging, you can use step commands like F10 (step over), F11 (step into), and Shift + F11 (step out) to navigate through your code one line at a time.

- **Inspecting Variables**: Visual Studio provides a "Watch" window where you can add variables to monitor their values as your app runs. You can also hover over variables in your code to see their current values.

- **Immediate Window**: The Immediate window allows you to execute code interactively while debugging. You can evaluate expressions and run methods to test specific code segments.

Debugging Xamarin.Android

When debugging Xamarin.Android apps in Visual Studio, you have access to various debugging tools and options:

- **Android Emulators**: You can use Android emulators to test and debug your app on virtual devices with different configurations. Visual Studio provides seamless integration with Android emulators.

- **Device Debugging**: To debug on physical Android devices, you need to enable Developer Mode and USB debugging on the device. Visual Studio can deploy and debug directly on connected Android devices.

- **Logcat**: Android's logging system, known as Logcat, allows you to view logs generated by your app. You can access Logcat logs through the Android Device Monitor or Android Profiler in Visual Studio.

Debugging Xamarin.iOS

Debugging Xamarin.iOS apps in Visual Studio is also straightforward:

- **iOS Simulator**: You can use the iOS Simulator to run and debug your app on virtual iOS devices. Visual Studio offers a smooth debugging experience with the iOS Simulator.

- **Physical iOS Devices**: To debug on physical iOS devices, you need a Mac with Xamarin installed. Visual Studio connects to the Mac for deployment and debugging.

- **Output Window**: Visual Studio provides an Output window where you can view build and debug output, including any error messages or warnings.

Common Debugging Scenarios

Here are some common scenarios where debugging is invaluable:

- **UI Issues**: Debugging helps identify layout and rendering problems, ensuring your app's user interface looks and behaves as expected.

- **Crash Analysis**: Debugging helps pinpoint the source of crashes or exceptions in your app, allowing you to fix them promptly.

- **Performance Optimization**: Profiling and debugging tools assist in optimizing your app's performance by identifying bottlenecks and memory leaks.

- **Testing Different Scenarios**: Debugging helps you simulate different scenarios, such as various device orientations, screen sizes, and network conditions, to ensure your app handles them gracefully.

Debugging Best Practices

To make debugging more effective:

- **Use Version Control**: Keep your codebase under version control. This allows you to track changes and easily revert to a stable state if needed.

- **Write Unit Tests**: Implement unit tests to catch issues early in the development process. Visual Studio supports various unit testing frameworks for Xamarin apps.

- **Use Logging**: Incorporate logging into your code to capture important information, even in production. Log messages can be invaluable when diagnosing issues reported by users.

- **Keep Dependencies Updated**: Regularly update Xamarin and third-party libraries to leverage bug fixes and improvements.

In conclusion, debugging is an essential skill for mobile app developers using Xamarin and Visual Studio. By mastering debugging techniques and tools, you can efficiently identify and resolve issues, ensuring your apps provide a seamless user experience on both Android and iOS devices.

8.4 Mobile UI Design Principles

Designing a user-friendly and visually appealing user interface (UI) is a crucial aspect of mobile app development. In this section, we'll explore fundamental UI design principles and best practices to create engaging and effective mobile app interfaces.

1. User-Centered Design

Put your users at the center of your design process. Understand their needs, preferences, and behaviors through user research and feedback. Consider their goals and pain points when designing the app's UI. User-centered design ensures that your app is intuitive and serves its intended audience.

2. Consistency

Maintain a consistent design throughout your app. Use the same fonts, colors, and UI elements to create a cohesive and familiar experience. Consistency helps users navigate your app with ease and reduces confusion.

3. Simplicity

Simplicity is key to a successful mobile UI. Keep your design clean and uncluttered. Avoid unnecessary elements and features that can overwhelm users. Focus on delivering core functionality and content. A simple UI enhances usability and readability.

4. Navigation

Provide clear and intuitive navigation paths. Use standard navigation patterns such as tab bars, side menus, or bottom navigation bars. Users should be able to move between sections of your app effortlessly.

5. Responsive Design

Design for various screen sizes and orientations. Ensure that your app looks and functions well on different devices, from small smartphones to large tablets. Use responsive layouts and adapt your UI elements accordingly.

6. Touch-Friendly Interfaces

Mobile devices rely on touch interactions. Design touch-friendly elements, such as buttons and icons, with adequate spacing to prevent accidental taps. Consider the size of a user's finger when placing interactive elements.

7. Typography and Readability

Choose legible fonts and maintain proper text sizes. Ensure that text is easy to read, even on small screens. Use hierarchy and formatting (bold, italics, etc.) to emphasize important information.

8. Visual Hierarchy

Establish a clear visual hierarchy to guide users' attention. Use size, color, and positioning to highlight primary actions and content. Users should quickly understand the most important elements on each screen.

9. Feedback and Confirmation

Provide feedback for user actions. Use animations, notifications, or visual changes to confirm that an action has been completed successfully. Feedback reassures users and reduces uncertainty.

10. Accessibility

Make your app accessible to all users, including those with disabilities. Ensure that screen readers can interpret your UI elements and that colors have sufficient contrast. Accessibility features improve usability and inclusivity.

11. Performance

Optimize your UI for performance. Ensure smooth transitions and responsive interactions. Minimize loading times and prioritize content that users need immediately.

12. Testing and Iteration

Regularly test your UI with real users and gather feedback. Use usability testing to identify pain points and areas for improvement. Continuously iterate and refine your design based on user insights.

13. Platform Guidelines

Adhere to platform-specific design guidelines (e.g., Material Design for Android, Human Interface Guidelines for iOS). Following these guidelines ensures that your app feels native to the platform and aligns with user expectations.

14. Prototyping

Create interactive prototypes to visualize and test your UI design. Prototyping tools allow you to simulate user interactions and gather feedback early in the design process.

15. User Onboarding

Provide a smooth onboarding experience for new users. Guide them through essential app features and explain how to use your app effectively. Onboarding reduces user frustration and abandonment.

16. A/B Testing

Experiment with different UI variations using A/B testing. Compare user engagement and behavior to determine which design elements are more effective. A/B testing helps you make data-driven design decisions.

Incorporating these UI design principles and best practices into your mobile app development process can lead to a more engaging, user-friendly, and successful application. Remember that good design is an ongoing effort that evolves based on user feedback and changing trends.

8.5 Deploying to App Stores

After developing a mobile application, the next critical step is deploying it to app stores, such as the Apple App Store for iOS and Google Play Store for Android. This section provides an overview of the app deployment process, including the necessary preparations and steps involved.

1. App Store Registration

Before you can publish your app, you need developer accounts on the respective app stores. Register as a developer on the Apple App Store and Google Play Store. These accounts often require a one-time fee.

2. App Store Guidelines

Familiarize yourself with the guidelines and policies of the app stores. Each store has specific requirements for app content, design, and functionality. Ensure your app complies with these guidelines to avoid rejection.

3. App Icons and Screenshots

Prepare high-quality app icons and screenshots that showcase your app's features. These visuals are essential for attracting users on the app store. Follow the recommended sizes and formats for each platform.

4. App Store Optimization (ASO)

Optimize your app's listing for search engines within the app store. Use relevant keywords in your app's title and description to improve discoverability. ASO can significantly impact your app's visibility.

5. Testing and Debugging

Thoroughly test your app on real devices to identify and fix any issues. Check for compatibility with different OS versions and screen sizes. Ensure that your app functions as expected and doesn't crash.

6. Privacy Policy

Provide a clear and accessible privacy policy within your app, especially if it collects user data. Transparency regarding data usage is crucial for user trust and compliance with app store policies.

7. App Store Submission

Submit your app to the app store's review process. This process can take several days or even weeks. Be prepared for potential feedback and requests for changes from the app store's review team.

8. App Store Optimization (ASO)

Optimize your app's listing for search engines within the app store. Use relevant keywords in your app's title and description to improve discoverability. ASO can significantly impact your app's visibility.

9. Launch Plan

Plan your app's launch carefully. Decide on a launch date, and consider promotional strategies to attract initial users. Launching with a well-thought-out marketing plan can boost your app's visibility.

10. User Support and Feedback

Be prepared to provide user support and respond to feedback and reviews on the app store. Engage with users, address their concerns, and use their feedback to improve your app.

11. App Updates

Continue to improve your app by releasing regular updates. Address bugs, add new features, and stay updated with the latest OS versions and device capabilities. Consistent updates demonstrate your commitment to the app's quality.

12. Marketing and Promotion

Promote your app through various channels, such as social media, email marketing, and online advertising. Consider collaborating with influencers or app review websites to increase exposure.

13. Analytics and Monitoring

Implement analytics tools to track user behavior, app performance, and user engagement. Monitor key metrics to gain insights into your app's performance and make data-driven decisions.

14. App Monetization

If your app includes in-app purchases or advertisements, implement monetization strategies carefully. Balance revenue generation with providing value to users to maintain their satisfaction.

15. Legal Considerations

Ensure that your app complies with legal regulations, including copyright and intellectual property laws. Consult legal experts if needed to protect your app and its content.

16. Internationalization

Consider translating your app into multiple languages to expand your user base. Make your app accessible to users from different regions by offering content in their preferred languages.

Deploying your mobile app to app stores is a significant milestone in your development journey. Remember that the success of your app also depends on how well you market, maintain, and engage with your user base post-launch. Keep an eye on user feedback and continuously work on enhancing your app's features and usability.

Chapter 9: Visual Studio Extensions and Customization

9.1 Exploring the Visual Studio Marketplace

The Visual Studio Marketplace is a central hub for extensions, tools, and customizations that enhance your Visual Studio experience. It offers a vast array of extensions created by both Microsoft and the community, allowing you to tailor Visual Studio to your specific needs.

Navigating the Marketplace

To access the Visual Studio Marketplace, open Visual Studio and go to the "Extensions" menu. Click on "Manage Extensions," and in the Extensions window, you'll find the "Online" category. This category provides access to the Visual Studio Marketplace. You can also visit the Marketplace website directly in your web browser.

Search and Discover Extensions

The Marketplace allows you to search for extensions by keywords, categories, and tags. You can explore popular extensions, new arrivals, and those recommended for your development environment. Additionally, you can read user reviews and ratings to assess the quality and relevance of an extension.

Installing Extensions

To install an extension, simply click the "Install" button on its Marketplace page or in the Extensions window in Visual Studio. Visual Studio will download and install the extension automatically.

Some extensions may require you to restart Visual Studio to take effect.

Managing Installed Extensions

You can manage your installed extensions through the Extensions window. From there, you can enable, disable, uninstall, or update extensions. Keeping your extensions up-to-date ensures compatibility with the latest Visual Studio updates and improvements.

Popular Extension Categories

The Visual Studio Marketplace offers extensions across various categories, including:

- Productivity: Extensions that enhance your coding efficiency, such as code snippets, code generators, and intelligent code completion tools.

- Debugging and Diagnostics: Tools that assist in debugging, profiling, and diagnosing issues in your projects.

- Source Control: Extensions for integrating with source control systems like Git, TFS, and GitHub.

- Testing and Quality Assurance: Extensions for writing unit tests, conducting code reviews, and ensuring code quality.

- Web Development: Tools and frameworks for web development, including support for popular front-end and back-end technologies.

- Cloud and Azure: Extensions that streamline cloud development and Azure integration.

- Mobile Development: Tools and templates for building mobile applications on various platforms.

Creating Your Own Extensions

If you have specific needs that are not met by existing extensions, you can create your own Visual Studio extensions using the Visual Studio Extensibility (VSIX) project template. This allows you to customize Visual Studio to match your workflow precisely.

Community Contributions and Collaboration

The Visual Studio community actively contributes to the Marketplace by creating and sharing extensions. You can also collaborate with other developers by contributing to open-source extensions or creating collaborative tools through Live Share, a built-in feature of Visual Studio.

The Visual Studio Marketplace is a valuable resource for tailoring your development environment and enhancing your productivity. Exploring and utilizing extensions from the Marketplace can help you streamline your workflow, discover new tools, and adapt Visual Studio to your unique development needs.

9.2 Installing and Managing Extensions

Once you've explored the Visual Studio Marketplace and found extensions that fit your development needs, the next step is to install and manage these extensions effectively. Installing and managing extensions is straightforward and can greatly enhance your development environment. In this section, we'll cover the key steps and best practices for installing and managing Visual Studio extensions.

Installing Extensions

Installing an extension from the Visual Studio Marketplace is a simple process:

1. **Navigate to the Extension**: Find the extension you want to install in the Visual Studio Marketplace.
2. **Click "Install"**: On the extension's page, click the "Install" button. If you're installing from within Visual Studio, it will prompt you to confirm the installation.

3. **Review Permissions**: Visual Studio may request certain permissions for the extension, such as accessing your files or interacting with other tools. Review these permissions and click "Accept" to proceed with the installation.
4. **Installation Process**: Visual Studio will download and install the extension. Depending on the extension's complexity, this may take a moment. Once installed, you may need to restart Visual Studio for the changes to take effect.
5. **Extension Enabled**: After installation, the extension will be enabled by default. You can see it in the "Extensions" window.

Managing Installed Extensions

As you install more extensions, it's essential to manage them effectively to ensure they don't conflict with one another and to keep them up-to-date:

1. **Access the Extensions Window**: To manage your installed extensions, go to the "Extensions" menu in Visual Studio and select "Manage Extensions." Here, you'll find a list of all your installed extensions.
2. **Enabling and Disabling**: You can enable or disable extensions as needed. Disabling an extension temporarily deactivates it without uninstalling it. This can be useful if you want to troubleshoot issues or if you only need the extension for specific tasks.
3. **Uninstalling Extensions**: If you no longer need an extension, you can uninstall it by selecting it in the Extensions window and clicking the "Uninstall" button. Uninstalling an extension will remove it from Visual Studio.

4. **Updating Extensions**: Developers regularly release updates to their extensions to improve functionality and compatibility with new versions of Visual Studio. It's crucial to keep your extensions up-to-date to ensure a smooth development experience. In the Extensions window, you can see which extensions have updates available and install them with a single click.

Handling Extension Conflicts

Sometimes, multiple extensions may conflict with each other, leading to unexpected behavior in Visual Studio. If you encounter issues, consider the following steps:

- **Check for Updates**: Ensure that all your installed extensions are up-to-date. Developers may release updates to address conflicts or compatibility issues.

- **Disable Extensions**: Temporarily disable extensions one by one to identify which one is causing the conflict. Once you've identified the problematic extension, you can troubleshoot or contact the extension developer for assistance.

- **Review Documentation**: Extension developers often provide documentation or support resources that can help resolve conflicts or issues. Check the extension's documentation or the Visual Studio Marketplace page for troubleshooting guidance.

- **Contact Support**: If you can't resolve the conflict on your own, consider reaching out to the extension developer's support channels or forums for assistance.

Practices for Extension Management

To maintain a stable and efficient development environment, consider these best practices:

- **Regularly Review Installed Extensions**: Periodically review your list of installed extensions to ensure you're only using those that are essential to your workflow. Uninstall any unused or redundant extensions.

- **Backup Settings**: Before making significant changes to your extensions, consider backing up your Visual Studio settings using the "Export Settings" feature. This allows you to restore your configuration if needed.

- **Stay Informed**: Keep an eye on updates and news related to your favorite extensions. Subscribe to extension newsletters or follow the extension developers on social media to stay informed about new features and updates.

Installing and managing extensions is a fundamental aspect of customizing Visual Studio to meet your development requirements. By following best practices and staying organized, you can enhance your productivity and create a tailored development environment that suits your unique needs.

9.3 Customizing the IDE

Customizing the Integrated Development Environment (IDE) is a powerful way to tailor Visual Studio to your specific workflow and preferences. Visual Studio offers a range of customization options, allowing you to adjust the appearance, behavior, and functionality of the IDE to meet your needs. In this section, we'll explore how you can customize Visual Studio to create a personalized and efficient development environment.

Customizing Visual Studio Appearance

1. **Themes**: Visual Studio offers a variety of themes, including light and dark themes, as well as high-contrast options. You can change the theme by going to Tools > Options > Environment > General > Color Theme.
2. **Font and Colors**: Customize the font size and colors for various elements in the code editor. This is particularly useful for enhancing code readability. Navigate to Tools > Options > Environment > Fonts and Colors.
3. **Window Layouts**: Create custom window layouts to arrange tool windows and code editor panes to your liking. You can save and switch between different layouts as needed.
4. **Toolbox**: Customize the Toolbox to include your frequently used controls, snippets, and components. Right-click in the Toolbox and select "Choose Items" to add or remove items.

Customizing Keyboard Shortcuts

1. **Keybindings**: Visual Studio allows you to customize keyboard shortcuts for various commands. Go to Tools > Options > Environment > Keyboard to remap shortcuts or create your own.
2. **Export and Import Settings**: You can export your keyboard shortcuts and import them into another instance of Visual Studio or share them with colleagues.

Extensions and Add-ons

1. **Extensions**: As discussed in previous sections, you can extend Visual Studio's functionality by installing extensions from the Visual Studio Marketplace. These extensions can add features, tools, and support for different programming languages.
2. **Custom Snippets**: Create custom code snippets for repetitive tasks by going to Tools > Code Snippets Manager. You can also download and install snippet libraries created by others.

Code Editor Customization

1. **Editor Settings**: Customize the behavior of the code editor, such as auto-indentation, tab size, and code formatting. These settings can be found in Tools > Options > Text Editor.
2. **Editor Extensions**: Install extensions like ReSharper, which offer advanced code analysis, refactoring tools, and code navigation enhancements.

Customizing Tool Windows

1. **Solution Explorer**: Customize the way Solution Explorer displays your project structure and files. You can filter files, group items, and sort them as per your preference.
2. **Properties Window**: Adjust the properties window to show the properties that are most relevant to your current development task.

Customizing Debugging

1. **Debugger Display**: Customize how objects are displayed during debugging by creating DebuggerDisplay attributes in your code.
2. **Debugging Tools**: Visual Studio provides various debugging tools and extensions that you can customize to improve your debugging experience.

Workspace Customization

1. **Window Layouts**: Save and load different window layouts depending on your tasks, such as debugging, coding, or designing.
2. **Environment Settings**: Customize general environment settings, such as startup behavior, default directories, and external tools integration.

Version Control Customization

1. **Git Integration**: If you're using Git for version control, customize Git settings and integration to align with your workflow.

Customizing Project Templates

1. **Project Templates**: You can create custom project templates for specific project types, enabling you to start new projects with your predefined settings and structures.
2. **Item Templates**: Similarly, create item templates for common code snippets, classes, or files that you often use.

Customizing Work Item Tracking

1. **Work Item Templates**: If you're using Team Foundation Server (TFS) or Azure DevOps for work item tracking, customize work item templates to fit your team's processes and requirements.
2. **Process Customization**: Tailor the Agile, Scrum, or CMMI processes to match your team's development methodology.

Customizing Visual Studio to align with your coding style, preferences, and workflow is essential for enhancing your productivity and overall development experience. By taking advantage of the numerous customization options available, you can create a development environment that feels intuitive and efficient for your specific needs.

9.4 Creating Your Own Extensions

In Visual Studio, creating your own extensions can greatly enhance your development environment by adding custom functionality tailored to your specific needs. These extensions can range from simple code snippets to more complex tools and features. In this section, we'll explore how to create your own Visual Studio extensions, empowering you to extend the IDE in ways that optimize your workflow.

Types of Extensions

Visual Studio supports various types of extensions, including:

1. **Code Snippets**: These are small pieces of reusable code that you can quickly insert into your projects. Creating

custom code snippets can save time on repetitive tasks.

2. **Item Templates**: Item templates allow you to create custom project items with predefined code and structure. This is useful for enforcing coding standards or creating reusable components.
3. **Project Templates**: Customize project templates to create new projects with predefined settings, references, and configurations. This can streamline project setup for specific scenarios.
4. **Visual Studio Add-ins**: Add-ins are extensions that can provide additional features, integrate with external tools, or automate tasks within Visual Studio. They can be created using various programming languages, including C#.
5. **Visual Studio Extensions**: Visual Studio extensions can be more comprehensive and may include UI elements, tool windows, and integration with external services or APIs.

Creating Code Snippets

Creating custom code snippets is a straightforward way to extend Visual Studio's functionality. You can define your own snippets for common code patterns or frequently used blocks of code.

To create a code snippet:

1. Go to File > New > File and select "Code Snippet" from the template options.
2. Define the snippet's code and specify where it should be inserted in your code files. You can use placeholders for dynamic values that will be filled in when the snippet is used.
3. Save the snippet with a .snippet file extension.

4. To use the snippet, simply type its shortcut in the code editor and press Tab to insert it.

Creating Item Templates

Item templates allow you to create custom project items with predefined code and structure. These can be useful for standardizing the creation of specific files or components in your projects.

To create an item template:

1. Create a new project or open an existing one.
2. Add a new item to your project and configure it as needed.
3. Once the item is set up the way you want, right-click it in Solution Explorer, and choose "Export Template."
4. Follow the wizard to create the item template. You can specify template parameters that users can customize when adding the item to their projects.
5. Save the template.
6. Users can then add your custom item template to their projects via the "Add New Item" dialog in Visual Studio.

Creating Visual Studio Extensions

Creating full-fledged Visual Studio extensions is more advanced but offers significant flexibility. You can create extensions to add custom tool windows, menu items, commands, and integration with external services.

Here are the general steps to create a Visual Studio extension:

1. Install the Visual Studio Extensibility workload during Visual Studio installation.
2. Create a new Visual Studio Extensibility project.

3. Define the extension's functionality, including any UI elements or commands it should provide.
4. Implement the extension's logic using C# or other supported languages.
5. Build and debug the extension within Visual Studio.
6. Package the extension as a Visual Studio extension (VSIX) for distribution.
7. Publish the extension to the Visual Studio Marketplace or share it with your team.

Creating extensions allows you to tailor Visual Studio to your specific requirements and automate repetitive tasks, making your development workflow more efficient.

By creating your own extensions, you can fully customize Visual Studio to match your coding style, project requirements, and development process, ultimately boosting your productivity and improving your overall development experience.

9.5 Community Contributions and Resources

The Visual Studio community is a vibrant and collaborative ecosystem of developers, educators, and enthusiasts. Leveraging community contributions and resources can greatly enhance your experience with Visual Studio. In this section, we'll explore the various ways you can benefit from the collective knowledge and support of the Visual Studio community.

1. Online Forums and Communities

Participating in online forums and communities dedicated to Visual Studio is an excellent way to seek help, share knowledge, and connect with other developers facing similar challenges. Some popular platforms and communities include:

- **Stack Overflow**: Stack Overflow has a dedicated section for Visual Studio-related questions and answers. You can ask questions, provide answers, and learn from others' experiences.

- **Visual Studio Developer Community**: Microsoft hosts an official Visual Studio Developer Community where you can engage with experts, report issues, and find solutions to problems.

- **GitHub**: GitHub is home to numerous open-source projects related to Visual Studio. You can explore and contribute to projects, report issues, and collaborate with developers worldwide.

- **Reddit**: The Visual Studio subreddit is a place for discussions, announcements, and sharing resources related to Visual Studio.

2. Visual Studio Extensions

The Visual Studio Marketplace is a treasure trove of extensions and add-ons created by developers for developers. You can find extensions that enhance your coding experience, improve productivity, and add new features to Visual Studio. Popular extensions include code analyzers, productivity tools, and theme customizations.

3. Blogs and Tutorials

Many developers and technology experts maintain blogs and tutorials that cover various aspects of Visual Studio. These resources can provide valuable insights, tips, and tricks for using Visual Studio more effectively. Look for blogs, YouTube channels, and online courses that cater to your specific interests within Visual Studio development.

4. GitHub Repositories

GitHub hosts repositories containing sample projects, code snippets, and templates related to Visual Studio development. Exploring these repositories can help you understand best practices, learn from real-world code, and kickstart your own projects.

5. User Groups and Meetups

Joining local or online Visual Studio user groups and attending meetups can provide networking opportunities, workshops, and access to experienced developers who are passionate about Visual Studio and its ecosystem. These groups often organize events, hackathons, and presentations on Visual Studio-related topics.

6. Documentation and Official Resources

Don't forget to consult the official Visual Studio documentation, tutorials, and official blogs provided by Microsoft. These resources are regularly updated and offer comprehensive information on Visual Studio features, best practices, and the latest updates.

7. GitHub Discussions

Many open-source projects related to Visual Studio use GitHub Discussions as a platform for asking questions, sharing ideas, and discussing project-related matters. Engaging in these discussions can provide you with insights into specific projects and the chance to interact with their maintainers.

8. Social Media

Follow Visual Studio and related hashtags on social media platforms like Twitter, LinkedIn, and Facebook. You can stay updated on the latest news, tips, and community events related to Visual Studio.

9. Contributing to Open Source

If you're interested in giving back to the Visual Studio community, consider contributing to open-source projects related to Visual Studio or developing your own extensions and tools. Open source is a collaborative environment where your skills and contributions can have a significant impact.

In conclusion, the Visual Studio community offers a wealth of resources and opportunities to enhance your skills and make the most of this powerful development environment. Whether you're seeking help, sharing your expertise, or exploring new extensions, the collective knowledge of the community can be a valuable asset in your journey as a Visual Studio developer.

Chapter 10: Testing and Quality Assurance

10.1 Introduction to Automated Testing in Visual Studio

Automated testing is a fundamental practice in software development that helps ensure the quality, reliability, and correctness of your applications. In Visual Studio, you have access to a robust set of tools and frameworks to implement automated testing for your projects. This section provides an introduction to automated testing concepts and the various testing frameworks available in Visual Studio.

What Is Automated Testing?

Automated testing involves the use of scripts and testing frameworks to automatically execute test cases on your software applications. These test cases are designed to verify that your code functions correctly and that it meets specified requirements. Automated tests can be executed repeatedly and consistently, making them essential for maintaining software quality during development and beyond.

Benefits of Automated Testing

Automated testing offers several advantages for software development:

1. **Improved Quality:** Automated tests can catch bugs and issues early in the development cycle, reducing the likelihood of defects reaching production.
2. **Faster Feedback:** Automated tests provide quick feedback to developers, helping them identify and fix problems

promptly.

3. **Regression Testing:** Automated tests can be easily rerun to ensure that new changes haven't introduced regressions or broken existing functionality.
4. **Continuous Integration:** Automated tests are integral to continuous integration and continuous delivery (CI/CD) pipelines, where they help validate code changes before deployment.
5. **Documentation:** Test cases serve as living documentation, providing insights into the expected behavior of the software.

Testing Frameworks in Visual Studio

Visual Studio supports multiple testing frameworks that enable you to create and run automated tests. Some of the popular testing frameworks compatible with Visual Studio include:

- **MSTest:** Microsoft's MSTest framework is built into Visual Studio and offers a simple and intuitive way to write and run tests. It supports unit testing and can be used for various test types.

- **NUnit:** NUnit is a popular open-source testing framework that provides a flexible and extensible platform for writing unit tests in .NET projects.

- **xUnit:** xUnit is another open-source testing framework known for its simplicity and extensibility. It's widely used for unit testing in .NET Core and .NET 5+ projects.

- **SpecFlow:** SpecFlow is a framework that supports behavior-driven development (BDD) and enables you to write executable specifications using Gherkin language.

- **Coded UI Test:** Visual Studio's Coded UI Test framework allows you to create automated UI tests by recording and playing back interactions with your application's user interface.

Writing Your First Automated Test

To get started with automated testing in Visual Studio, you need to create a test project within your solution. Here's a high-level overview of the steps involved in writing your first automated test:

1. **Create a Test Project:** In Visual Studio, add a new test project to your solution. You can choose the appropriate testing framework for your project.
2. **Write Test Cases:** Create test methods within your test project. These methods should contain the test logic and assertions that verify the correctness of your code.
3. **Run Tests:** Use Visual Studio's test explorer to discover and run your tests. The test explorer provides a convenient interface for managing and executing your test suite.
4. **Analyze Results:** After running the tests, Visual Studio provides detailed reports on test outcomes. You can see which tests passed, failed, or encountered errors.

Test-Driven Development (TDD)

Test-driven development (TDD) is a software development approach where you write tests before writing the actual code. TDD follows a cycle known as the "Red-Green-Refactor" cycle:

1. **Red:** Write a failing test case that defines the behavior you want to implement.
2. **Green:** Write the minimum code required to make the test pass.

3. **Refactor:** Refactor the code to improve its structure and maintainability while ensuring that the test continues to pass.

TDD helps ensure that your code is thoroughly tested from the outset and can lead to more robust and maintainable software.

In the subsequent sections of this chapter, we will dive deeper into various testing frameworks, explore advanced testing techniques, and discuss strategies for integrating automated testing into your development workflow. Automated testing is a critical aspect of modern software development, and Visual Studio provides you with the tools to excel in this area.

10.2 Unit Testing Frameworks

Unit testing is a fundamental component of automated testing in software development. It involves testing individual units or components of your code in isolation to ensure they function as expected. Unit tests are typically small and focus on specific parts of your codebase, such as functions, methods, or classes. Visual Studio supports various unit testing frameworks that enable you to create and execute unit tests efficiently. In this section, we will explore some of the popular unit testing frameworks available within Visual Studio.

MSTest

MSTest is Microsoft's built-in unit testing framework for Visual Studio. It is widely used for writing and executing unit tests in .NET projects. MSTest provides a straightforward and familiar way to create unit tests, making it an excellent choice for developers using

Visual Studio. Here's a basic example of a unit test written using MSTest:

```
using Microsoft.VisualStudio.TestTools.UnitTesting;

[TestClass]

public class CalculatorTests

{

[TestMethod]

public void Add_WhenGivenTwoNumbers_ReturnsSum()

{

// Arrange

Calculator calculator = new Calculator();

// Act

int result = calculator.Add(3, 5);

// Assert

Assert.AreEqual(8, result);

}

}
```

In the example above, we have a test class CalculatorTests with a test method Add_WhenGivenTwoNumbers_ReturnsSum. The test method follows the "Arrange, Act, Assert" pattern:

- **Arrange:** Set up the necessary objects and data.

- **Act:** Perform the action or operation to be tested.
- **Assert:** Verify that the expected outcome matches the actual result.

MSTest provides a set of assertion methods like Assert.AreEqual, Assert.IsTrue, and Assert.IsFalse to validate test outcomes.

NUnit

NUnit is a popular open-source unit testing framework compatible with Visual Studio. It offers a more extensive set of features and greater flexibility for writing unit tests. NUnit supports parameterized tests, test fixtures, and various attribute-based test configurations. Here's a simple NUnit test example:

```
using NUnit.Framework;

[TestFixture]

public class CalculatorTests

{

[Test]

public void Add_WhenGivenTwoNumbers_ReturnsSum()

{

// Arrange

Calculator calculator = new Calculator();

// Act

int result = calculator.Add(3, 5);
```

```
// Assert
Assert.AreEqual(8, result);
}
}
```

NUnit uses attributes like [TestFixture] and [Test] to define test classes and test methods, respectively. It provides a rich set of assertion methods similar to MSTest.

xUnit

xUnit is another open-source unit testing framework that has gained popularity in the .NET Core and .NET 5+ ecosystem. It follows a more modern and extensible design. Writing unit tests with xUnit involves using attributes such as [Fact] and [Theory]. Here's a basic xUnit test example:

```
using Xunit;
public class CalculatorTests
{
[Fact]
public void Add_WhenGivenTwoNumbers_ReturnsSum()
{
// Arrange
Calculator calculator = new Calculator();
// Act
```

```
int result = calculator.Add(3, 5);

// Assert

Assert.Equal(8, result);

}

}
```

In this xUnit example, we use the [Fact] attribute to denote a fact-based test. xUnit also supports theory-based tests using the [Theory] attribute, allowing you to test multiple input combinations with a single test method.

These are just a few examples of the unit testing frameworks available in Visual Studio. The choice of framework depends on your project's requirements and your familiarity with the framework's features and conventions. Unit testing is a crucial practice for ensuring the correctness of your code, and Visual Studio provides the tools and integrations to make it an integral part of your development workflow. In the next sections, we will explore more advanced testing topics and best practices for unit testing in Visual Studio.

10.3 Integration and Functional Testing

Integration testing and functional testing are essential components of the software testing process. While unit testing focuses on testing individual units or components in isolation, integration and functional testing involve testing the interactions between various components and verifying that the software behaves correctly as a whole.

Integration Testing

Integration testing ensures that different parts of your software work together seamlessly when combined. It aims to identify issues related to data flow, communication between modules, and the integration of external services or components. Visual Studio offers several tools and frameworks to facilitate integration testing:

1. Web and Load Testing: Visual Studio provides built-in tools for creating and running web tests and load tests. Web tests allow you to record and play back user interactions with a web application, while load tests help you assess your application's performance under various loads.

2. Azure DevOps Test Plans: Azure DevOps (formerly known as Visual Studio Team Services) includes test plans that enable you to manage, track, and execute your integration tests. You can associate test cases with user stories, requirements, and test suites to ensure comprehensive test coverage.

3. Third-Party Testing Frameworks: Visual Studio integrates with popular third-party testing frameworks like Selenium, Appium, and SpecFlow. These frameworks are widely used for automated testing of web applications, mobile apps, and behavior-driven development (BDD) scenarios.

Integration testing often involves setting up test environments that mimic production configurations. Tools like Docker and Azure DevTest Labs can help create isolated test environments for integration testing.

Functional Testing

Functional testing focuses on evaluating whether the software functions correctly from the end user's perspective. It verifies that the application meets its specified requirements and behaves as expected. Visual Studio provides various approaches to perform functional testing:

1. Coded UI Tests: Coded UI Tests allow you to create automated tests by recording user actions and generating code. These tests can interact with the user interface of your application, making them suitable for testing Windows desktop applications.

2. App Center Test: Visual Studio App Center (now part of Azure DevOps) offers cloud-based testing services for mobile apps. It supports UI testing on real devices and simulators/emulators for Android and iOS platforms.

3. Manual Testing: Visual Studio Test Professional provides tools for manual testing. Testers can create test plans, execute test cases, and report defects using this integrated toolset.

4. Automated Testing with Third-Party Tools: Visual Studio integrates with third-party functional testing tools such as Selenium, WinAppDriver, and Xamarin Test Cloud for testing web, desktop, and mobile applications.

In addition to these tools, Visual Studio allows you to create custom test adapters and extensions for specialized testing scenarios.

When planning integration and functional testing, it's crucial to define clear test cases, test data, and expected outcomes. Test automation can significantly speed up the testing process and provide repeatability, especially for regression testing.

Overall, Visual Studio provides a comprehensive set of tools and integrations to support integration and functional testing, ensuring the reliability and quality of your software applications. In the next section, we will explore code coverage analysis and its role in software testing.

10.4 Code Coverage and Analysis

Code coverage analysis is a critical aspect of software testing that measures how much of your code is exercised by your tests. It helps identify untested code paths and can be a valuable indicator of the effectiveness of your test suite. Visual Studio provides robust tools for code coverage analysis, enabling you to assess the quality and coverage of your tests.

Understanding Code Coverage

Code coverage is typically expressed as a percentage and represents the portion of your codebase that is executed during test runs. There are several key metrics associated with code coverage:

1. **Line Coverage:** This metric measures the percentage of executable lines of code that were executed by your tests. It's a fundamental indicator of how well your tests exercise the codebase.
2. **Branch Coverage:** Branch coverage goes beyond line coverage and focuses on the different decision branches within your code, such as if statements and loops. It measures the percentage of decision points that were taken during test execution.

3. **Statement Coverage:** Statement coverage is similar to line coverage but considers individual statements within lines. It's a finer-grained metric that helps identify specific statements that were missed by tests.
4. **Function and Method Coverage:** This metric assesses the percentage of functions or methods in your codebase that were called during testing. It's particularly important in object-oriented programming languages like C#.

Using Visual Studio for Code Coverage

Visual Studio offers built-in support for code coverage analysis, making it easy to assess the quality of your tests. Here's how to use it:

1. **Instrumentation:** Before running your tests, you need to enable code coverage instrumentation. You can do this in the test settings or configuration of your project. Visual Studio will instrument your binaries to track code execution.
2. **Run Tests:** Execute your test suite as you normally would, either through the Test Explorer or the command line. Visual Studio will collect data on which portions of your code were executed.
3. **View Code Coverage Results:** After running your tests, you can view the code coverage results. Visual Studio provides interactive reports that highlight covered and uncovered code. You can see which lines, branches, and functions were tested.
4. **Analyze and Improve:** Analyze the code coverage results to identify areas with low coverage. Focus on writing additional tests to cover these areas and improve the overall coverage of your codebase.

Benefits of Code Coverage

Code coverage analysis offers several benefits in the software development process:

- **Quality Assurance:** It ensures that your tests adequately validate your code and reduces the risk of undetected defects.

- **Documentation:** Code coverage reports serve as documentation, showing which parts of your code are tested and which are not.

- **Test Optimization:** It helps you optimize your test suite by identifying redundant or ineffective tests.

- **Regression Testing:** Code coverage can help you identify regressions when making changes to your codebase.

- **Code Review:** Developers can use code coverage reports during code reviews to ensure that new code is adequately tested.

While achieving 100% code coverage is not always necessary or practical, code coverage analysis is a valuable tool for improving the effectiveness of your testing efforts. It provides insights into areas that may require additional attention and helps maintain code quality throughout the development lifecycle.

10.5 Continuous Integration and Deployment

Continuous Integration (CI) and Continuous Deployment (CD) are essential practices in modern software development. They streamline the process of building, testing, and deploying software, allowing development teams to deliver updates and features more rapidly and reliably. In this section, we'll explore how Visual Studio facilitates CI/CD pipelines and best practices for implementing them.

Understanding Continuous Integration (CI)

Continuous Integration is the practice of automatically building and testing code changes as soon as they are committed to a version control repository, such as Git. The main goals of CI are:

1. **Early Detection of Issues:** CI pipelines run automated tests (unit tests, integration tests, etc.) and code analysis tools whenever code changes are made. This ensures that issues are detected and addressed early in the development process.
2. **Consistency:** CI promotes a consistent and reproducible build process, reducing the "it works on my machine" problem.
3. **Collaboration:** CI encourages collaboration by integrating changes from multiple developers into a shared codebase frequently. It helps avoid merge conflicts and ensures that the codebase is always in a deployable state.

Setting Up CI in Visual Studio

Visual Studio provides robust support for setting up CI pipelines. Here are the general steps to configure CI:

1. **Version Control:** Ensure your project is hosted in a version control system like Git or Azure DevOps Repos.
2. **CI Service:** Choose a CI service that integrates with Visual Studio, such as Azure DevOps Pipelines, GitHub Actions, or Jenkins.
3. **Pipeline Configuration:** Create a configuration file (e.g., YAML file) that defines your CI pipeline. This file specifies the build steps, test scripts, and deployment tasks.
4. **Trigger:** Configure the pipeline to trigger automatically when code changes are pushed to the repository.
5. **Build and Test:** Define the build and test stages in your pipeline. Visual Studio provides templates for common project types, making it easier to set up.
6. **Artifact Publishing:** If your application requires build artifacts (e.g., executables or deployment packages), configure the pipeline to publish them.
7. **Notifications:** Set up notifications so that the development team is informed about the status of CI runs.

Continuous Deployment (CD)

Continuous Deployment takes CI a step further by automating the deployment of code changes to production or staging environments. The primary benefits of CD include:

1. **Rapid Releases:** CD enables you to release new features, bug fixes, and improvements to users quickly and with confidence.
2. **Reduced Manual Intervention:** Manual deployment processes are error-prone. CD automates deployments, reducing the risk of human error.
3. **Rollbacks:** CD pipelines often include automated rollback mechanisms in case a deployment fails or causes

issues in the production environment.

Implementing CD in Visual Studio

Visual Studio can be integrated with CD services like Azure DevOps Release Pipelines or third-party tools like Octopus Deploy. Here's a general approach to setting up CD:

1. **Artifacts:** Use the artifacts produced by your CI pipeline as the input for the CD pipeline.
2. **CD Pipeline:** Create a CD pipeline that defines the deployment steps, target environments, and rollback strategies.
3. **Environment Configuration:** Configure environment-specific settings and connection strings in the CD pipeline, allowing you to deploy to different environments (e.g., development, staging, production) with ease.
4. **Approvals:** Depending on your organization's policies, you can include approval gates in the CD pipeline, ensuring that changes are reviewed before deployment to production.
5. **Monitoring and Telemetry:** Implement monitoring and telemetry solutions to track the health and performance of your applications in production.
6. **Security and Compliance:** Ensure that your CD pipeline adheres to security and compliance standards, especially when dealing with sensitive data or regulated industries.

Visual Studio provides features like Azure Resource Manager templates and Azure DevOps services that make it seamless to set up CD pipelines for Azure-based applications. However, CD can be configured for a wide range of deployment targets, including on-premises servers and various cloud providers.

Best Practices for CI/CD

Here are some best practices to follow when implementing CI/CD with Visual Studio:

- **Automate Everything:** Automate as much of the process as possible, including build, testing, deployment, and rollback.

- **Keep Builds Clean:** Ensure that the build process is clean, reproducible, and free from external dependencies.

- **Version Everything:** Use version control for all code, configurations, and scripts to track changes and enable rollbacks.

- **Monitor and Measure:** Implement monitoring and telemetry to detect issues in production quickly.

- **Practice Infrastructure as Code (IaC):** Use Infrastructure as Code tools (e.g., Azure Resource Manager templates, Terraform) to manage infrastructure configurations alongside your code.

- **Security and Compliance:** Incorporate security and compliance checks into your pipelines to identify vulnerabilities early.

- **Documentation:** Document your CI/CD processes, pipeline configurations, and deployment procedures to ensure that the team can understand and maintain them effectively.

In conclusion, Visual Studio offers robust tools and integrations for implementing CI/CD pipelines, enabling development teams to streamline the development and deployment of software applications. By following best practices and automating key processes, you can achieve rapid, reliable, and secure software delivery.

Chapter 11: Collaborating with Teams in Visual Studio

Section 11.1: Using Team Foundation Server (TFS)

Collaboration is a crucial aspect of software development, and Visual Studio provides powerful tools for team collaboration. One of the key tools for collaborative development in Visual Studio is Team Foundation Server (TFS). TFS is a centralized source code management and project management system that facilitates collaboration among team members, version control, and project tracking. In this section, we will explore how to effectively use Team Foundation Server in your development workflow.

Understanding Team Foundation Server (TFS)

Team Foundation Server, often abbreviated as TFS, is a comprehensive collaboration platform provided by Microsoft. It offers a wide range of features for managing and tracking software projects. TFS includes version control, build automation, release management, work item tracking, and more. It can be hosted on-premises or in the cloud using Azure DevOps Services.

Setting Up Team Foundation Server

Before you can start using TFS for collaboration, you need to set up a TFS server or sign up for Azure DevOps Services. Setting up TFS involves installing and configuring the server, creating team projects, and defining access permissions for team members. Azure DevOps Services, on the other hand, is a cloud-based platform that provides similar capabilities without the need for on-premises server installation.

Creating and Managing Team Projects

Once TFS is set up, you can create team projects to organize your software development efforts. Each team project serves as a container for your source code, work items, and project-related artifacts. You can define project templates, customize process workflows, and configure team dashboards to suit your team's needs.

Version Control with TFS

One of the primary features of TFS is its robust version control system. TFS offers two version control options: Team Foundation Version Control (TFVC) and Git. TFVC is a centralized version control system that uses check-in and check-out operations, while Git is a distributed version control system known for its flexibility and branching capabilities. You can choose the version control system that best fits your project's requirements.

Work Item Tracking and Agile Planning

TFS provides tools for tracking work items such as user stories, bugs, tasks, and features. You can use TFS to plan and manage your project using agile methodologies like Scrum or Kanban. Work items can be assigned to team members, prioritized, and tracked through various states, ensuring transparency and progress monitoring.

Continuous Integration and Build Automation

TFS integrates seamlessly with build automation tools, allowing you to set up continuous integration (CI) pipelines. CI ensures that your code is automatically built, tested, and deployed whenever changes are committed to the version control system. This practice helps catch and address issues early in the development process.

Collaborative Coding with Visual Studio Live Share

In addition to TFS, Visual Studio provides another collaborative tool called Live Share. Live Share enables real-time collaborative coding sessions, allowing team members to edit code together, debug collaboratively, and share their development environment. It's a valuable tool for remote teams and pair programming.

Conclusion

Team Foundation Server (TFS) is a powerful platform for collaboration and project management in Visual Studio. By effectively using TFS, teams can streamline their development processes, improve code quality, and enhance collaboration among team members. In the next sections, we will explore other collaborative tools and practices in Visual Studio.

This concludes our overview of using Team Foundation Server (TFS) for collaborative development in Visual Studio. In the following sections, we will delve into other aspects of collaborating with teams in Visual Studio, including version control with Git, work item tracking, and best practices for team development.

Section 11.2: Collaborative Coding with Live Share

Collaboration among team members, especially in a distributed or remote work environment, is essential for successful software development. Visual Studio provides a powerful feature called Live Share that facilitates real-time collaborative coding sessions. In this section, we will explore how to use Live Share effectively for collaborative development.

What is Visual Studio Live Share?

Visual Studio Live Share is an extension for Visual Studio that enables developers to collaborate in real time, regardless of their physical location. With Live Share, you can share your development environment, code, debugging sessions, and even terminals with other team members. It's a valuable tool for pair programming, code reviews, and troubleshooting code together.

Getting Started with Live Share

To get started with Live Share, you need Visual Studio 2019 or later, as well as the Live Share extension installed. Once you have these prerequisites, follow these steps:

1. Open your project in Visual Studio.
2. Click on the "Live Share" button in the status bar at the bottom of the Visual Studio window.
3. Sign in with your Microsoft account or the account associated with your Visual Studio subscription.
4. After signing in, you'll receive a link that you can share with your team members. They can join the Live Share session using this link.

Collaborative Coding Features

Live Share provides several collaborative coding features:

1. Real-Time Code Editing

Team members can simultaneously edit code in the same file. You can see each other's cursors and selections in real time. This feature is particularly useful for pair programming or solving complex coding challenges together.

2. Debugging Together

Live Share allows for collaborative debugging sessions. Team members can set breakpoints, step through code, and inspect variables together. It's an excellent way to troubleshoot issues as a team.

3. Shared Terminals

You can share your terminal with other participants in the Live Share session. This is helpful when you need to run scripts or commands that affect the development environment.

4. Read-Only Mode

You can control the level of access for each participant. If you want someone to review your code without making changes, you can set them to read-only mode.

5. Code Comments and Annotations

Live Share allows participants to leave comments and annotations in the code. This is handy for providing feedback or explaining code sections.

Advanced Features

Live Share offers advanced features like guest access for those who don't have Visual Studio installed, support for multiple programming languages, and integration with Visual Studio Code.

Security and Privacy

Security is a top priority for Live Share. Only participants with the session link can join, and you can revoke access at any time. Additionally, Live Share ensures that sensitive information like credentials is not shared.

Conclusion

Visual Studio Live Share is a powerful tool for collaborative coding in Visual Studio. It enhances teamwork, productivity, and the overall development experience. Whether your team is co-located or distributed across the globe, Live Share enables seamless collaboration and real-time problem-solving. In the next sections, we will explore other collaboration tools and best practices in Visual Studio.

Section 11.3: Version Control with Git and Visual Studio

Version control is a fundamental aspect of modern software development, enabling teams to manage changes to their codebase, collaborate effectively, and track the history of their project. Git is one of the most popular version control systems, and Visual Studio provides robust integration with Git. In this section, we will explore how to use Git within Visual Studio for version control.

Git Basics

Git is a distributed version control system that allows developers to track changes to their codebase over time. It uses a branching model that enables developers to work on features, bug fixes, and improvements in isolation. Key Git concepts include:

- **Repository (Repo)**: A Git repository is a directory that contains your project's files and all the information needed to track changes to those files.

- **Commit**: A commit is a snapshot of your project at a specific point in time. Commits record changes to one or more files, along with a commit message describing the changes.

- **Branch**: A branch is a lightweight movable pointer to a commit. Developers can create branches to work on specific features or fixes without affecting the main codebase.

- **Merge**: Merging is the process of integrating changes from one branch into another, typically from a feature branch to the main branch.

- **Pull Request (PR)**: A pull request is a mechanism for submitting and reviewing code changes. It allows team members to discuss and review the proposed changes before merging them.

Git in Visual Studio

Visual Studio provides a rich set of tools and features for working with Git:

1. Git Integration

Visual Studio has built-in Git integration, allowing you to create, clone, and manage Git repositories directly within the IDE.

2. Team Explorer

The Team Explorer window in Visual Studio provides a centralized location for managing Git repositories, viewing commit history, creating branches, and initiating pull requests.

3. Git Branching and Merging

You can easily create and switch between Git branches in Visual Studio. Merging and resolving conflicts are also streamlined processes.

4. Pull Requests

Visual Studio supports creating and reviewing pull requests from within the IDE. You can view and comment on changes, initiate code reviews, and approve or reject pull requests.

5. Git History and Annotations

The Git History window allows you to visualize the commit history of your project, view file annotations to see who made specific changes, and compare different versions of your code.

Common Git Workflows

Here are a few common Git workflows you can follow in Visual Studio:

1. Feature Branch Workflow

In this workflow, each new feature or bug fix is developed in its own branch. Developers create a branch, make changes, commit them, and then create a pull request to merge their changes into the main branch.

2. Git Flow Workflow

Git Flow is a branching model that defines specific branch names and their purposes. It distinguishes between feature branches, release branches, and the main development branch.

3. GitHub Flow Workflow

GitHub Flow is a simplified workflow focused on continuous delivery. Developers create feature branches, make changes, push them to the main repository, and create pull requests for code review.

Conclusion

Version control with Git and Visual Studio is essential for managing collaborative software development projects. Whether you are working on a small team or a large-scale project, Git provides the tools to track changes, collaborate effectively, and maintain code quality. In the next sections, we will explore other aspects of collaborative development in Visual Studio.

Section 11.4: Managing Work Items and Tracking Progress

In software development projects, managing work items and tracking progress is crucial for maintaining transparency, collaboration, and efficient project delivery. Visual Studio offers tools and features to help teams manage work items, track issues, and monitor the status of tasks. In this section, we will explore how to effectively manage work items in Visual Studio.

Work Items and Agile Methodologies

Visual Studio supports Agile methodologies such as Scrum and Kanban, making it easy for teams to plan, prioritize, and execute work. Work items represent tasks, user stories, bugs, and other units of work in your project. Key concepts related to work items include:

- **User Stories**: User stories represent features or functionality from the end user's perspective. They are often used to capture requirements and define the scope of work.

- **Tasks**: Tasks are smaller units of work that make up user stories. They represent the specific actions needed to complete a user story.

- **Bugs**: Bugs track defects or issues in the software. They can be created by developers, testers, or stakeholders.

Work Item Tracking in Visual Studio

Visual Studio provides tools for creating, managing, and tracking work items:

1. Work Item Types

You can define custom work item types to suit your project's needs. For example, you can create work item types for requirements, features, tasks, and bugs.

2. Backlogs

The Backlog view allows you to prioritize and organize work items. You can add, update, and remove items from the backlog to plan upcoming sprints or iterations.

3. Boards

Boards in Visual Studio provide a visual representation of work items. You can use the Kanban board to move work items through different stages, such as "To Do," "In Progress," and "Done."

4. Queries

Work item queries allow you to filter and search for specific items. You can create queries based on various criteria, such as work item type, assigned team member, or iteration.

5. Dashboards and Reports

Visual Studio provides customizable dashboards and reports to track project progress and view key metrics. You can create widgets to display relevant data.

Agile Planning and Execution

Visual Studio facilitates Agile planning and execution through the following features:

1. Sprint Planning

Teams can plan their sprints by selecting work items from the backlog and assigning them to specific iterations. This helps in setting sprint goals and estimating the amount of work to be done.

2. Capacity Planning

Capacity planning allows teams to allocate work to team members based on their capacity. It helps in ensuring a balanced workload and realistic planning.

3. Task Boards

Task boards provide a visual representation of work item progress. Team members can move tasks across columns as they work on them, making it easy to see the status of each item.

Integration with Version Control

Visual Studio's integration with Git and other version control systems ensures that work item changes are linked to code changes. This traceability helps in understanding which code changes are associated with specific work items and vice versa.

Conclusion

Effective work item management and tracking are essential components of successful software development projects. Visual Studio's robust tools for work item management, Agile planning, and integration with version control systems make it a valuable platform for teams to collaborate, monitor progress, and deliver high-quality software on schedule. In the following sections, we will explore additional aspects of collaborative development in Visual Studio.

Section 11.5: Best Practices for Team Development

Collaborative software development is a complex endeavor that requires effective coordination, communication, and adherence to best practices. In this section, we'll explore some of the best practices for team development in Visual Studio, which can help ensure a smooth and productive development process.

1. Version Control

Use version control systems like Git integrated with Visual Studio to track changes to your codebase. This allows team members to work on different aspects of the project simultaneously without conflicts. Make frequent commits with descriptive commit messages to provide context about changes.

```
# Commit changes in Git

git add .

git commit -m "Added user authentication feature"

git push origin main
```

2. Code Reviews

Implement a code review process to maintain code quality. Visual Studio's integration with Git and tools like Azure DevOps facilitates code reviews. Encourage team members to review each other's code for correctness, maintainability, and adherence to coding standards.

3. Continuous Integration (CI)

Set up a CI pipeline to automate the build and testing process. Tools like Azure DevOps or Jenkins can be integrated with Visual Studio projects. CI ensures that code changes are continuously validated, reducing integration issues.

4. Continuous Deployment (CD)

Implement CD pipelines to automate the deployment process. When code changes pass CI tests, they can automatically be deployed to staging or production environments. CD reduces manual deployment errors and accelerates delivery.

5. Coding Standards

Establish coding standards and conventions that all team members should follow. Visual Studio allows you to define and enforce code style rules using tools like Roslyn analyzers and EditorConfig files.

6. Documentation

Maintain thorough documentation for your project. This includes code comments, README files, and user documentation. Visual Studio supports generating XML documentation comments that can be used to auto-generate API documentation.

7. Agile Methodologies

Adopt Agile methodologies like Scrum or Kanban to manage work items effectively. Use Visual Studio's Agile planning tools to create backlogs, plan sprints, and track progress.

8. Testing

Implement a comprehensive testing strategy, including unit testing, integration testing, and functional testing. Visual Studio provides testing frameworks and tools to support testing efforts.

```
// Example unit test in Visual Studio with MSTest

[TestClass]

public class MyTests

{

[TestMethod]

public void TestAddition()

{

// Arrange

int a = 5;

int b = 3;

int expected = 8;

// Act

int result = Calculator.Add(a, b);

// Assert

Assert.AreEqual(expected, result);

}

}
```

9. Task Tracking

Use Visual Studio's work item tracking and boards to manage tasks efficiently. Regularly update work items' status, and ensure that team members have a clear view of the project's progress.

10. Communication

Maintain open and effective communication channels within the team. Hold regular stand-up meetings, sprint planning sessions, and retrospectives to ensure everyone is aligned and can provide feedback.

11. Security

Prioritize security throughout development. Perform security reviews, vulnerability assessments, and incorporate security best practices into your codebase.

12. Performance Optimization

Regularly monitor and optimize the performance of your application. Visual Studio's profiling and diagnostic tools can help identify performance bottlenecks.

13. Backup and Disaster Recovery

Implement robust backup and disaster recovery strategies to safeguard your project's data and ensure business continuity.

By adhering to these best practices, development teams using Visual Studio can work more efficiently, deliver high-quality software, and minimize the risks associated with collaborative software development projects. Successful team development is not only about writing code but also about how effectively teams collaborate and manage the entire software development lifecycle.

Chapter 12: Visual Studio and Cloud Integration

Section 12.1: Connecting to Azure Services

In today's cloud-centric world, integrating cloud services into your Visual Studio projects can significantly enhance scalability, flexibility, and the overall capabilities of your applications. Microsoft Azure, a popular cloud platform, offers a wide range of services that can be seamlessly integrated with Visual Studio. In this section, we'll explore how to connect your Visual Studio projects to Azure services.

Azure Dev Tools for Visual Studio

Microsoft provides a set of Azure Dev Tools for Visual Studio, which streamlines the process of connecting your projects to Azure services. Here's how to get started:

1. **Azure Account**: Ensure that you have an active Azure account. If not, sign up for one on the Azure portal (https://portal.azure.com/).
2. **Install Visual Studio**: If you haven't already, install Visual Studio (the Community, Professional, or Enterprise edition) on your development machine.
3. **Azure Dev Tools Extension**: Open Visual Studio and go to the Extensions menu. Search for "Azure Dev Tools" and install the Azure Dev Tools for Visual Studio extension.
4. **Sign In**: Click on the "Sign In" button within Visual Studio, and log in with your Azure account credentials.
5. **Azure Services**: Once signed in, you can access various Azure services directly from Visual Studio. These services

include Azure App Service for web apps, Azure SQL Database, Azure Functions, Azure Storage, and more.

Creating Azure Resources

Now that you're connected to Azure, you can create and manage Azure resources from within Visual Studio. Here's how to create an Azure Web App as an example:

1. **Open Visual Studio**: Launch Visual Studio and open your project or create a new one.
2. **Add Azure Resources**: Right-click on your project in the Solution Explorer, and select "Add" > "Azure Resource Manager." This will open a wizard to add Azure resources to your project.
3. **Select Resource Type**: Choose the type of Azure resource you want to add (e.g., Web App).
4. **Configure Settings**: Configure the settings for your Azure resource, such as the name, location, and resource group.
5. **Review and Create**: Review your settings and click "Create" to provision the Azure resource.

Publishing to Azure

Once you've created Azure resources, you can publish your application to Azure directly from Visual Studio. Here's how to do it:

1. **Right-Click on Project**: Right-click on your project in Solution Explorer and select "Publish."
2. **Select Azure**: Choose "Azure" as the target for publishing.
3. **Choose Existing Azure App Service or Create New**: You can either choose an existing Azure App Service or create a new one.

4. **Publish**: Click the "Publish" button to deploy your application to Azure.

Visual Studio will package your application and deploy it to the selected Azure App Service. You can then access your application via its Azure URL.

Azure SDKs and Libraries

Visual Studio also provides a range of SDKs and libraries that simplify interaction with Azure services in your code. You can use these libraries to access Azure Storage, Azure Cosmos DB, Azure Cognitive Services, and more.

For example, to work with Azure Storage, you can use the Azure.Storage.Blobs library to manage blobs and containers:

```
using Azure.Storage.Blobs;

// Connect to the Azure Storage account

BlobServiceClient serviceClient = new BlobServiceClient(connectionString);

// Create a container

BlobContainerClient containerClient = serviceClient.GetBlobContainerClient("mycontainer");

// Upload a blob

BlobClient blobClient = containerClient.GetBlobClient("myblob");

await blobClient.UploadAsync("Hello, Azure!");

// Download a blob
```

```
BlobDownloadInfo blob = await blobClient.DownloadAsync();

string content = await new StreamReader(blob.Content).ReadToEndAsync();
```

In this section, we've covered the fundamentals of connecting your Visual Studio projects to Azure services. Azure integration offers a wide array of possibilities, from hosting web applications to leveraging AI and machine learning services, making it a valuable addition to your development toolkit.

Section 12.2: Developing Cloud Applications

Developing cloud applications in Visual Studio allows you to harness the power of cloud computing for scalability, reliability, and accessibility. In this section, we will explore the process of building cloud applications using Visual Studio and Microsoft Azure.

Choosing the Right Cloud Service Model

Before diving into development, it's essential to understand the different cloud service models available:

1. **Infrastructure as a Service (IaaS)**: In this model, you manage virtual machines (VMs) hosted in the cloud. You have control over the operating system, but responsibilities like patching and maintenance fall on you.
2. **Platform as a Service (PaaS)**: PaaS provides a platform for application development without worrying about infrastructure management. Azure App Service and Azure Functions are examples of PaaS offerings.
3. **Serverless Computing**: Azure Functions and AWS Lambda are serverless computing platforms that allow you to run code in response to events without managing

servers.

4. **Containers**: Docker and Kubernetes are popular for containerizing applications and managing them at scale.

Choosing the right service model depends on your application's requirements and your level of control over the environment.

Developing with Azure App Service

Azure App Service is a powerful PaaS offering for building and hosting web applications, APIs, and mobile app backends. Here's how to get started:

1. **Create an Azure App Service**: In Visual Studio, use the Azure SDK to create a new Azure App Service. You can select the runtime stack (e.g., .NET, Node.js, Python) and the type of application (e.g., web app, API).
2. **Code Your Application**: Develop your application using Visual Studio as you normally would. You can take advantage of Azure-specific libraries and tools for integration.
3. **Testing Locally**: Visual Studio provides tools to test your application locally before deploying it to Azure. This ensures your code works as expected.
4. **Publish to Azure**: Once your application is ready, right-click on the project and select "Publish." You can choose your Azure App Service as the target, and Visual Studio will handle the deployment.

Azure Functions for Serverless Applications

For serverless applications, Azure Functions offer a flexible way to run code in response to various triggers. Here's how to work with Azure Functions in Visual Studio:

1. **Create an Azure Function Project**: Use the Azure Functions project template in Visual Studio to get started. You can choose a trigger (e.g., HTTP, timer, queue) that activates your function.
2. **Code Your Function**: Write the code for your function. Azure Functions are typically short-lived and stateless, designed to perform a specific task.
3. **Testing Locally**: Visual Studio provides a local development environment for testing your Azure Functions before deploying them.
4. **Deploy to Azure**: You can publish your Azure Functions directly to Azure from Visual Studio. It handles the deployment and scaling of your functions.

Containerized Applications

Containerization allows you to package your application and its dependencies into a consistent environment. You can use Visual Studio to create Docker containers for your applications:

1. **Dockerize Your Application**: Visual Studio includes Docker support, enabling you to create Docker containers for your applications. You can choose a base image and customize it as needed.
2. **Debugging in Containers**: Visual Studio allows you to debug your code running inside Docker containers, making it easier to diagnose issues.
3. **Container Orchestration**: If you're managing multiple containers, tools like Kubernetes can be used to orchestrate and scale your containers in Azure Kubernetes Service (AKS).

Monitoring and Scaling

After deploying your cloud application, it's crucial to monitor its performance and scale resources as needed. Azure offers various monitoring and scaling tools to help you optimize your application's performance and cost.

In this section, we've explored the process of developing cloud applications using Visual Studio and Azure. Whether you're building web applications, serverless functions, or containerized solutions, Visual Studio provides the tools and integration needed to streamline your development workflow in the cloud.

Section 12.3: Managing Cloud Resources

In this section, we will delve into the critical aspect of managing cloud resources when developing cloud applications in Visual Studio. Proper resource management ensures the efficient operation of your applications, cost optimization, and security compliance.

Azure Resource Groups

Azure Resource Groups provide a way to organize and manage related Azure resources. When creating cloud applications, it's common to have various resources such as virtual machines, databases, storage accounts, and more. Resource Groups help you group these resources for easier management and monitoring.

Here's how to work with Resource Groups in Visual Studio:

1. **Create a Resource Group**: You can create a new Resource Group directly from Visual Studio using the Azure SDK. Specify a name, region, and optional tags.
2. **Organize Resources**: When creating or configuring Azure

resources, you can specify which Resource Group they belong to. This simplifies resource organization.

3. **Access Control**: Azure provides role-based access control (RBAC) to manage who can access and modify resources within a Resource Group.
4. **Monitoring**: Resource Groups allow you to monitor the health and performance of all resources they contain from a single dashboard.

Azure Resource Manager (ARM) Templates

ARM templates are JSON files that define the resources you need for your application. They enable infrastructure as code (IaC), allowing you to define and deploy your entire infrastructure programmatically. Visual Studio provides tools for working with ARM templates:

1. **Template Authoring**: Visual Studio includes a template authoring experience, making it easier to create and edit ARM templates. You can use the ARM template project template to get started.
2. **Parameterization**: ARM templates support parameterization, allowing you to customize deployments for different environments (e.g., development, staging, production).
3. **Deployment**: You can use Visual Studio to deploy ARM templates to Azure. This ensures consistent and repeatable deployments of your infrastructure.

Azure DevTest Labs

Azure DevTest Labs is a service that allows you to easily create and manage environments for development and testing. It helps control costs and provides a consistent environment for your development teams. In Visual Studio, you can integrate with DevTest Labs:

1. **Creating Lab Environments**: You can create lab environments with specific configurations, such as VM sizes, software installations, and policies, directly from Visual Studio.
2. **Resource Cleanup**: DevTest Labs can automatically deprovision resources when they're not in use, helping you save on costs.
3. **Integration with Visual Studio**: Visual Studio integrates with DevTest Labs to enable developers to request and use lab environments as needed.

Resource Tagging

Tagging resources is a best practice for resource management. Tags are name-value pairs that you can assign to resources for categorization, tracking, and cost allocation. Visual Studio allows you to:

1. **Assign Tags**: You can assign tags to resources during resource creation or by editing existing resources.
2. **Search and Filter**: Visual Studio provides tools to search and filter resources based on their tags, making it easier to manage and monitor resources with specific criteria.
3. **Cost Reporting**: Tags are essential for cost allocation and reporting, helping you track how resources contribute to your cloud expenses.

Resource Locks

Azure Resource Locks are a security feature that prevents accidental deletion or modification of critical resources. You can use Visual Studio to:

1. **Apply Locks**: Visual Studio allows you to apply read-only or delete locks to resources. This ensures that critical resources are protected from accidental changes.
2. **Role-Based Access Control (RBAC)**: Resource Locks can work in conjunction with RBAC to control who can apply or remove locks on resources.

Properly managing cloud resources is fundamental to the success of your cloud applications. With Visual Studio's integrated tools and Azure's resource management features, you can effectively organize, deploy, monitor, and secure your cloud resources, ensuring the reliability and cost-effectiveness of your applications.

Section 12.4: Cloud Deployment and Monitoring

In this section, we will explore cloud deployment strategies and monitoring techniques for cloud applications developed in Visual Studio. Deployment and monitoring are crucial aspects of ensuring the availability, scalability, and reliability of your cloud-based solutions.

Cloud Deployment Strategies

When deploying cloud applications, you have several deployment strategies to choose from, depending on your requirements:

1. **Continuous Deployment (CD)**: Implement CD pipelines

to automate the deployment process whenever code changes are pushed to the repository. Visual Studio can integrate with various CI/CD tools, including Azure DevOps, Jenkins, and GitHub Actions.
2. **Blue-Green Deployment**: Create two identical environments (blue and green). Deploy new versions to the green environment while the blue environment handles production traffic. Once the green environment is validated, switch traffic to it.
3. **Canary Deployment**: Gradually roll out new features or updates to a subset of users before deploying to the entire user base. Visual Studio can assist in feature flag management for canary releases.
4. **Traffic Manager**: Use Azure Traffic Manager to distribute traffic across multiple regions or deployments, improving availability and fault tolerance.

Azure DevOps Integration

Visual Studio seamlessly integrates with Azure DevOps (formerly known as Visual Studio Team Services or VSTS) for end-to-end application lifecycle management. Azure DevOps offers features like version control, continuous integration, continuous deployment, and work item tracking.

You can use Visual Studio to:

1. **Create Azure DevOps Projects**: Create new Azure DevOps projects directly from Visual Studio to manage your source code and development pipelines.
2. **Source Control Integration**: Visual Studio provides built-in integration with Git, allowing you to easily connect your projects to Azure DevOps Git repositories.

3. **Continuous Integration**: Set up CI/CD pipelines in Azure DevOps to automate build and release processes. Visual Studio solutions can be built and deployed using Azure Pipelines.

Azure Application Insights

Azure Application Insights is a powerful monitoring and diagnostics service for cloud applications. It helps you track application performance, detect and diagnose issues, and understand user behavior. Visual Studio provides tools to integrate Application Insights into your projects:

1. **Instrumentation**: Visual Studio allows you to instrument your code with Application Insights SDKs to collect telemetry data. This data can include exceptions, custom events, and performance metrics.
2. **Dashboard and Alerts**: Create custom dashboards to monitor key performance indicators and set up alerts to be notified of issues in real-time.
3. **Trace and Debug**: Visual Studio's integration with Application Insights enables you to trace requests, diagnose performance bottlenecks, and troubleshoot issues effectively.
4. **User Analytics**: Gain insights into user behavior, such as session durations, user flows, and error rates, to improve the user experience.

Azure Monitor

Azure Monitor is a comprehensive monitoring service for Azure resources and applications. It provides a unified platform for collecting, analyzing, and acting on telemetry data from various sources. Visual Studio can be used in conjunction with Azure Monitor to:

1. **Application Performance Monitoring (APM)**: Visual Studio integrates with Azure Monitor's APM capabilities to help you track and analyze application performance, including response times, dependencies, and code-level insights.
2. **Log Analytics**: Visual Studio allows you to query and analyze log data collected by Azure Monitor using Kusto Query Language (KQL). This enables advanced troubleshooting and root cause analysis.
3. **Alerts and Auto-scaling**: Set up alerts based on metrics and logs to proactively respond to issues. Visual Studio provides tools for configuring auto-scaling to dynamically adjust resources based on demand.

Third-party Monitoring Solutions

Visual Studio is compatible with a wide range of third-party monitoring and observability tools. You can integrate these tools into your cloud applications to gain additional insights and capabilities. Some popular third-party monitoring solutions include:

1. **New Relic**: Visual Studio supports New Relic integration for application monitoring, error tracking, and performance optimization.
2. **Datadog**: Integrate Datadog to gain real-time visibility into your applications and infrastructure, with support for metrics, traces, and logs.
3. **Prometheus and Grafana**: Visual Studio can be configured to export metrics to Prometheus and use Grafana for visualization and alerting in Kubernetes

environments.

4. **Splunk**: Integrate Splunk for log aggregation, analysis, and real-time monitoring of your applications and infrastructure.

Selecting the right deployment strategy and monitoring solution is essential for the success of your cloud applications. Visual Studio, in combination with Azure DevOps, Azure Application Insights, Azure Monitor, and third-party tools, provides a comprehensive set of options to ensure your applications are deployed smoothly and monitored effectively.

Section 12.5: Security Considerations in Cloud Development

Security is a critical aspect of cloud development, and it's essential to safeguard your applications and data when working with cloud platforms like Microsoft Azure. In this section, we'll explore important security considerations and best practices for cloud-based applications developed in Visual Studio.

Data Encryption

One of the fundamental principles of cloud security is encrypting data both in transit and at rest:

- **Transport Layer Security (TLS)**: Always use TLS/SSL to encrypt data in transit. Visual Studio and Azure offer tools and services for managing SSL certificates and configuring HTTPS endpoints for your applications.

- **Azure Key Vault**: Azure Key Vault allows you to securely manage keys, secrets, and certificates used for data encryption. Visual Studio integrates with Azure Key Vault for easy access to these resources.

Identity and Access Management

Properly managing identities and access to cloud resources is vital:

- **Azure Active Directory (Azure AD)**: Visual Studio seamlessly integrates with Azure AD for identity management. Implement Azure AD authentication and authorization to control access to your applications.

- **Role-Based Access Control (RBAC)**: Use RBAC in Azure to assign permissions to users and service principals. Visual Studio's Azure SDK provides tools for managing RBAC roles programmatically.

Security Patching and Updates

Keeping your cloud infrastructure and applications up to date with security patches is crucial:

- **Azure Update Management**: Use Azure Update Management to automate patching and update processes for virtual machines and other Azure resources. Visual Studio can help you schedule and manage updates.

Threat Detection and Monitoring

Detecting and responding to security threats is essential:

- **Azure Security Center**: Visual Studio integrates with Azure Security Center, which provides advanced threat detection and security monitoring. Implement security policies and use advanced threat protection features.

- **Application Insights**: Utilize Application Insights to monitor and detect anomalies in your application's behavior. Visual Studio supports integrating Application Insights into your projects for real-time monitoring.

Compliance and Auditing

Compliance with industry standards and regulations is often necessary:

- **Azure Policy**: Implement Azure Policy to enforce compliance requirements for your resources. Visual Studio helps you define and manage Azure Policy definitions.

Secure Coding Practices

Adopt secure coding practices to prevent common vulnerabilities:

- **OWASP Top Ten**: Familiarize yourself with the OWASP Top Ten list of web application vulnerabilities and use Visual Studio's code analysis tools to identify and fix potential issues.

- **Static Code Analysis**: Visual Studio includes static code analysis tools that can identify security issues during development. Use these tools to catch vulnerabilities early in the development process.

Secure DevOps

Incorporate security into your DevOps practices:

- **DevSecOps**: Promote a DevSecOps culture by integrating security into your DevOps pipelines. Visual

Studio can be used with Azure DevOps and other CI/CD tools to automate security checks.

- **Container Security**: If you use containerization with Docker or Kubernetes, ensure container images are scanned for vulnerabilities using tools like Azure Container Registry scanning.

Security Awareness and Training

Invest in security awareness and training for your development team:

- **Security Training**: Provide security training to developers to raise awareness about common threats and best practices. Visual Studio offers resources and extensions for secure coding training.

- **Azure Security Learning Paths**: Azure provides learning paths and documentation on secure application development practices.

Incident Response Plan

Develop an incident response plan to handle security incidents effectively:

- **Azure Security Center Playbooks**: Use Azure Security Center playbooks to automate incident response actions. Visual Studio can be used to develop custom playbooks.

Remember that security is an ongoing process, and staying updated on emerging threats and best practices is essential. Visual Studio, in combination with Azure's security services, provides the tools and capabilities you need to build secure and resilient cloud applications.

Chapter 13: Advanced Programming Techniques

In this chapter, we delve into advanced programming techniques that can take your development skills to the next level. These techniques are essential for building robust and efficient applications. In Section 13.1, we'll explore the concept of design patterns, which are reusable solutions to common software design problems.

Section 13.1: Understanding Design Patterns

Design patterns are tried-and-tested solutions to recurring design problems in software development. They provide a structured approach to solving problems and can significantly improve the maintainability and scalability of your code. Let's dive into some of the most commonly used design patterns.

Creational Design Patterns

1. **Singleton Pattern**: The Singleton pattern ensures that a class has only one instance and provides a global point of access to that instance. It's useful when you want to limit the number of instances of a class.
2. **Factory Method Pattern**: The Factory Method pattern defines an interface for creating an object but allows subclasses to alter the type of objects that will be created. It's useful for creating objects without specifying the exact class of object that will be created.
3. **Abstract Factory Pattern**: The Abstract Factory pattern provides an interface for creating families of related or dependent objects without specifying their concrete classes. It's helpful for ensuring that the created objects

work together seamlessly.

Structural Design Patterns

1. **Adapter Pattern**: The Adapter pattern allows the interface of an existing class to be used as another interface. It's useful when you want to make an existing class work with others without modifying its source code.
2. **Decorator Pattern**: The Decorator pattern attaches additional responsibilities to an object dynamically. It's useful for extending the behavior of objects without subclassing.
3. **Composite Pattern**: The Composite pattern composes objects into tree structures to represent part-whole hierarchies. It's beneficial for treating both individual objects and compositions of objects uniformly.

Behavioral Design Patterns

1. **Observer Pattern**: The Observer pattern defines a one-to-many dependency between objects, where one object (the subject) maintains a list of its dependents (observers) and notifies them of state changes. It's useful for building loosely coupled systems.
2. **Strategy Pattern**: The Strategy pattern defines a family of algorithms, encapsulates each one, and makes them interchangeable. It's helpful for allowing clients to choose the algorithm that suits their needs at runtime.
3. **Command Pattern**: The Command pattern encapsulates a request as an object, thereby allowing for parameterization of clients with queues, requests, and operations. It's useful for implementing undo functionality and more.

Other Design Patterns

1. **MVC (Model-View-Controller) Pattern**: MVC is an architectural pattern that separates an application into three interconnected components: Model, View, and Controller. It's widely used in building user interfaces.
2. **Dependency Injection Pattern**: Dependency Injection is a technique where the dependencies of a class are provided from the outside, typically through constructor injection or property injection. It promotes loose coupling and testability.

Understanding and applying these design patterns can greatly enhance your ability to design and develop scalable, maintainable, and flexible software. Each pattern has its use cases, and knowing when and how to apply them is a valuable skill for any developer.

In the following sections, we will explore more advanced programming topics, including asynchronous programming, advanced data structures, security implementation, and memory management optimization. These topics will further deepen your knowledge and proficiency in software development.

Section 13.2: Asynchronous Programming and Threading

Asynchronous programming is a crucial aspect of modern software development, especially in applications that need to perform non-blocking operations or efficiently utilize available hardware resources. In this section, we will explore the concepts of asynchronous programming and threading.

Understanding Asynchronous Programming

Asynchronous programming allows a program to execute tasks concurrently without blocking the main application thread. This is particularly important for tasks that involve I/O operations, such as reading from or writing to files, making network requests, or querying a database. By performing these operations asynchronously, you can keep your application responsive and avoid freezing the user interface.

Asynchronous Programming in C

In C#, you can use the async and await keywords to write asynchronous code. Here's a basic example of how asynchronous programming works in C#:

```
public async Task<string> DownloadDataAsync(string url)

{

HttpClient httpClient = new HttpClient();

HttpResponseMessage response = await httpClient.GetAsync(url);

if (response.IsSuccessStatusCode)

{

string data = await response.Content.ReadAsStringAsync();

return data;

}

return null;

}
```

In this example, the DownloadDataAsync method uses the async keyword to indicate that it's an asynchronous method. The await keyword is used to asynchronously wait for the completion of the GetAsync and ReadAsStringAsync operations, allowing the application to remain responsive.

Threading and Parallelism

Threading is another technique used to achieve concurrency in software. Threads are lightweight processes within an application that can execute code independently. They are suitable for tasks that can be parallelized, such as performing complex calculations or processing large datasets.

Using Threads in C

In C#, you can work with threads using the System.Threading namespace. Here's a simple example of creating and running a new thread:

```
using System;

using System.Threading;

public class ThreadExample

{

public static void Main(string[] args)

{

// Create a new thread and start it

Thread thread = new Thread(WorkerMethod);
```

```
thread.Start();

// Main thread continues executing other tasks

Console.WriteLine("Main thread is doing some work...");

}

private static void WorkerMethod()

{

// Simulate some work

Thread.Sleep(2000);

// Work is done

Console.WriteLine("Worker thread has finished.");

}

}
```

In this example, we create a new thread using the Thread class and start it with Start(). The main thread continues its work while the worker thread executes WorkerMethod asynchronously.

Choosing Between Asynchronous Programming and Threading

When deciding whether to use asynchronous programming or threading, consider the nature of your tasks. Asynchronous programming is typically more suitable for I/O-bound operations, while threading is better for CPU-bound tasks. You can also use a combination of both approaches when dealing with complex scenarios.

In the following sections, we will explore more advanced topics related to asynchronous programming and threading, including synchronization, parallel programming, and best practices for concurrency control. These concepts are crucial for building high-performance and responsive applications.

Section 13.3: Advanced Data Structures

In software development, data structures play a pivotal role in organizing and managing data efficiently. While basic data structures like arrays, lists, and dictionaries are commonly used, there are advanced data structures that provide specific advantages for various scenarios. In this section, we'll explore some of these advanced data structures and understand their applications.

1. Hash Tables

A hash table (or hash map) is a data structure that allows you to store key-value pairs. It provides fast access to values based on their keys, making it efficient for tasks like dictionary implementations and caching.

In C#, you can use the Dictionary<TKey, TValue> class to work with hash tables:

```
Dictionary<string, int> studentGrades = new Dictionary<string, int>();

studentGrades["Alice"] = 95;

studentGrades["Bob"] = 89;

int aliceGrade = studentGrades["Alice"]; // Retrieves the value associated with the key "Alice"
```

2. Linked Lists

Linked lists are dynamic data structures where each element (node) contains data and a reference (pointer) to the next node. Linked lists excel at insertions and deletions in the middle of the list, unlike arrays, which require shifting elements.

Here's a basic implementation of a singly linked list in C#:

```
public class ListNode<T>

{

public T Value { get; set; }

public ListNode<T> Next { get; set; }

public ListNode(T value)

{

Value = value;

}

}

public class LinkedList<T>

{

public ListNode<T> Head { get; private set; }

public void Add(T value)

{

var newNode = new ListNode<T>(value);
```

```
newNode.Next = Head;

Head = newNode;

}

}
```

3. Trees

Trees are hierarchical data structures with nodes connected by edges. They are widely used in applications like file systems, parsing expressions, and hierarchical data storage.

One common type of tree is the binary tree, where each node has at most two children. Here's an example of a binary tree in C#:

```
public class TreeNode<T>

{

public T Value { get; set; }

public TreeNode<T> Left { get; set; }

public TreeNode<T> Right { get; set; }

public TreeNode(T value)

{

Value = value;

}

}
```

4. Graphs

Graphs are versatile data structures used to represent relationships between entities. They consist of nodes (vertices) connected by edges. Graphs are used in a wide range of applications, including social networks, network routing, and recommendation systems.

In C#, you can use libraries like QuickGraph to work with graphs efficiently.

5. Heaps

A heap is a specialized tree-based data structure that satisfies the heap property. Heaps are used for tasks like implementing priority queues and sorting algorithms. Binary heaps, in particular, are commonly used.

Here's an example of a binary min-heap in C#:

```
using System;

using System.Collections.Generic;

var minHeap = new MinHeap<int>();

minHeap.Insert(10);

minHeap.Insert(15);

minHeap.Insert(30);

minHeap.Insert(5);

int min = minHeap.ExtractMin(); // Removes and returns the minimum value (5)
```

These advanced data structures provide solutions to complex data organization and manipulation problems. Choosing the right data structure for a specific task is essential for efficient and effective software development.

Section 13.4: Implementing Security in Applications

Security is a paramount concern in software development, and it's essential to consider security measures throughout the development lifecycle. In this section, we'll explore various aspects of implementing security in applications, including authentication, authorization, data encryption, and best practices.

1. Authentication and Authorization

Authentication is the process of verifying the identity of users, ensuring they are who they claim to be. Authorization, on the other hand, determines what actions and resources a user is allowed to access after they have been authenticated.

In .NET applications, you can implement authentication and authorization using libraries like ASP.NET Identity or third-party solutions like IdentityServer4. These frameworks provide tools for user management, role-based access control, and token-based authentication.

Here's a simplified example of how authentication and authorization work in ASP.NET Core:

```
[Authorize(Roles = "Admin")]

public class AdminController : Controller

{
```

```
// Only authenticated users with the "Admin" role can access this controller.

}
```

2. Data Encryption

Protecting sensitive data is crucial. Encryption is the process of converting data into a format that can only be deciphered with the appropriate decryption key. .NET provides libraries like System.Security.Cryptography for encryption and decryption tasks.

Here's an example of encrypting data in C#:

```
using System;

using System.Security.Cryptography;

using System.Text;

public static string Encrypt(string plainText, string key)

{

using (Aes aesAlg = Aes.Create())

{

aesAlg.Key = Encoding.UTF8.GetBytes(key);

aesAlg.IV = new byte[16]; // Initialization Vector (IV) for AES encryption

ICryptoTransform encryptor = aesAlg.CreateEncryptor(aesAlg.Key, aesAlg.IV);

using (MemoryStream msEncrypt = new MemoryStream())
```

```
{
using (CryptoStream csEncrypt = new CryptoStream(msEncrypt, encryptor, CryptoStreamMode.Write))
{
using (StreamWriter swEncrypt = new StreamWriter(csEncrypt))
{
swEncrypt.Write(plainText);
}
}
return Convert.ToBase64String(msEncrypt.ToArray());
}
}
}
```

3. Secure Coding Practices

Secure coding practices are essential for writing secure applications. Some key principles include:

- Input validation: Always validate and sanitize user inputs to prevent injection attacks like SQL injection and Cross-Site Scripting (XSS).
- Error handling: Implement proper error handling to avoid exposing sensitive information in error messages.

- Least privilege: Grant the minimum necessary permissions to users and components to limit potential damage in case of a breach.

- Regular updates: Keep all software components, libraries, and dependencies up to date to address security vulnerabilities.

- Security testing: Perform regular security testing, including penetration testing and code reviews, to identify and fix vulnerabilities.

4. Authentication Protocols

When implementing authentication, you may encounter various protocols like OAuth 2.0 and OpenID Connect for web applications. OAuth 2.0 allows third-party applications to access resources on behalf of a user, while OpenID Connect provides identity and authentication services.

In .NET, libraries like IdentityServer4 simplify the implementation of these protocols, allowing you to secure your applications effectively.

5. Identity and Access Management (IAM)

For larger applications and organizations, consider using Identity and Access Management (IAM) solutions like Azure Active Directory or AWS Identity and Access Management. These services provide centralized user management, authentication, and authorization for multiple applications.

Implementing security measures in your applications is an ongoing process that requires vigilance and continuous improvement. By following best practices and using the tools and libraries available in the .NET ecosystem, you can enhance the security of your software and protect sensitive data from threats and vulnerabilities.

Section 13.5: Memory Management and Optimization

Memory management plays a crucial role in the performance and stability of software applications. In this section, we'll explore memory management and optimization techniques in the context of .NET development.

1. Understanding Memory Management in .NET

In the .NET runtime, memory management is primarily handled by the Garbage Collector (GC). The GC is responsible for allocating and releasing memory, ensuring that objects that are no longer in use are reclaimed to prevent memory leaks.

.NET uses a generational garbage collection approach, where objects are categorized into different generations based on their age. This allows the GC to focus on collecting short-lived objects more frequently while leaving long-lived objects relatively untouched.

2. Memory Profiling and Analysis

To optimize memory usage in your application, it's essential to profile and analyze memory usage patterns. There are several tools available, such as the Visual Studio Profiler, JetBrains dotMemory, and ANTS Memory Profiler, that can help identify memory leaks, excessive allocations, and inefficient memory usage.

Memory profilers can provide insights into object lifetimes, memory traffic, and memory fragmentation, helping you pinpoint areas of improvement.

3. Managing Large Data Sets

In applications dealing with large data sets, efficient memory management becomes even more critical. Consider using streaming and pagination techniques to process data in smaller, manageable chunks rather than loading the entire data set into memory.

For example, when working with large databases, use database query pagination or the Entity Framework's Take and Skip methods to retrieve and process data in smaller portions.

4. Disposing of Resources

Properly disposing of resources, such as file handles, network connections, and database connections, is essential for memory management. Neglecting to release resources can lead to resource leaks and increased memory consumption.

The IDisposable pattern in .NET allows you to implement resource cleanup using the using statement or by explicitly calling the Dispose method. Here's an example of using the using statement to ensure resource disposal:

```
using (FileStream fs = new FileStream("example.txt", FileMode.Open))
{
// Use the FileStream
} // The FileStream is automatically disposed here
```

5. Optimizing Data Structures

Choosing the right data structures can significantly impact memory usage and application performance. For example, using a List<T>

may be suitable for small collections, but for large datasets, a more memory-efficient data structure like HashSet<T> or Dictionary<TKey, TValue> may be a better choice.

Additionally, consider using data structures from the System.Collections.Concurrent namespace for multi-threaded applications to reduce synchronization overhead.

6. Finalizers and Resource Cleanup

Finalizers in .NET allow you to perform resource cleanup when an object is garbage-collected. However, relying solely on finalizers can lead to non-deterministic resource cleanup and increased memory pressure. Whenever possible, prefer the IDisposable pattern for deterministic cleanup.

7. Memory Pressure and Monitoring

Monitoring memory usage and pressure is essential for proactive memory management. Tools like Windows Performance Monitor (PerfMon) and application-specific monitoring solutions can help you track memory usage, garbage collection activity, and potential memory-related issues in real-time.

8. Memory Optimization Techniques

There are several memory optimization techniques you can employ, such as object pooling, lazy loading, and reducing unnecessary object allocations. For example, consider reusing objects instead of creating new ones when possible, especially for frequently used objects.

// Object pooling example

```
var pool = new ObjectPool<MyObject>(() => new MyObject(), 10); // Create a pool with a maximum of 10 objects

MyObject obj = pool.Get(); // Get an object from the pool

// ...

pool.Release(obj); // Return the object to the pool for reuse
```

9. Testing and Profiling

Regular testing and profiling of your application's memory usage are essential to identify and address memory-related issues. Incorporate memory profiling into your development and testing processes to catch problems early and ensure efficient memory management.

By implementing these memory management and optimization techniques in your .NET applications, you can enhance their performance, stability, and resource utilization, ultimately providing a better user experience and reducing the risk of memory-related issues.

Chapter 14: Working with Graphics and Game Development

Section 14.1: Introduction to Graphics Programming

Graphics programming is a fascinating and creative field that allows developers to create visually stunning applications, including games, simulations, multimedia applications, and more. In this section, we'll introduce you to the fundamentals of graphics programming, which will serve as a foundation for understanding more advanced topics related to game development and graphics.

1. Understanding Graphics Programming

Graphics programming involves manipulating and rendering visual elements on a computer screen. It encompasses various aspects, including 2D and 3D rendering, image processing, animation, and interaction with input devices.

2. Graphics Libraries and APIs

To work with graphics, developers often use graphics libraries and APIs (Application Programming Interfaces) that provide functions and tools for rendering graphics. Some popular graphics libraries and APIs include DirectX, OpenGL, Vulkan, and WebGL for 3D graphics, and libraries like SDL (Simple DirectMedia Layer) for 2D graphics.

3. Coordinate Systems

In graphics programming, understanding coordinate systems is crucial. The coordinate system defines how points are positioned on the screen. The most common coordinate system for 2D graphics is the Cartesian coordinate system, where the origin (0,0) is at the top-left corner of the screen.

4. Drawing Primitives

Graphics programming involves drawing basic geometric shapes, known as primitives. Common primitives include points, lines, triangles, rectangles, and circles. These primitives serve as building blocks for creating complex images.

5. Color and Shading

Color plays a significant role in graphics. In digital graphics, colors are represented using combinations of red, green, and blue (RGB) values. Additionally, shading and lighting techniques are used to give depth and realism to rendered objects.

6. Transformations

Transformations are operations that modify the position, size, or orientation of objects in the graphics scene. Common transformations include translation (movement), rotation, scaling, and shearing.

7. Rasterization

Rasterization is the process of converting vector-based graphics (described by shapes and lines) into a raster or pixel-based image that can be displayed on the screen. Rasterization involves determining which pixels should be filled to represent the shapes accurately.

8. Rendering Pipeline

Graphics programming follows a rendering pipeline, which is a series of stages that transform 3D data into 2D images. These stages include geometry processing, vertex shading, pixel shading, and rasterization.

9. Graphics Hardware

Modern graphics programming heavily relies on dedicated graphics hardware, such as Graphics Processing Units (GPUs). GPUs are highly parallel processors optimized for rendering graphics quickly and efficiently.

10. Game Development and Graphics

Graphics programming is essential in game development. Games require rendering complex 3D scenes, handling animations, and providing immersive visual experiences. Game engines like Unity and Unreal Engine offer tools and frameworks to simplify graphics programming in the context of game development.

11. Graphics Programming Languages

Graphics programming can be done using various programming languages, including C++, C#, Java, and Python. The choice of language often depends on the specific graphics library or API being used and the platform of the application.

12. Getting Started

To get started with graphics programming, you'll need to choose a graphics library or framework that suits your project's requirements. Learning resources, tutorials, and sample code are available for most popular libraries, making it easier to start creating graphics-rich applications and games.

In this chapter, we'll delve deeper into graphics programming, exploring topics such as 2D and 3D graphics rendering, shaders, texture mapping, and more. Whether you're interested in creating visually stunning games or developing graphics-intensive applications, this chapter will provide you with the foundational knowledge needed to embark on your graphics programming journey.

Section 14.2: Using DirectX and Unity in Visual Studio

Graphics programming often involves leveraging powerful libraries and engines to simplify the development process and take advantage of hardware acceleration. Two widely used tools in graphics and game development are DirectX and Unity. In this section, we'll explore how Visual Studio can be used effectively with both of these tools.

1. DirectX with Visual Studio

DirectX is a collection of APIs developed by Microsoft for multimedia and game development, particularly for Windows platforms. It provides a low-level interface for tasks like 2D and 3D graphics rendering, audio processing, and input handling.

When working with DirectX in Visual Studio:

- **Development Environment**: Visual Studio provides a robust development environment for DirectX applications. You can create DirectX projects, access documentation, and use debugging tools.

- **DirectX SDK**: To work with DirectX, you'll need the DirectX SDK, which contains the necessary headers, libraries, and tools. Visual Studio can integrate with the SDK, making it easier to manage dependencies.

- **Direct3D**: DirectX includes Direct3D, which is the component responsible for 3D graphics rendering. Visual Studio allows you to write, compile, and debug Direct3D applications efficiently.

- **Shader Development**: Shaders are essential for graphics programming. Visual Studio offers features for developing and debugging HLSL (High-Level Shading Language) shaders, which are used in Direct3D.

- **Graphics Debugging**: Visual Studio's debugging capabilities extend to DirectX applications. You can set breakpoints, inspect variables, and analyze frame-by-frame rendering for debugging graphics-related issues.

- **Performance Profiling**: Profiling tools in Visual Studio help optimize DirectX applications. You can identify performance bottlenecks and improve the efficiency of your graphics code.

2. Unity with Visual Studio

Unity is a popular game engine that simplifies game development across multiple platforms. It provides a high-level environment for creating 2D and 3D games, including a visual editor, physics simulation, and scripting support.

When working with Unity in Visual Studio:

- **Integration**: Visual Studio seamlessly integrates with Unity, allowing you to write C# scripts that control game logic. You can use Visual Studio as your primary code editor for Unity projects.

- **Debugging**: Visual Studio provides debugging tools for Unity projects. You can set breakpoints, step through code, and inspect variables while your Unity game is running.

- **Scripting**: Unity primarily uses C# for scripting. Visual Studio offers code completion, IntelliSense, and code navigation features that enhance the scripting experience.

- **Unity Package Manager**: Visual Studio integrates with Unity Package Manager, which simplifies the process of managing external libraries and assets for your Unity project.

- **Performance Analysis**: Profiling and performance analysis tools in Visual Studio help you identify bottlenecks in your Unity game. You can optimize performance by analyzing CPU and memory usage.

- **Version Control**: Visual Studio supports version control systems like Git, which is commonly used with Unity projects for collaborative development.

3. Choosing the Right Tool

The choice between DirectX and Unity depends on your project's requirements and your familiarity with these tools. DirectX is ideal for developers who require fine-grained control over graphics and want to create custom rendering engines. Unity, on the other hand, is a versatile solution for game development, offering a wide range of built-in features.

In this section, we've introduced the integration of DirectX and Unity with Visual Studio. In subsequent chapters, we'll explore more advanced graphics programming topics and delve deeper into these tools to help you create captivating visual experiences in your applications and games.

Section 14.3: Developing 2D and 3D Games

Game development is a fascinating and creative field that has gained immense popularity over the years. In this section, we'll dive into the world of 2D and 3D game development using Visual Studio and explore the fundamental concepts you need to know.

1. Choosing a Game Engine

Before you start developing a game, you'll need to decide whether to build your own custom engine or use an existing game engine. Game engines like Unity, Unreal Engine, and Godot provide a wide range of tools and resources for game development and can significantly speed up the development process.

- **Unity**: Unity is a powerful and versatile game engine that supports both 2D and 3D game development. It offers a visual editor, a scripting environment using C#, and a wide range of assets and plugins.

- **Unreal Engine**: Unreal Engine is known for its stunning graphics and is popular for developing high-quality 3D games. It uses the Blueprint visual scripting system and C++ for programming.

• **Godot**: Godot is an open-source game engine that is gaining popularity for its simplicity and ease of use. It features a custom scripting language called GDScript, which is similar to Python.

2. Game Development with Visual Studio

Visual Studio provides excellent support for game development, irrespective of the game engine you choose. Here's how you can use Visual Studio effectively:

• **IDE Integration**: Most game engines, including Unity and Unreal Engine, offer seamless integration with Visual Studio. You can write and debug your game code directly in Visual Studio.

• **Scripting**: Game development often involves scripting to control game logic. Visual Studio offers advanced code editing features like syntax highlighting, code completion, and debugging for various scripting languages, including C#, C++, and GDScript.

• **Asset Management**: Visual Studio can be used to manage game assets, such as textures, models, and audio files, through version control systems like Git.

• **Debugging**: Debugging is crucial in game development to identify and fix issues. Visual Studio's debugging tools can help you track down and resolve bugs efficiently.

• **Performance Profiling**: Profiling your game's performance is essential for optimization. Visual Studio provides profiling tools to analyze CPU and memory usage, helping you improve your game's performance.

3. Graphics and Game Design

Creating captivating graphics and game design is a vital aspect of game development. Visual Studio can help you in the following ways:

- **Shader Development**: If you're working on a 3D game, you may need to write shaders to control how objects are rendered. Visual Studio provides support for writing and debugging shaders.

- **Asset Creation**: Visual Studio can be used alongside graphics software like Adobe Photoshop, Blender, or Maya for creating and editing game assets.

- **Game Design Documents**: You can use Visual Studio to create and maintain game design documents, outlining the game's mechanics, story, and objectives.

4. Testing and Debugging

Thorough testing and debugging are critical in game development to ensure a smooth player experience. Visual Studio offers various testing and debugging tools, including unit testing frameworks, which can be used to validate different aspects of your game.

5. Deployment and Distribution

Finally, Visual Studio can assist you in packaging and deploying your game to various platforms, whether it's for PC, console, mobile, or web. You can configure build pipelines and automate deployment processes to streamline the release of your game.

In conclusion, game development is a challenging but rewarding field. Visual Studio, coupled with a suitable game engine, can empower you to create stunning 2D and 3D games. Whether you're an indie developer or part of a larger game studio, the tools and features provided by Visual Studio can significantly enhance your game development workflow.

Section 14.4: Graphics Debugging and Performance

Graphics debugging and performance optimization are crucial aspects of game development. In this section, we will explore how Visual Studio can help you identify and resolve graphics-related issues and improve the performance of your games.

1. Graphics Debugging Tools

Visual Studio provides several tools for graphics debugging, which are particularly valuable when working with 3D games:

- **Graphics Debugger**: You can use the Graphics Debugger to inspect and debug the rendering process of your game. It allows you to view individual draw calls, shaders, and textures in real-time, helping you identify rendering issues.

- **GPU Usage Profiling**: Visual Studio's GPU Usage Profiling tool enables you to analyze how much time your game spends on the GPU. It helps identify GPU bottlenecks and optimize rendering code.

- **Shader Debugging**: When working with custom shaders, Visual Studio supports shader debugging, allowing you to step through shader code, set breakpoints, and inspect variable values during rendering.

2. Performance Profiling

Optimizing your game's performance is essential to ensure smooth gameplay experiences. Visual Studio offers various profiling tools:

- **CPU Usage Profiling**: Visual Studio's CPU Usage Profiler helps you identify performance bottlenecks on the CPU side. It provides insights into CPU usage by different functions and code regions, allowing you to focus on optimization efforts effectively.

- **Memory Usage Profiling**: Memory management is critical for game performance. Visual Studio can profile your game's memory usage, helping you detect memory leaks and inefficient memory allocation patterns.

- **Frame Rate Analysis**: For real-time rendering, maintaining a consistent frame rate is crucial. Visual Studio allows you to analyze frame times and frame rate variations, helping you pinpoint performance drops.

3. Debugging Graphics-Related Issues

When dealing with graphics-related issues in your game, Visual Studio can be your ally:

- **Breakpoints**: You can set breakpoints in your rendering code to pause the game at specific points and inspect variables and data structures, making it easier to catch and diagnose rendering problems.

- **Conditional Breakpoints**: Use conditional breakpoints to break execution only when certain conditions are met, such as when a specific rendering error occurs.

- **Immediate Window**: The Immediate Window in Visual Studio enables you to execute code during debugging sessions. You can use it to interactively test and modify rendering-related code.

4. Optimizing Graphics Performance

To improve graphics performance, consider the following techniques:

- **Batching**: Minimize the number of draw calls by batching objects that share the same materials or shaders. This reduces CPU overhead and improves rendering efficiency.

- **Level of Detail (LOD)**: Implement LOD systems to render simpler models or textures for distant objects, reducing GPU workload.

- **Texture Compression**: Use texture compression formats to reduce texture memory usage and GPU bandwidth requirements.

- **Culling**: Implement frustum and occlusion culling techniques to skip rendering of objects that are not visible to the camera.

- **GPU Instancing**: Utilize GPU instancing to efficiently render multiple instances of the same object with a single draw call.

- **Shader Optimization**: Profile and optimize your shaders to ensure they run efficiently on the GPU. Reduce unnecessary calculations and texture fetches.

5. Cross-Platform Considerations

If you're targeting multiple platforms (e.g., PC, consoles, mobile), keep in mind that each platform may have different graphics capabilities and limitations. Visual Studio allows you to configure and build your game for various platforms and perform platform-specific optimizations.

In conclusion, graphics debugging and performance optimization are integral parts of game development. Visual Studio provides a suite of tools and features to help you identify and resolve graphics-related issues and ensure your game runs smoothly. By utilizing these tools and applying optimization techniques, you can create games that offer exceptional visual quality and performance on a wide range of platforms.

Section 14.5: Publishing and Monetizing Games

Publishing and monetizing your games is a crucial step in the game development process. This section covers various aspects of bringing your game to market, making it accessible to players, and generating revenue from your hard work.

1. Choosing a Distribution Platform

Selecting the right distribution platform is essential for your game's success. Popular platforms for publishing games include:

- **Steam**: Steam is one of the largest digital distribution platforms for PC gaming. It offers a wide audience and tools for selling and marketing your game.

- **Epic Games Store**: The Epic Games Store provides a curated selection of games and offers competitive revenue-sharing models for developers.

- **Apple App Store and Google Play**: For mobile games, these platforms are the primary marketplaces. Each has its guidelines, revenue models, and audience.

- **Console Platforms**: If you're developing for consoles like PlayStation, Xbox, or Nintendo Switch, you'll need to partner with the platform holders for publishing.

2. Game Monetization Models

Choosing the right monetization model for your game is crucial. Some common models include:

- **Paid Games**: Players purchase your game upfront. This model works well for premium and high-quality titles.

- **Free-to-Play (F2P)**: Games are free to download and play, but you generate revenue through in-app purchases, advertisements, or microtransactions.

- **In-App Purchases (IAPs)**: Players can buy virtual items, cosmetics, or premium content within the game.

- **Ads**: You earn revenue by displaying ads to players. Common ad formats include interstitials, banners, and rewarded videos.

3. Game Marketing and Promotion

Effective marketing and promotion are essential to reach your target audience:

- **Create a Website**: Build a dedicated website for your game to showcase trailers, screenshots, and gameplay information.

- **Social Media**: Leverage platforms like Twitter, Facebook, Instagram, and YouTube to create a community around your game.

- **Press Releases**: Distribute press releases to gaming media outlets and influencers to generate interest and coverage.

- **Beta Testing**: Run beta tests to gather feedback and generate early buzz. Encourage players to sign up for beta access.

- **App Store Optimization (ASO)**: Optimize your game's listing on app stores with relevant keywords, appealing screenshots, and a compelling description.

4. Game Localization

Consider localizing your game for different regions and languages. Localization can significantly expand your potential player base.

5. User Support and Updates

Maintaining a positive relationship with your players is crucial:

- **Customer Support**: Offer timely and helpful customer support to address player inquiries, bug reports, and issues.

- **Regular Updates**: Continuously improve your game by releasing updates, new content, and bug fixes. Engaging with your player community can help you prioritize updates effectively.

6. Protecting Your Intellectual Property (IP)

Ensure you have the necessary legal protections for your game and its assets. Consult with legal experts to understand copyright, trademark, and licensing issues.

7. Monitoring and Analytics

Use analytics tools to track player behavior, engagement, and monetization. This data can guide your decisions regarding game updates, marketing strategies, and monetization adjustments.

8. Revenue Sharing and Payment Processing

Understand the revenue-sharing models of the distribution platforms you choose. Ensure you have a reliable payment processing system in place to receive your earnings.

9. Game Reviews and Ratings

Encourage players to leave reviews and ratings on app stores and gaming platforms. Positive reviews can boost your game's visibility and credibility.

10. Community Building

Foster a community of dedicated players around your game. Engage with your community through forums, social media, and in-game events.

11. Adaptation and Long-Term Planning

Be prepared to adapt your game's strategy based on player feedback, market trends, and evolving platforms. Long-term planning can help your game remain relevant and profitable.

In conclusion, publishing and monetizing your game is a multifaceted process that requires careful planning and execution. By choosing the right distribution platform, monetization model, and marketing strategies, as well as providing excellent customer support and maintaining a dedicated player community, you can increase the chances of your game's success in the competitive gaming industry. Keep monitoring your game's performance and be ready to adapt to changes in the market to maximize your game's potential.

Chapter 15: Scripting and Automation in Visual Studio

Scripting and automation are powerful techniques to streamline repetitive tasks, enhance productivity, and ensure consistent processes in Visual Studio. In this chapter, we'll explore various scripting and automation methods to help you work more efficiently within the integrated development environment.

Section 15.1: Automating Tasks with MSBuild

MSBuild (Microsoft Build Engine) is a platform for building applications in Visual Studio. It's primarily used to compile and build projects, but it can also be extended to automate various development tasks. Below are some key aspects of automating tasks with MSBuild:

1. Understanding MSBuild Scripts

MSBuild scripts are XML-based files with a .proj or .targets extension. They define how your project or solution should be built, including the order of compilation, references, and output locations.

```
<Project xmlns="http://schemas.microsoft.com/developer/msbuild/2003">

<PropertyGroup>

<Configuration>Debug</Configuration>

<Platform>AnyCPU</Platform>

</PropertyGroup>

<ItemGroup>

<Compile Include="Program.cs" />

</ItemGroup>

<Target Name="Build">

<Csc Sources="@(Compile)" OutputAssembly="MyApp.exe" />

</Target>
```

```
</Project>
```

2. Command-Line Execution

You can execute MSBuild scripts from the command line using the msbuild command followed by the path to your .proj or .targets file.

```
msbuild MyProject.proj
```

3. Customizing Build Targets

MSBuild allows you to create custom build targets within your script. These targets define specific actions you want to automate, such as copying files, running tests, or generating documentation.

```
<Target Name="CustomTarget">

<Copy SourceFiles="@(FilesToCopy)" DestinationFolder="Output" />

</Target>
```

4. Using Properties and Items

Properties and items in MSBuild scripts provide flexibility. Properties hold values like build configurations, while items are collections of files or resources.

```
<PropertyGroup>

<OutputPath>bin\$(Configuration)\</OutputPath>

</PropertyGroup>

<ItemGroup>
```

```
<FilesToCopy Include="Data\*.txt" />

</ItemGroup>
```

5. Conditionals and Flow Control

MSBuild supports conditionals and flow control statements like Choose, When, and Otherwise, allowing you to define different behaviors based on conditions.

```
<Choose>

<When Condition="'$(Configuration)' == 'Debug'">

<!—Debug-specific actions—>

</When>

<When Condition="'$(Configuration)' == 'Release'">

<!—Release-specific actions—>

</When>

</Choose>
```

6. Task Execution

Tasks are the building blocks of MSBuild scripts. They perform actions such as compiling code, copying files, or running external tools. Many built-in tasks are available, and you can create custom tasks when needed.

```
<Target Name="Compile">
```

```
<Csc Sources="@(Compile)"
OutputAssembly="$(OutputPath)MyApp.exe" />

</Target>
```

*7. **Logging and Output***

MSBuild provides detailed logging options, allowing you to capture information about each step of the build process. You can specify the level of verbosity to control the amount of output.

```
msbuild MyProject.proj /verbosity:diagnostic
```

*8. **Integration with Visual Studio***

MSBuild is tightly integrated with Visual Studio, ensuring that projects built within the IDE are consistent with your automated builds. You can also customize build events and pre-/post-build actions.

Automating tasks with MSBuild can save significant development time, improve code quality, and ensure consistent builds across development and deployment environments. Whether you're compiling code, running tests, or performing custom actions, MSBuild is a versatile tool for automating tasks in Visual Studio.

Section 15.2: Customizing Build Processes

Customizing build processes is essential for adapting Visual Studio to your specific project requirements and ensuring smooth development workflows. In this section, we'll explore various techniques and tools to tailor the build process to your needs.

1. MSBuild Properties and Targets

MSBuild, as discussed in the previous section, offers extensive customization capabilities. You can define properties and targets in your project file (.csproj, .vbproj, etc.) to control various aspects of the build process. Properties allow you to set values like output paths, while targets define specific actions during the build.

For instance, you can customize the build process by altering the BeforeBuild and AfterBuild targets. These targets execute specific tasks before and after the build, respectively. This customization can be beneficial for tasks like code generation, file copying, or ensuring data migrations before building your project.

```
<Target Name="BeforeBuild">

<!—Custom tasks to execute before building—>

</Target>

<Target Name="AfterBuild">

<!—Custom tasks to execute after building—>

</Target>
```

2. Using Visual Studio Macros

Visual Studio provides macros that allow you to automate tasks and customize the build process further. Macros are snippets of code that can be executed before or after the build. These macros are written in Visual Basic and can access Visual Studio's object model.

For example, you can create a macro that automatically increments the version number of your assembly before each build:

```
Public Sub IncrementVersionNumber()
```

Dim project **As** Project = DTE.Solution.Projects.Item(1)

Dim propertyGroup **As** PropertyGroup = project.ConfigurationManager.ActiveConfiguration.PropertyGroups.Ite

Dim assemblyInfoFile **As** String = propertyGroup.Item("AssemblyInfoFile")

'Increment version number logic here...

'Save the modified AssemblyInfo file

My.Computer.FileSystem.WriteAllText(assemblyInfoFile, assemblyInfoContents, **False**)

End Sub

You can access and create macros by navigating to "Tools" > "Macros" > "Macro Explorer."

3. Visual Studio Extensibility

Visual Studio's extensibility framework allows you to create custom extensions (also known as add-ins or packages) that can modify and extend the build process. You can use the Visual Studio SDK (Software Development Kit) to develop extensions in various programming languages, including C# and VB.NET.

Extensions can add new menu commands, tool windows, and build events. They can even interact with project files and solution items. This flexibility enables you to create tailored solutions for specific development requirements.

4. Third-Party Build Tools

In addition to MSBuild, Visual Studio supports integration with third-party build tools and task runners like Grunt, Gulp, and Webpack. These tools are particularly useful for web development projects and can be configured to run custom scripts and tasks as part of the build process.

You can install and configure these tools using popular package managers like npm (Node Package Manager) or Yarn. Once set up, they can automate tasks like minification, bundling, and asset optimization, enhancing your web development workflow.

5. CI/CD Pipelines

For automated and continuous integration and deployment (CI/CD) pipelines, you can use dedicated tools like Azure DevOps, Jenkins, or GitHub Actions. These platforms allow you to define custom build and deployment processes through configuration files or scripts.

CI/CD pipelines enable automated testing, building, and deployment of your applications in a controlled and repeatable manner. They are particularly valuable when working on large projects with multiple contributors and frequent code changes.

Customizing the build process in Visual Studio empowers you to adapt the development environment to your project's unique needs. Whether it's tweaking build targets, using macros, developing extensions, integrating third-party tools, or setting up CI/CD pipelines, customization ensures efficient and consistent development workflows. By tailoring the build process, you can streamline tasks, improve code quality, and optimize the deployment pipeline for your projects.

Section 15.3: Scripting with PowerShell

PowerShell is a powerful scripting language that can be harnessed to automate various tasks and processes within Visual Studio. In this section, we'll explore how to leverage PowerShell scripts for automation and customization of development workflows.

1. Understanding PowerShell

PowerShell is a task automation and configuration management framework from Microsoft, known for its command-line interface and scripting capabilities. It is particularly valuable for managing Windows-based systems and applications, making it an excellent choice for automating tasks in Visual Studio.

PowerShell scripts are saved with a .ps1 file extension and can be executed from the command line or integrated into Visual Studio projects.

2. Running PowerShell Scripts

You can run PowerShell scripts directly from the command line or within Visual Studio. To execute a script, open a PowerShell console or the integrated terminal in Visual Studio and use the following command:

```
.\YourScript.ps1
```

Visual Studio provides the "Package Manager Console," which is a PowerShell environment specifically tailored for managing NuGet packages and running scripts related to your project. You can access it by going to "View" > "Other Windows" > "Package Manager Console."

3. Automating Tasks

PowerShell enables you to automate various development tasks in Visual Studio, such as:

- **Building Projects**: You can create scripts that build your solutions or projects with specific configurations, platforms, and targets.

- **NuGet Package Management**: PowerShell can automate the installation, updating, or removal of NuGet packages for your projects.

- **File Operations**: You can script file and folder operations like copying, moving, renaming, and deleting files, which can be handy for managing project assets.

- **Code Generation**: PowerShell can generate code snippets, classes, or files based on predefined templates, streamlining repetitive coding tasks.

- **Version Control**: You can create scripts to interact with version control systems like Git or TFS, automating commits, pulls, or branching operations.

4. Integration with Visual Studio

To integrate PowerShell scripts into your Visual Studio projects, you can create custom build events or post-build scripts that execute PowerShell commands. This integration allows you to trigger scripts as part of the build process or other project-related events.

For example, you can create a PowerShell script that minifies JavaScript and CSS files after a successful build:

```
# Minify JavaScript files
Get-ChildItem -Path .\Scripts\*.js | ForEach-Object {
# Minify logic here...
}
# Minify CSS files
Get-ChildItem -Path .\Content\*.css | ForEach-Object {
# Minify logic here...
}
```

5. PowerShell Modules and Libraries

PowerShell offers a wide range of modules and libraries that can be imported and utilized in your scripts. These modules extend the functionality of PowerShell and can be particularly beneficial for tasks like interacting with databases, web services, or cloud platforms.

You can import modules using the Import-Module cmdlet or install them via the PowerShell Gallery, a central repository for PowerShell modules.

6. Error Handling and Logging

PowerShell provides robust error handling and logging mechanisms, allowing you to capture and log errors, exceptions, and script output. This is crucial for debugging and troubleshooting automation scripts, ensuring that you can identify and address issues effectively.

By mastering PowerShell scripting, you can significantly enhance your productivity within Visual Studio, automate repetitive tasks, and customize your development environment to suit your specific requirements. Whether it's automating builds, managing NuGet packages, generating code, or integrating with version control systems, PowerShell is a versatile tool for streamlining your development workflows.

Section 15.4: Using the Command Line Interface

The command line interface (CLI) is a text-based way to interact with Visual Studio, offering developers powerful tools and commands to perform various tasks efficiently. In this section, we'll delve into the Visual Studio CLI, exploring how it can enhance your development workflow.

1. Understanding the Visual Studio CLI

The Visual Studio CLI, often referred to as devenv.exe (short for Development Environment), allows you to control and manage Visual Studio from the command line. It's a versatile tool that enables you to perform actions such as building solutions, running tests, and even opening projects.

2. Accessing the Visual Studio CLI

To access the Visual Studio CLI, open a command prompt or terminal window, navigate to the Visual Studio installation directory, and locate the devenv.exe executable. The exact path may vary depending on your Visual Studio version and installation options.

For example, if you're using Visual Studio 2019 and it's installed in the default location, you can access the CLI by running the following command:

"C:\Program Files (x86)\Microsoft Visual Studio\2019\Community\Common7\IDE\devenv.exe"

3. Common CLI Commands

Here are some common commands you can execute using the Visual Studio CLI:

- **Open a Solution or Project**: You can use the CLI to open a specific solution or project file directly from the command line. For example:

  devenv.exe YourSolution.sln

- **Build a Solution**: To build a solution, use the /build switch followed by the solution file path:

  devenv.exe YourSolution.sln /build

- **Run Tests**: If you have unit tests in your project, you can run them from the CLI using the /RunTests switch:

  devenv.exe YourSolution.sln /RunTests

- **Install Extensions**: You can use the CLI to install Visual Studio extensions (VSIX files) with the /InstallVsix switch:

  devenv.exe /InstallVsix YourExtension.vsix

- **Set Environment Variables**: You can set environment variables for Visual Studio using the /SetEnvironment switch:

  devenv.exe /SetEnvironment "MyVar=Value"

- **Execute Macros**: If you have Visual Studio macros, you can execute them from the CLI:

devenv.exe /Command "Macros.MyMacro"

- **Silent Installation**: For automated installations, you can use the /InstallVSTemplates switch to suppress user prompts:

devenv.exe /InstallVSTemplates

4. Customizing CLI Commands

You can create custom CLI scripts or batch files to automate repetitive tasks or complex workflows in Visual Studio. These scripts can combine various CLI commands to perform specific actions tailored to your project's needs.

5. Batch Processing and Automation

The Visual Studio CLI is highly useful for batch processing and automation scenarios. You can integrate CLI commands into your build scripts, continuous integration (CI) pipelines, or deployment processes to ensure consistency and repeatability in your development workflows.

For example, you can create a batch script that automates the build and deployment of your application whenever changes are pushed to a repository.

@echo off

devenv.exe YourSolution.sln /build

xcopy /s /y /i "Output*" "\\Server\DeploymentFolder"

6. Error Handling and Logging

When using the Visual Studio CLI in automated workflows, it's essential to implement error handling and logging mechanisms. This ensures that any issues or failures are properly documented and can be addressed promptly.

By mastering the Visual Studio CLI, you can significantly enhance your development productivity, automate tasks, and integrate Visual Studio seamlessly into your development pipeline. Whether you're building, testing, deploying, or customizing your development environment, the CLI is a valuable tool for streamlining your Visual Studio workflows.

Section 15.5: Continuous Integration Automation

Continuous Integration (CI) is a software development practice where code changes are automatically built, tested, and integrated into the project on a frequent basis. This section explores how you can implement CI automation in Visual Studio, ensuring that your codebase remains stable and ready for deployment.

1. Setting Up CI Pipelines

To enable CI in Visual Studio, you'll need to set up CI pipelines using CI/CD (Continuous Integration/Continuous Deployment) tools like Azure DevOps, Jenkins, or GitHub Actions. These tools allow you to define build and test processes for your project.

Here's an example of a simple CI pipeline configuration using Azure DevOps:

```
trigger:
```

- main *# Define the branch to trigger the pipeline*

pool:

vmImage: 'windows-latest'

jobs:

- job: Build

steps:

- task: UseDotNet@2

inputs:

packageType: 'sdk'

version: '3.x' *# Specify the .NET SDK version*

installationPath: $(Agent.ToolsDirectory)/dotnet

- script: dotnet restore

displayName: 'Restore Dependencies'

- script: dotnet build—configuration Release

displayName: 'Build Solution'

- task: PublishPipelineArtifact@1

inputs:

targetPath: '$(System.DefaultWorkingDirectory)/bin/Release/netcoreapp3.1'

artifactName: 'drop'

This YAML pipeline configuration specifies that the CI pipeline should trigger on changes to the main branch. It then defines steps for restoring dependencies, building the solution, and publishing the build artifacts.

2. Automated Testing

In addition to building the project, CI pipelines should include automated testing to ensure the code's quality and correctness. Popular testing frameworks like MSTest, NUnit, or xUnit can be integrated into CI pipelines to run unit tests, integration tests, and other types of tests.

Here's an example of adding a testing step to the CI pipeline:

- script: dotnet test—configuration Release—logger trx

displayName: 'Run Tests'

This step uses dotnet test to run tests and generate a test results file in TRX format.

3. Continuous Deployment

CI pipelines can also include steps for continuous deployment. Once the code passes all tests and builds successfully, it can be automatically deployed to staging or production environments.

Deployment steps can vary depending on your project's requirements. You might use Azure Web Apps, Docker containers, or other deployment targets. Tools like Azure DevOps Release Pipelines or GitHub Actions can assist in configuring deployment workflows.

4. Monitoring and Notifications

To ensure CI runs smoothly, it's crucial to set up monitoring and notifications. CI/CD tools often provide dashboards and alerting mechanisms to track the status of builds and deployments.

Notifications can be sent via email, Slack, or other communication channels to inform the team about the build and deployment results. This helps in quickly identifying and addressing any issues.

5. Branch Policies and Pull Requests

In CI, branch policies and pull requests play a vital role in maintaining code quality. Policies can enforce code reviews, automated tests, and status checks before allowing changes to be merged into the main branch. This ensures that only validated and tested code is integrated.

6. Conclusion

Continuous Integration automation is a fundamental practice for modern software development. By implementing CI pipelines, you can accelerate development cycles, catch bugs early, and deliver high-quality software to your users with confidence. Visual Studio integrates seamlessly with various CI/CD tools, allowing you to tailor your CI workflow to your project's needs.

Chapter 16: Visual Studio and the Internet of Things (IoT)

16.1 Setting Up for IoT Projects

In this section, we will explore how to set up your development environment in Visual Studio for Internet of Things (IoT) projects. IoT is a rapidly growing field where devices and sensors are connected to the internet, enabling them to collect and exchange data. Visual Studio provides tools and support for IoT development, allowing you to create applications for a wide range of IoT devices.

16.1.1 Choosing the Right IoT Platform

Before you start your IoT project in Visual Studio, it's essential to choose the right IoT platform. The choice of platform depends on your specific project requirements. Common IoT platforms include Raspberry Pi, Arduino, Windows IoT Core, and various microcontrollers. Visual Studio supports many of these platforms, so you need to select the one that best suits your project.

16.1.2 Installing Visual Studio Extensions

To begin IoT development in Visual Studio, you may need to install extensions that support your chosen IoT platform. These extensions typically include project templates, debugging tools, and device emulators. You can install these extensions from the Visual Studio Marketplace or using the Visual Studio Installer.

16.1.3 Configuring IoT Devices

Once you've installed the necessary extensions, you'll need to configure your IoT devices. This involves setting up the development environment on your hardware, ensuring that it's connected to your development machine, and configuring communication protocols if required.

16.1.4 Creating an IoT Project

With your development environment and devices set up, it's time to create your IoT project in Visual Studio. You can choose from various project templates, depending on your platform and programming language preferences. Visual Studio provides templates for C#, Python, and other languages commonly used in IoT development.

16.1.5 Writing Code for IoT

IoT projects typically involve writing code to interact with sensors, actuators, and communication protocols. Visual Studio offers a robust code editor with features like IntelliSense and code debugging to make your development process smoother. You can leverage libraries and SDKs specific to your IoT platform to simplify coding.

16.1.6 Debugging IoT Applications

Debugging IoT applications is a crucial part of development. Visual Studio provides debugging tools that allow you to monitor and troubleshoot your IoT code as it runs on your devices. You can set breakpoints, inspect variables, and use the device emulator for testing.

16.1.7 Deploying IoT Solutions

Once your IoT application is ready, you need to deploy it to your IoT devices. Visual Studio simplifies the deployment process, enabling you to push your code and configurations to your hardware seamlessly. You can also use remote debugging to troubleshoot issues on the device.

16.1.8 Testing and Monitoring

Testing IoT applications involves verifying that your devices and sensors are working correctly. You can use various testing frameworks and tools to ensure the reliability and functionality of your IoT solutions. Additionally, implementing monitoring and analytics helps you collect data from your devices for further analysis.

16.1.9 IoT Security Considerations

Security is a critical aspect of IoT development. When working with IoT devices, it's essential to implement security measures to protect data and devices from potential threats. Visual Studio provides resources and guidance on IoT security best practices.

In summary, setting up for IoT projects in Visual Studio involves choosing the right platform, installing extensions, configuring devices, creating projects, writing code, debugging, deploying, testing, and ensuring security. With the right tools and knowledge, you can embark on your IoT journey using Visual Studio's powerful development environment.

16.2 Developing for Windows IoT Core

In this section, we will focus on developing for Windows IoT Core using Visual Studio. Windows IoT Core is a version of Windows 10 designed for small, low-cost devices in the Internet of Things (IoT) ecosystem. It provides a familiar Windows development environment for building IoT applications and solutions.

16.2.1 Windows IoT Core Overview

Windows IoT Core is a lightweight, headless version of Windows 10 that is optimized for IoT scenarios. It is designed to run on devices with limited resources, making it suitable for a wide range of IoT hardware. Windows IoT Core offers built-in security features, connectivity options, and support for various programming languages.

16.2.2 Setting Up Windows IoT Core

Before you can start developing for Windows IoT Core, you need to set up your IoT device with Windows IoT Core. Microsoft provides detailed instructions on how to install Windows IoT Core on supported hardware platforms, such as Raspberry Pi. Once your device is prepared, you can connect it to your development machine.

16.2.3 Installing the Windows IoT Core Extension

To develop for Windows IoT Core in Visual Studio, you'll need to install the Windows IoT Core Project Templates extension. This extension provides project templates and tools necessary for IoT development. You can download and install it directly from Visual Studio.

16.2.4 Creating a Windows IoT Core Project

With the extension installed, you can create a new Windows IoT Core project in Visual Studio. These projects come with predefined templates for various IoT scenarios, including background applications and IoT solutions. You can choose the appropriate template based on your project requirements.

16.2.5 Writing Code for Windows IoT Core

Windows IoT Core projects in Visual Studio support multiple programming languages, including C#, C++, and Python. You can leverage the Universal Windows Platform (UWP) APIs to interact with hardware peripherals and sensors on your IoT device. Visual Studio's code editor provides syntax highlighting, IntelliSense, and debugging capabilities to streamline your coding process.

16.2.6 Building User Interfaces

If your IoT solution requires a user interface, you can design and build it using XAML and the UWP framework. Visual Studio offers a visual designer for XAML, making it easier to create responsive and user-friendly interfaces for your IoT applications.

16.2.7 Debugging and Deploying

Visual Studio provides robust debugging and deployment tools for Windows IoT Core projects. You can set breakpoints, inspect variables, and even perform remote debugging on your IoT device. Deploying your application to the device is straightforward, and you can monitor its execution in real-time.

16.2.8 IoT Connectivity

IoT solutions often require connectivity to the cloud or other devices. Windows IoT Core offers support for various communication protocols and IoT services. Visual Studio allows you to integrate connectivity features seamlessly into your IoT applications.

16.2.9 Security and Updates

Security is a paramount concern in IoT development. Windows IoT Core provides security features to protect your devices and data. Regular updates and patches ensure that your IoT devices remain secure against emerging threats. Visual Studio assists in managing security configurations and updates.

In conclusion, developing for Windows IoT Core with Visual Studio offers a powerful and familiar environment for creating IoT applications. It provides tools for setting up, coding, debugging, and deploying IoT solutions on a wide range of supported hardware. Whether you're building IoT prototypes or commercial solutions, Visual Studio simplifies the development process for Windows IoT Core.

16.3 Working with Raspberry Pi and Arduino

Raspberry Pi and Arduino are two popular hardware platforms for IoT development, and in this section, we will explore how to work with them in conjunction with Windows IoT Core and Visual Studio.

16.3.1 Raspberry Pi and Windows IoT Core

Raspberry Pi is a versatile single-board computer that can run Windows IoT Core. To get started, you'll need a compatible Raspberry Pi model and an SD card. Here are the key steps:

1. **Prepare the SD Card**: You'll need to flash a Windows IoT Core image onto your SD card. Microsoft provides tools and documentation to guide you through this process.
2. **Connect Hardware**: Connect your Raspberry Pi to peripherals like a display, keyboard, and mouse. Ensure it

has an internet connection, either via Ethernet or Wi-Fi.
3. **Access the Device Portal**: Windows IoT Core provides a web-based Device Portal that allows you to configure and manage your Raspberry Pi remotely. You can access it using a web browser by entering the Pi's IP address.
4. **Install Visual Studio**: Install Visual Studio on your development machine if you haven't already. Make sure you have the Windows IoT Core Project Templates extension installed.
5. **Create a Project**: In Visual Studio, create a new Windows IoT Core project. Select the appropriate template based on your IoT scenario.
6. **Coding and Deployment**: Write your code using C# or another supported language. You can use the Universal Windows Platform (UWP) APIs to interact with hardware peripherals. Deploy your application to the Raspberry Pi using Visual Studio.
7. **Debugging**: Debug your application by setting breakpoints and monitoring its execution. Visual Studio supports remote debugging on the Raspberry Pi.
8. **IoT Connectivity**: If your project requires connectivity, you can use Raspberry Pi's built-in Wi-Fi or add external hardware modules for additional communication options.

16.3.2 Arduino and Windows IoT Core

Arduino is a popular microcontroller platform, and you can integrate it with Windows IoT Core to create IoT solutions. Here's how to work with Arduino in this context:

1. **Select an Arduino Board**: Choose an Arduino board that is compatible with Windows IoT Core. Some models have built-in compatibility, while others may require additional

components.

2. **Install Windows IoT Core on Raspberry Pi**: Although we're focusing on Arduino, you might still need a Raspberry Pi running Windows IoT Core as an intermediary between your Arduino and your development machine.
3. **Connect Arduino to Raspberry Pi**: Establish a physical connection between your Arduino board and the Raspberry Pi. This may involve wiring and configuring the appropriate pins.
4. **Use Serial Communication**: Arduino communicates with the Raspberry Pi (and ultimately with your IoT application) via serial communication. You can write code on both the Raspberry Pi (in C# or Python) and the Arduino (in Arduino's C/C++-like language) to enable this communication.
5. **Develop the IoT Application**: In Visual Studio, create a Windows IoT Core project that interfaces with the Arduino via serial communication. Write the code for your application, taking advantage of UWP APIs for IoT-related tasks.
6. **Deployment and Debugging**: Deploy your application to the Raspberry Pi and debug it using Visual Studio's debugging tools.
7. **IoT Connectivity**: Implement any required connectivity features, such as sending data from Arduino to the cloud or other IoT devices.

Working with Raspberry Pi and Arduino in Windows IoT Core projects opens up a world of possibilities for IoT development. These platforms provide various sensors and actuators, making them suitable for a wide range of applications, from home automation to industrial monitoring. By integrating them with Visual Studio and Windows IoT Core, you can harness their capabilities to create innovative IoT solutions.

16.4 IoT Prototyping and Testing

Prototyping and testing are critical phases in IoT development, allowing you to validate your ideas, identify issues, and refine your solutions. In this section, we'll explore IoT prototyping and testing methodologies and how Visual Studio can assist in these processes.

16.4.1 IoT Prototyping

IoT prototyping involves creating a preliminary version of your IoT solution to evaluate its feasibility and functionality. Here's how you can approach IoT prototyping:

1. **Define Objectives**: Clearly define the objectives of your IoT prototype. What problem is it solving? What features must it demonstrate? Having a clear goal will guide your prototype development.
2. **Select Hardware**: Choose the hardware components and sensors required for your prototype. Raspberry Pi, Arduino, and various sensors can be used. Visual Studio provides templates and libraries to work with common IoT hardware.
3. **Develop a Minimum Viable Product (MVP)**: Start by creating a minimal version of your IoT solution that focuses on core functionality. Use Visual Studio to write code for data acquisition, processing, and communication with the cloud or other devices.
4. **Design User Interface (UI)**: If your IoT solution includes a user interface, design a simple UI to interact with the

prototype. Visual Studio offers tools for designing UIs for IoT applications.

5. **Collect Data**: Use the prototype to collect real-world data. This data can be used for testing, refining algorithms, and demonstrating the solution's capabilities.
6. **Iterate**: Based on feedback and insights from the prototype, iterate on your design and code. Make improvements and enhancements as needed.
7. **Document**: Document the hardware components, software architecture, and code. Proper documentation is crucial for future development and troubleshooting.

16.4.2 IoT Testing

IoT testing ensures that your IoT solution functions correctly, reliably, and securely. Here are some aspects of IoT testing:

1. **Functional Testing**: Test the basic functionality of your IoT solution. Verify that data is collected, processed, and transmitted as expected. Use Visual Studio's debugging and testing tools to identify and fix issues.
2. **Security Testing**: IoT devices are potential targets for security breaches. Conduct security testing to identify vulnerabilities and implement measures to secure your solution. Visual Studio provides tools for code analysis and security testing.
3. **Scalability Testing**: If your IoT solution is intended to scale, perform scalability testing to ensure it can handle increasing loads. Simulate large numbers of devices and data points to assess performance.
4. **Compatibility Testing**: Ensure that your IoT solution works with different devices, browsers, and platforms. Visual Studio allows you to test compatibility across

various configurations.

5. **Usability Testing**: If your IoT solution has a user interface, conduct usability testing to assess user-friendliness. Visual Studio provides tools for UI testing and automation.
6. **Edge Cases and Failures**: Test how your IoT solution handles edge cases and failures. What happens when sensors malfunction or connectivity is lost? Visual Studio's testing framework can help simulate these scenarios.
7. **Load and Stress Testing**: Assess how your IoT solution performs under heavy loads and stress conditions. Visual Studio's load testing tools can help simulate these scenarios.
8. **Data Validation**: Validate incoming data to ensure it meets expected criteria. Visual Studio can assist in creating data validation routines.
9. **Data Integrity and Reliability**: Verify that data is transmitted and stored reliably and with integrity. Visual Studio's testing tools can help validate data flows.
10. **End-to-End Testing**: Test the entire IoT ecosystem, from devices to cloud services and back-end systems. Visual Studio allows for end-to-end testing and monitoring.

By following IoT prototyping and testing best practices, you can increase the chances of success in your IoT projects. Visual Studio's comprehensive set of tools and features can streamline the development and testing processes, helping you build robust and reliable IoT solutions.

16.5 Deploying IoT Solutions

Deploying IoT solutions is a crucial step in bringing your projects to life and making them accessible to users. In this section, we will explore the deployment process for IoT solutions and how Visual Studio can assist in this journey.

16.5.1 Preparing for Deployment

Before deploying your IoT solution, you need to ensure that it is ready for production use. Here are some key steps to prepare for deployment:

1. **Testing and Validation**: Thoroughly test your IoT solution to identify and resolve any issues. Make sure it performs as expected under real-world conditions.
2. **Security**: Implement security measures to protect your IoT devices and data. Use encryption, authentication, and authorization mechanisms to safeguard your solution.
3. **Scalability**: Consider the scalability of your solution. Ensure that it can handle a growing number of devices and data points.
4. **Compliance**: Check if your IoT solution complies with industry standards and regulations. Depending on the application, you may need to adhere to specific guidelines.
5. **Data Backup and Recovery**: Implement data backup and recovery mechanisms to protect against data loss. Ensure that you can recover data in case of hardware failures or other issues.

16.5.2 Choosing the Deployment Model

IoT solutions can be deployed in various ways, depending on your requirements. Here are some common deployment models:

1. **Edge Deployment**: In this model, IoT devices process data locally on the edge and send only relevant information to the cloud. It reduces latency and can be suitable for

applications requiring real-time processing.

2. **Cloud Deployment**: IoT data is sent directly to the cloud for processing and storage. This model offers scalability and centralization of data but may have higher latency.
3. **Hybrid Deployment**: A combination of edge and cloud deployment, this model allows you to take advantage of local processing while still benefiting from cloud resources.

16.5.3 Deploying with Visual Studio

Visual Studio provides tools and features to facilitate the deployment of IoT solutions. Here's how you can use Visual Studio for IoT deployment:

1. **Configuration Management**: Visual Studio allows you to manage configuration settings for your IoT devices. You can define variables and settings that can be updated remotely.
2. **Remote Monitoring**: Visual Studio's IoT Hub integration enables remote monitoring and management of IoT devices. You can monitor device health, update firmware, and troubleshoot issues.
3. **Continuous Integration/Continuous Deployment (CI/CD)**: Implement CI/CD pipelines in Visual Studio to automate the deployment process. This ensures that changes to your IoT solution are deployed consistently and quickly.
4. **Containerization**: Use containerization technologies like Docker to package your IoT applications. Visual Studio supports container development and deployment for IoT scenarios.
5. **Device Provisioning**: Visual Studio provides tools for device provisioning, making it easier to onboard new

devices securely.

6. **Firmware Updates**: Visual Studio allows you to manage and deploy firmware updates to your IoT devices. This is essential for keeping devices up-to-date and secure.
7. **Monitoring and Diagnostics**: Visual Studio provides tools for monitoring the health and performance of your deployed IoT solution. You can set up alerts and diagnostics for proactive issue resolution.
8. **Edge Deployment**: For edge deployments, Visual Studio can help you package and deploy containerized workloads to edge devices such as Raspberry Pi or Azure IoT Edge devices.

16.5.4 Post-Deployment Considerations

After deploying your IoT solution, it's essential to monitor its performance and gather insights for ongoing improvements. Here are some post-deployment considerations:

1. **Monitoring**: Continuously monitor the health and performance of your IoT devices and the overall solution. Visual Studio's monitoring tools and Azure services can assist in this regard.
2. **Analytics**: Use data analytics tools to gain insights from the data generated by your IoT solution. Analyzing data can lead to optimizations and enhancements.
3. **User Feedback**: Collect feedback from users and stakeholders to identify areas for improvement. Consider user experience and satisfaction.
4. **Security Updates**: Stay vigilant about security updates and vulnerabilities. Regularly update your IoT devices and the cloud infrastructure to address security issues.
5. **Scalability**: As your IoT solution grows, ensure that it can

scale to meet increasing demands. Monitor performance and scalability metrics.

6. **Cost Optimization**: Optimize costs by monitoring resource usage and adjusting your IoT solution's configuration as needed. Azure offers tools for cost management.
7. **Documentation**: Keep documentation up-to-date with the latest configurations, procedures, and troubleshooting guidelines.

By following these deployment best practices and leveraging Visual Studio's capabilities, you can successfully deploy and maintain your IoT solutions, ensuring they deliver value and perform reliably in the field.

17.1 Integrating AI and ML Tools

Artificial Intelligence (AI) and Machine Learning (ML) have become integral parts of software development, enabling applications to make intelligent decisions, analyze data, and provide predictive capabilities. In this section, we will explore how Visual Studio facilitates the integration of AI and ML tools into your projects.

AI and ML in Modern Software

AI and ML are transforming various industries by automating tasks, making predictions, and providing insights from large datasets. Whether you are working on healthcare applications, finance, e-commerce, or any other domain, integrating AI and ML can offer significant advantages. Here are some common use cases:

- **Recommendation Systems**: Implement recommendation algorithms to suggest products, content, or services to users based on their preferences and behavior.

- **Predictive Maintenance**: Use ML models to predict equipment failures or maintenance needs, reducing downtime and maintenance costs.

- **Natural Language Processing (NLP)**: Develop applications that understand and process human language, enabling chatbots, sentiment analysis, and language translation.

- **Image and Video Analysis**: Utilize computer vision techniques to analyze images and videos, enabling applications like facial recognition, object detection, and medical image analysis.

- **Anomaly Detection**: Detect anomalies or unusual patterns in data, which is valuable for fraud detection, security, and quality control.

17.1.1 AI and ML Tools in Visual Studio

Visual Studio provides robust support for AI and ML development, making it easier to build, train, and deploy models. Here are some key features and tools available:

1. Azure Machine Learning: Visual Studio integrates with Azure Machine Learning, allowing you to create, train, and deploy ML models in the cloud. You can use Azure ML services directly within Visual Studio.

2. ML.NET: ML.NET is an open-source, cross-platform machine learning framework that integrates seamlessly with Visual Studio. You can build custom ML models using C# and .NET, making it accessible to .NET developers.

3. Python Integration: Visual Studio provides excellent support for Python, a widely-used language for AI and ML. You can use Python libraries like TensorFlow, PyTorch, and scikit-learn directly in Visual Studio projects.

4. Data Science Workloads: Visual Studio offers tools for data scientists, including Jupyter Notebook integration, data exploration, and data visualization.

5. Model Evaluation: You can evaluate the performance of ML models using built-in tools and metrics. Visual Studio helps you analyze model accuracy, precision, recall, and more.

6. Model Deployment: Visual Studio supports deploying ML models to various platforms, including web services, mobile apps, and IoT devices. Azure Machine Learning simplifies the deployment process.

17.1.2 Getting Started with AI and ML in Visual Studio

To start integrating AI and ML into your Visual Studio projects, follow these steps:

1. **Choose Your Language**: Decide whether you want to work with C#, Python, or another language. Visual Studio supports multiple languages for AI and ML development.
2. **Select Your Framework**: Depending on your project's requirements, choose a machine learning framework like ML.NET, TensorFlow, or PyTorch. Install the necessary packages or libraries.
3. **Data Preparation**: Prepare your data for training by cleaning, preprocessing, and splitting it into training and testing sets.
4. **Model Building**: Create and train your machine learning model using the selected framework. Visual Studio provides code templates and tools to streamline this process.
5. **Model Evaluation**: Evaluate the model's performance using metrics relevant to your problem, such as accuracy or mean squared error.
6. **Deployment**: Deploy your trained model to your application, whether it's a web service, desktop application, or mobile app. Azure Machine Learning can assist in model deployment.
7. **Monitoring and Maintenance**: Continuously monitor your deployed model's performance and retrain it as needed to ensure accuracy and relevance.

Visual Studio's integration with AI and ML tools simplifies the development process and allows you to leverage the power of machine learning in your applications. Whether you are a beginner or an experienced data scientist, Visual Studio provides the necessary tools and workflows to get started with AI and ML development.

17.2 Using ML.NET for Machine Learning

ML.NET is an open-source, cross-platform machine learning framework developed by Microsoft. It is specifically designed for .NET developers, allowing them to build custom machine learning models using C# and .NET languages. In this section, we will explore the capabilities of ML.NET and how you can leverage it for your machine learning projects in Visual Studio.

Introduction to ML.NET

ML.NET empowers .NET developers to integrate machine learning into their applications without requiring expertise in complex ML algorithms or frameworks. Here are some key features and advantages of ML.NET:

- **Ease of Use**: ML.NET provides a high-level API that simplifies the process of creating, training, and deploying machine learning models. Developers can work with familiar C# code.

- **Custom Models**: You can build custom machine learning models tailored to your specific problem domain. ML.NET supports both supervised and unsupervised learning scenarios.

- **Integration with Visual Studio**: ML.NET seamlessly integrates with Visual Studio, making it easy to develop, debug, and test machine learning models within your projects.

- **Cross-Platform**: ML.NET is cross-platform and can be used on Windows, macOS, and Linux, enabling you to create machine learning solutions for various platforms.

Getting Started with ML.NET

To start using ML.NET in Visual Studio, follow these steps:

1. **Install the ML.NET NuGet Package**: Open your Visual Studio project and install the Microsoft.ML NuGet package. This package contains the necessary libraries and tools for ML.NET.
2. **Data Preparation**: Prepare your dataset for machine learning. ML.NET supports various data formats, including CSV, JSON, and databases. Load and preprocess your data using C#.
3. **Define Your Model**: Create a machine learning model using ML.NET's API. Define the features and labels in your dataset, choose the algorithm, and configure hyperparameters.
4. **Data Pipeline**: Build a data pipeline that includes data loading, transformation, and training. ML.NET provides a fluent API for defining these pipelines.
5. **Training**: Train your machine learning model on your dataset. Use the .Fit() method to initiate the training process.
6. **Evaluation**: Evaluate the model's performance using metrics like accuracy, precision, recall, and F1-score. ML.NET offers built-in evaluation tools.
7. **Prediction**: Once your model is trained and evaluated, you can use it to make predictions on new data. ML.NET's API simplifies the prediction process.

Here is an example of building a simple binary classification model using ML.NET to predict whether an email is spam or not:

// Define your data class

```
public class SpamData

{

[LoadColumn(0)] public string Label;

[LoadColumn(1)] public string Text;

}

// Load your data

var data = mlContext.Data.LoadFromTextFile<SpamData>("spam.csv", separatorChar: ',');

// Define a data pipeline

var pipeline = mlContext.Transforms.Text.FeaturizeText("Features", "Text")

.Append(mlContext.Transforms.CopyColumns("Label", "Label"))

.Append(mlContext.Transforms.NormalizeMinMax("Features"))

.Append(mlContext.BinaryClassification.Trainers.SdcaLogisticRegressio

// Train the model

var model = pipeline.Fit(data);

// Evaluate the model

var metrics = mlContext.BinaryClassification.Evaluate(model, data);

Console.WriteLine($"Accuracy: {metrics.Accuracy}");
```

ML.NET simplifies the machine learning workflow, making it accessible to .NET developers. Whether you are working on classification, regression, clustering, or other ML tasks, ML.NET provides the tools and flexibility you need to create custom models and integrate them into your Visual Studio projects seamlessly.

ML.NET and Visual Studio Integration

ML.NET offers deep integration with Visual Studio, allowing you to leverage the full power of the IDE for machine learning development. You can use Visual Studio's debugging, testing, and code editing features to streamline your ML.NET projects. Additionally, ML.NET Model Builder, a Visual Studio extension, provides a visual interface for building and training ML models, making the process even more accessible to developers.

In summary, ML.NET is a valuable tool for .NET developers interested in machine learning. It enables you to build custom ML models using C# and integrates seamlessly with Visual Studio, simplifying the development and deployment of machine learning solutions. Whether you are a beginner or an experienced data scientist, ML.NET provides a user-friendly approach to machine learning in the .NET ecosystem.

17.3 Building AI-powered Applications

In this section, we will explore how to build AI-powered applications using the tools and frameworks available in Visual Studio. Artificial Intelligence (AI) has become increasingly important in modern software development, and integrating AI capabilities into your applications can enhance their functionality and provide more value to users.

AI Frameworks and Libraries

Visual Studio supports various AI frameworks and libraries, making it easier to develop AI-powered applications. Some of the popular frameworks and libraries include:

- **ML.NET**: As mentioned in the previous section, ML.NET is a machine learning framework designed for .NET developers. You can use ML.NET to create custom machine learning models for tasks such as image classification, sentiment analysis, and more.

- **TensorFlow.NET**: TensorFlow is a well-known open-source machine learning framework. TensorFlow.NET is a .NET binding for TensorFlow, allowing you to use TensorFlow models and features in your .NET applications.

- **Keras.NET**: Keras is a high-level neural networks API. Keras.NET provides a .NET interface for building and training deep learning models using Keras.

- **OpenCV**: OpenCV is a popular computer vision library. Visual Studio provides support for integrating OpenCV into your applications, enabling you to perform image and video analysis.

AI-Powered Application Scenarios

Here are some common scenarios where you can leverage AI to enhance your applications:

1. Image and Video Analysis

You can use AI to analyze images and videos, extract information, and make decisions based on visual data. For example, you can build applications that detect objects in images, recognize faces, or analyze medical images.

2. Natural Language Processing (NLP)

NLP techniques enable your applications to understand and process human language. You can create chatbots, language translation tools, sentiment analysis applications, and more using NLP models.

3. Predictive Analytics

AI can be used for predictive analytics, where your application makes predictions or recommendations based on historical data. For instance, you can build recommendation systems, predictive maintenance applications, and financial forecasting tools.

4. Voice Recognition

Voice recognition technology allows your applications to understand and respond to spoken language. This is useful for creating virtual assistants, voice-controlled applications, and accessibility features.

Building AI-Powered Applications in Visual Studio

To build AI-powered applications in Visual Studio, follow these general steps:

1. **Choose an AI Framework**: Select the AI framework or

library that best suits your application's requirements. ML.NET is a good choice for .NET developers, while TensorFlow.NET and Keras.NET provide more extensive deep learning capabilities.

2. **Data Preparation**: Gather and preprocess data for training and evaluation. High-quality data is crucial for training accurate AI models.
3. **Model Development**: Create or select a suitable AI model architecture for your application. You may need to fine-tune existing models or build custom ones.
4. **Training**: Train your AI model using relevant datasets. This step involves optimizing model parameters to achieve the desired accuracy.
5. **Integration**: Integrate the trained AI model into your application code. Visual Studio's code editing and debugging features can help you with this process.
6. **Testing and Evaluation**: Test your AI-powered application thoroughly. Use appropriate evaluation metrics to measure the model's performance.
7. **Deployment**: Deploy your AI-powered application to the target environment, whether it's a web server, desktop application, or mobile device.
8. **Monitoring and Maintenance**: Continuously monitor the application's performance and update the AI model as needed. AI models may require retraining over time to adapt to changing data patterns.

Below is a simplified example of using ML.NET to create an AI-powered sentiment analysis application:

// Load a pre-trained sentiment analysis model

```
var model = mlContext.Model.Load("sentiment_model.zip", out var modelSchema);

// Make predictions

var predictions = model.Transform(data);

// Retrieve sentiment labels

var sentiments = predictions.GetColumn<string>("Sentiment");

// Process the sentiments and provide feedback to the user

foreach (var sentiment in sentiments)

{

Console.WriteLine($"Sentiment: {sentiment}");

}
```

This code demonstrates how to load a pre-trained sentiment analysis model and use it to analyze sentiments in a given dataset.

In conclusion, Visual Studio provides a robust environment for building AI-powered applications. Whether you are working with machine learning, deep learning, computer vision, or NLP, Visual Studio's integration with AI frameworks and libraries makes it easier to develop intelligent applications that can provide valuable insights and automation to users.

17.4 Data Analysis and Visualization

Data analysis and visualization are integral parts of AI and machine learning projects. In this section, we'll explore how Visual Studio facilitates data analysis and visualization tasks, helping you gain insights from your data and present them effectively.

Data Analysis Tools in Visual Studio

Visual Studio offers various tools and extensions that simplify data analysis:

1. **Python Integration**: Visual Studio provides robust support for Python, a popular language for data analysis. You can use Python libraries like NumPy, pandas, and matplotlib directly within Visual Studio to process and analyze data.
2. **R Tools for Visual Studio (RTVS)**: RTVS is an extension that adds R language support to Visual Studio. R is widely used for statistical analysis, and RTVS provides an interactive development environment for data scientists.
3. **SQL Server Data Tools (SSDT)**: If your data resides in SQL Server databases, SSDT allows you to design, develop, and deploy database projects. It also provides tools for querying and analyzing data.

Data Visualization with Visual Studio

Effective data visualization helps in conveying insights to stakeholders. Visual Studio supports several libraries and tools for data visualization:

1. **Matplotlib**: Matplotlib is a popular Python library for creating static, animated, or interactive visualizations. You can use it within Visual Studio to generate various types of charts and graphs.
2. **Power BI Integration**: Power BI is a powerful business intelligence tool. Visual Studio allows you to integrate Power BI reports and dashboards into your applications, providing interactive data visualizations.
3. **SQL Server Reporting Services (SSRS)**: SSRS is a tool

for creating, deploying, and managing reports. Visual Studio provides project templates for developing SSRS reports, making it easy to design and present data effectively.

Data Analysis Workflow

Here's a simplified workflow for data analysis in Visual Studio:

1. **Data Collection**: Gather relevant data from various sources, such as databases, APIs, or flat files, and import it into your data analysis environment.
2. **Data Preprocessing**: Clean and preprocess the data to handle missing values, outliers, and format inconsistencies. Visual Studio's data manipulation tools (e.g., pandas or R functions) can assist in this step.
3. **Exploratory Data Analysis (EDA)**: Use statistical techniques and visualization libraries to explore the data's characteristics. Identify patterns, correlations, and outliers.
4. **Model Building**: If your analysis requires predictive modeling or machine learning, develop and train your models using appropriate algorithms. Visual Studio's support for Python and R makes it easy to build and evaluate models.
5. **Data Visualization**: Create informative visualizations (e.g., charts, graphs, and reports) to communicate your findings effectively. Matplotlib, Power BI, or SSRS can help in this regard.
6. **Insights and Reporting**: Document your analysis results, insights, and recommendations in reports or dashboards. Tools like Power BI and SSRS provide reporting capabilities.

Example Data Visualization (Matplotlib)

```
import matplotlib.pyplot as plt

import numpy as np

# Sample data

x = np.arange(0, 10, 0.1)

y = np.sin(x)

# Create a line chart

plt.plot(x, y)

plt.title("Sine Wave")

plt.xlabel("X-axis")

plt.ylabel("Y-axis")

plt.show()
```

In this example, we use Matplotlib within Visual Studio to create a simple line chart of a sine wave. Matplotlib offers extensive customization options for creating more complex visualizations.

Visual Studio's data analysis and visualization capabilities empower data scientists and analysts to gain insights from data efficiently and present their findings effectively to stakeholders, making it a valuable tool for AI and machine learning projects.

17.5 Ethical Considerations in AI Development

As the field of artificial intelligence (AI) continues to advance, it brings both opportunities and challenges. One critical aspect that developers, data scientists, and organizations must consider is ethics. In this section, we'll explore the ethical considerations in AI development and how Visual Studio can support ethical practices.

Ethical Challenges in AI

AI technologies, particularly machine learning, can raise several ethical challenges:

1. **Bias and Fairness**: AI models can inherit biases from training data, resulting in unfair or discriminatory outcomes, especially in applications involving sensitive attributes like race or gender.
2. **Transparency**: Complex AI models, such as deep neural networks, can be challenging to interpret, making it difficult to understand their decision-making processes.
3. **Privacy**: AI systems often process large amounts of personal data. Ensuring data privacy and protection is crucial to prevent unauthorized access or misuse.
4. **Accountability**: Determining who is responsible when an AI system makes a harmful decision or error can be complex. The lack of clear accountability can lead to legal and ethical dilemmas.
5. **Security**: AI systems can be vulnerable to attacks, including adversarial attacks that manipulate input data to deceive the model.

Ethical AI Development Practices

Visual Studio can assist developers in implementing ethical AI practices:

1. **Data Ethics**: Visual Studio's data analysis capabilities enable data scientists to detect and mitigate biases in training data. Tools for data preprocessing and fairness evaluation can help address bias issues.
2. **Interpretability**: Visual Studio offers tools for model interpretability and visualization. Developers can use these tools to make AI models more transparent and understandable.
3. **Privacy Protection**: Visual Studio supports secure coding practices, including data encryption, access control, and secure data storage, to protect user data and privacy.
4. **Accountability and Documentation**: Developers can use Visual Studio's version control and documentation features to keep track of changes, model versions, and development decisions, aiding in accountability.
5. **Security**: Visual Studio's security analysis tools can help identify vulnerabilities in code and design. Developers can follow secure coding practices to protect AI systems from attacks.

Ethical AI Checklist

Developers can follow this ethical AI checklist within Visual Studio:

1. **Understand the Data**: Thoroughly analyze and understand the training data, identifying potential biases or sensitive attributes.
2. **Bias Mitigation**: Implement bias mitigation techniques during data preprocessing and model training.

3. **Transparency**: Use model interpretability tools to make AI model decisions more transparent and interpretable.
4. **Privacy Protection**: Ensure that user data is anonymized, encrypted, and stored securely, following data protection regulations.
5. **Accountability**: Maintain clear documentation of development decisions, model versions, and responsible parties.
6. **Security**: Regularly assess and improve the security of AI systems to prevent unauthorized access and adversarial attacks.
7. **User Consent**: Implement mechanisms for obtaining user consent when collecting and processing data.
8. **Fairness Testing**: Continuously test AI systems for fairness and bias using real-world data and user feedback.
9. **Feedback Loop**: Establish a feedback loop to gather user input and improve AI system behavior over time.
10. **Ethics Training**: Educate development teams about ethical AI practices and encourage ethical decision-making.

Incorporating ethics into AI development is not only a best practice but also a legal and societal requirement. Visual Studio, with its development, analysis, and documentation tools, can play a pivotal role in ensuring that AI systems are developed and deployed ethically, aligning technology with human values and societal norms.

18.1 Enhancing Productivity in Visual Studio

In the fast-paced world of software development, productivity is paramount. Visual Studio provides a plethora of features and tools that can significantly boost your productivity as a developer. In this section, we'll explore various ways to enhance your productivity within the Visual Studio Integrated Development Environment (IDE).

Keyboard Shortcuts

One of the quickest ways to become more productive in Visual Studio is by mastering keyboard shortcuts. Instead of navigating through menus with your mouse, you can perform many actions with a simple key combination. Visual Studio offers a vast array of keyboard shortcuts for tasks like opening files, debugging, refactoring, and more.

Here are some essential keyboard shortcuts to get you started:

- **Ctrl + S**: Save the current file.
- **Ctrl + F5**: Build and run the project without debugging.
- **F5**: Build and run the project with debugging.
- **Ctrl + Z**: Undo the last action.
- **Ctrl + Shift + Z**: Redo the last undone action.
- **Ctrl + F**: Find text in the current document.
- **Ctrl + H**: Replace text in the current document.

- **Ctrl + K, Ctrl + C**: Comment out selected lines of code.
- **Ctrl + K, Ctrl + U**: Uncomment selected lines of code.

You can customize keyboard shortcuts and even import presets for different programming languages to optimize your workflow.

IntelliSense

Visual Studio's IntelliSense is a powerful code completion feature that saves you time by providing context-aware suggestions as you type. It not only completes variable and function names but also offers information about parameters, method signatures, and available properties and methods of objects. To trigger IntelliSense, press **Ctrl + Space** or simply continue typing to accept the suggested completion.

Code Snippets

Code snippets are predefined code templates that help you write common code blocks quickly. Visual Studio includes a library of built-in code snippets, and you can create custom snippets to match your development patterns. To insert a code snippet, type its shortcut and press **Tab** twice.

Templates and Project Wizards

Visual Studio provides project templates and wizards for various types of applications, such as web projects, desktop applications, and mobile apps. These templates set up the initial structure of your project, saving you from repetitive configuration work. When creating a new project, explore the available templates to kickstart your development.

Extensions and Add-ons

Visual Studio's extensibility allows you to enhance its functionality further. You can browse and install extensions from the Visual Studio Marketplace, which offers a wide range of tools and add-ons to improve your workflow. Whether you need additional code analysis tools, version control integrations, or project management extensions, the marketplace likely has what you're looking for.

Task Automation

Visual Studio supports task automation through tools like MSBuild and PowerShell. You can create build scripts and automate various development tasks to streamline your workflow. Automation reduces manual intervention, minimizes errors, and ensures consistency in your development process.

Debugging Tools

Efficient debugging is crucial for identifying and fixing issues in your code. Visual Studio offers a comprehensive set of debugging tools, including breakpoints, watch windows, call stacks, and real-time variable inspection. Learn to use these tools effectively to diagnose and resolve problems quickly.

Code Navigation

Navigating through large codebases can be challenging. Visual Studio simplifies this process with features like "Go To Definition" (**F12**) and "Find All References" (**Shift + F12**). You can also use the Solution Explorer and the Class View to explore project structures.

Version Control Integration

If you're working with version control systems like Git or Team Foundation Server (TFS), Visual Studio provides seamless integration. You can commit changes, view commit history, and resolve merge conflicts directly within the IDE.

Live Share

Visual Studio's Live Share feature enables collaborative coding in real-time. You can invite team members or collaborators to join your coding session, where they can view, edit, and debug code alongside you, regardless of their physical location.

These are just a few of the many ways you can enhance your productivity in Visual Studio. Exploring and mastering these features can make your development process smoother and more efficient, ultimately helping you deliver better software in less time.

18.2 Keyboard Shortcuts and Productivity Tools

In the previous section, we discussed the importance of keyboard shortcuts in enhancing your productivity in Visual Studio. Now, let's dive deeper into this topic and explore additional productivity tools and techniques that can make your development experience even more efficient.

Customizing Keyboard Shortcuts

While Visual Studio comes with a predefined set of keyboard shortcuts, you have the flexibility to customize them to match your workflow and preferences. To do this, navigate to Tools > Options > Environment > Keyboard in Visual Studio. Here, you can search for specific commands, assign new shortcuts, and even export or import shortcut settings.

Customizing keyboard shortcuts allows you to create a development environment tailored to your needs. You can assign shortcuts to frequently used commands, refactorings, and extensions you've installed from the Visual Studio Marketplace.

Keyboard Shortcut Reference

To view a comprehensive list of available keyboard shortcuts and their descriptions, you can use the Keyboard Shortcut Reference in Visual Studio. Access it by pressing **Ctrl + Q** to open the Quick Launch, then type "Keyboard Shortcuts" and press **Enter**. This reference provides a searchable list of commands and their associated keyboard shortcuts, making it easy to discover new shortcuts or remind yourself of existing ones.

Productivity Tools

Visual Studio offers a range of built-in productivity tools to help you write code more efficiently and catch errors early in the development process. Here are some notable productivity tools:

Code Analysis and Code Fix Suggestion

As you write code, Visual Studio's code analysis engine continually checks for code quality issues, potential bugs, and compliance with coding standards. When an issue is detected, a green squiggle line appears in the code editor, along with a light bulb icon. Clicking the light bulb presents suggestions for fixing the issue, and you can apply the suggested fix with a single click. This feature helps you maintain clean and error-free code.

IntelliCode

IntelliCode is an AI-assisted feature in Visual Studio that offers context-aware code completion suggestions. It analyzes your code and patterns within your project to provide more relevant IntelliSense suggestions. This can significantly speed up your coding by predicting the next code element you're likely to use.

Code Snippet Suggestions

Visual Studio can suggest code snippets based on your coding context. For instance, if you frequently use a specific code pattern, Visual Studio may suggest a code snippet that automates the generation of that pattern. This feature saves you time by reducing the need to manually type common code structures.

Live Unit Testing

Live Unit Testing is a powerful tool that runs your unit tests in the background as you write code. It displays real-time feedback in the code editor, showing which lines of code are covered by tests and their pass/fail status. This tool helps you identify issues early in development and ensures that your code remains testable.

Refactoring Tools

Visual Studio provides a wide range of refactoring tools that help you restructure your code for improved readability and maintainability. These tools include features like renaming variables, extracting methods, and encapsulating fields. The built-in refactoring capabilities make it easier to keep your codebase clean and organized.

Third-party Productivity Extensions

In addition to Visual Studio's built-in productivity tools, you can further enhance your development environment by installing third-party extensions from the Visual Studio Marketplace. These extensions can provide additional code analysis, project management, and debugging features tailored to your specific development needs.

By combining customizable keyboard shortcuts, built-in productivity tools, and third-party extensions, you can create a highly efficient development environment that maximizes your coding productivity in Visual Studio. Experiment with these tools and techniques to discover the ones that work best for your workflow.

18.3 Code Management Best Practices

Efficient code management is crucial for maintaining a scalable and maintainable software project. In this section, we'll explore a set of best practices and techniques to help you manage your code effectively in Visual Studio.

1. Modularization and Separation of Concerns

One of the fundamental principles of code management is the modularization of code into smaller, self-contained units. In Visual Studio, this often involves organizing your code into projects, classes, and functions with well-defined responsibilities. By separating concerns, you make your codebase more understandable and maintainable.

2. Version Control

Using a version control system (VCS) like Git is essential for tracking changes to your codebase, collaborating with other developers, and ensuring code integrity. Visual Studio provides built-in Git integration, allowing you to commit, branch, merge, and perform other VCS operations without leaving the IDE.

3. Code Documentation

Proper documentation is crucial for understanding code, especially in larger projects. Visual Studio supports XML documentation comments, allowing you to document classes, methods, and properties. Use these comments to describe the purpose of code elements, parameters, return values, and exceptions.

4. Code Reviews

Code reviews are an effective way to maintain code quality and identify issues early in the development process. Visual Studio offers features for conducting code reviews, such as the ability to comment on code changes, suggest improvements, and track review status.

5. Refactoring

Visual Studio provides a range of refactoring tools that help you improve code quality and maintainability. Use these tools to rename variables, extract methods, and restructure your code while ensuring that it remains error-free.

6. Unit Testing

Implementing unit tests is crucial for verifying the correctness of your code. Visual Studio supports various unit testing frameworks, such as MSTest, NUnit, and xUnit.NET. You can create and run unit tests directly from the IDE, ensuring that your code behaves as expected.

7. Continuous Integration and Continuous Deployment (CI/CD)

Automating your build, test, and deployment processes through CI/CD pipelines is essential for delivering software with confidence and efficiency. Visual Studio integrates with popular CI/CD platforms, allowing you to set up automated pipelines for building, testing, and deploying your applications.

8. Code Analysis

Visual Studio's code analysis tools help you identify code quality issues, potential bugs, and adherence to coding standards. Regularly run code analysis on your projects and address the reported issues to maintain a high level of code quality.

9. Code Reviews and Pull Requests

If you're using Git for version control, Visual Studio offers built-in support for code reviews and pull requests. This feature allows team members to review code changes, provide feedback, and ensure that code is thoroughly examined before it's merged into the main branch.

10. Code Metrics

Visual Studio can generate code metrics that provide insights into the complexity and maintainability of your code. Monitoring code metrics can help you identify areas that require refactoring or improvement.

11. Code Templates and Snippets

Take advantage of Visual Studio's code templates and snippets to speed up your coding process. You can create custom code snippets for frequently used code patterns or use built-in templates for common tasks.

12. Code Navigation

Efficient code navigation is crucial when working with large codebases. Visual Studio offers features like "Go To Definition," "Find All References," and "Navigate To" to help you quickly locate and understand code elements.

13. Code Analysis Rules

Customize code analysis rules to align with your project's coding standards and best practices. By enforcing consistent coding conventions, you can improve code quality and maintainability.

14. Continuous Learning

Stay up-to-date with the latest developments in software development by continuously learning and adapting. Visual Studio provides access to documentation, tutorials, and online resources to help you expand your knowledge and skills.

By incorporating these code management best practices into your development workflow in Visual Studio, you can ensure that your projects are well-organized, maintainable, and of high quality. These practices help you minimize technical debt, reduce bugs, and improve collaboration among team members.

18.4 Troubleshooting Common Issues

In software development, encountering issues and bugs is inevitable. Troubleshooting is a critical skill for developers, and Visual Studio provides several tools and techniques to help identify and resolve common problems efficiently. In this section, we'll explore some common issues you might encounter during development and how to troubleshoot them effectively.

1. Compilation Errors

Compilation errors are among the most common issues in software development. Visual Studio's built-in compiler and error-checking tools help you identify syntax errors, missing references, and other issues that prevent your code from building successfully. When you encounter compilation errors, review the error messages in the "Error List" window, which provides details about the problem's location and description. Clicking on an error message takes you to the corresponding line in the code, making it easier to fix the issue.

2. Runtime Exceptions

During runtime, your application might encounter exceptions that disrupt its normal execution. Visual Studio's debugging capabilities come in handy for troubleshooting runtime issues. You can set breakpoints in your code to pause execution at specific points, inspect variable values, and track the call stack to identify the source of exceptions. The "Immediate" window allows you to execute code snippets and inspect objects interactively during debugging.

3. Debugging Tools

Visual Studio offers various debugging tools that help you diagnose and fix issues efficiently. These tools include the "Watch" window for monitoring variable values, the "Locals" window for inspecting local variables, and the "Call Stack" window for tracing method calls. Additionally, you can use conditional breakpoints to break execution only when specific conditions are met.

4. IntelliSense and Code Completion

IntelliSense is a powerful feature in Visual Studio that provides real-time code suggestions, auto-completion, and quick documentation. If you encounter issues related to incorrect method names, missing namespaces, or undefined variables, IntelliSense can often help you identify and resolve them by providing suggestions as you type your code.

5. Version Control Conflicts

In team development scenarios using version control systems like Git, merge conflicts can arise when multiple developers modify the same file concurrently. Visual Studio's integrated Git tools assist in resolving conflicts by highlighting conflicting lines and offering options to accept changes from one branch or the other. Use the "Team Explorer" and "Changes" window to manage and resolve version control conflicts.

6. Performance Bottlenecks

If your application suffers from performance issues, Visual Studio's profiling and diagnostic tools can assist in identifying bottlenecks. The "Performance Profiler" tool allows you to analyze CPU and memory usage, track method execution times, and discover areas where optimizations are needed. Profiling reports help you pinpoint performance bottlenecks and make data-driven improvements.

7. Third-party Library Compatibility

When using third-party libraries or components, compatibility issues can arise, especially during updates or when switching to different versions. Visual Studio's "NuGet Package Manager" and "Manage NuGet Packages for Solution" dialog help you manage package dependencies and ensure that you're using compatible versions of libraries.

8. Browser Compatibility (Web Development)

In web development, cross-browser compatibility is a common concern. Visual Studio's web debugging tools, such as the "Browser Link" feature and the ability to choose different browser targets, assist in testing and debugging web applications across multiple browsers. Use these tools to identify and resolve rendering or functionality issues specific to certain browsers.

9. Data Connectivity Issues

For database-related issues, Visual Studio provides tools like Server Explorer and the Entity Framework Designer to manage database connections and schemas. If you encounter data connectivity problems, ensure that your connection strings are correctly configured and that the database server is accessible.

10. Documentation and Online Resources

When troubleshooting issues in Visual Studio, don't hesitate to consult documentation, online forums, and community resources. Visual Studio's "Help" menu provides access to extensive documentation, and online communities like Stack Overflow are excellent sources for finding solutions to common problems.

Remember that effective troubleshooting often requires a systematic approach. Reproduce the issue, gather relevant information, and use debugging tools and techniques to isolate and resolve the problem. Troubleshooting skills improve with experience, so don't be discouraged by challenges—each issue you encounter is an opportunity to learn and become a more proficient developer.

18.5 Staying Updated with Visual Studio

In the fast-paced world of software development, staying updated with the latest tools, technologies, and best practices is crucial to maintaining your productivity and ensuring that your projects are secure and efficient. Visual Studio, as a comprehensive integrated development environment (IDE), regularly receives updates, enhancements, and new features. In this section, we'll explore the importance of staying updated with Visual Studio and how to keep your development environment current.

1. Security Updates

One of the primary reasons to stay updated with Visual Studio is to receive security updates. Vulnerabilities and security threats are continuously evolving, and outdated software can become a target for malicious actors. Microsoft is committed to addressing security vulnerabilities promptly, and new versions of Visual Studio often include patches and security enhancements. Regularly updating your IDE helps protect your development environment and your projects from potential security risks.

2. Bug Fixes and Stability

Software development is prone to bugs and issues, and IDEs like Visual Studio are no exception. Each update typically includes bug fixes and stability improvements. By keeping your IDE up-to-date, you benefit from a more reliable development experience. An updated Visual Studio is less likely to encounter crashes, freezes, or other stability issues that can disrupt your workflow.

3. New Features and Productivity Enhancements

Visual Studio updates often introduce new features and productivity enhancements. These additions can streamline your development process, improve code quality, and boost your efficiency. Staying updated allows you to take advantage of these new tools and capabilities, making your development tasks more manageable and enjoyable.

4. Language and Platform Support

Programming languages and platforms evolve over time. Visual Studio updates usually include support for the latest language versions, frameworks, and platforms. If you're working with a cutting-edge technology or need to target a specific platform version, updating Visual Studio ensures that you have access to the necessary tools and compilers.

5. Compatibility with Third-party Tools

As your projects grow, you may rely on various third-party libraries, tools, and extensions. Some of these dependencies may require specific Visual Studio versions or extensions to function correctly. Regularly updating your IDE helps ensure compatibility with the latest versions of third-party tools, preventing conflicts and compatibility issues.

6. Performance Improvements

Visual Studio updates often include performance improvements that make your development environment faster and more responsive. Slow builds, code analysis, or debugging can significantly impact your productivity. By updating to the latest version, you can benefit from these performance optimizations.

7. Access to Online Services

Some Visual Studio features and integrations with cloud services may require updated IDE versions. Staying updated ensures that you have access to online services for code repositories, continuous integration, deployment, and more. This can be essential for modern software development practices like DevOps.

8. How to Stay Updated

To stay updated with Visual Studio, follow these steps:

- **Enable Automatic Updates:** Visual Studio provides an option to enable automatic updates. When enabled, the IDE checks for updates and installs them in the background, ensuring you're always on the latest version.

- **Check for Updates Manually:** You can manually check for updates by going to the "Help" menu and selecting "Check for Updates." Visual Studio will then prompt you to install any available updates.

- **Subscribe to Release Notes:** Subscribe to Visual Studio release notes and announcements to receive notifications about new versions and updates.

- **Consider Preview Versions:** Visual Studio often offers preview versions of upcoming releases. If you want to explore new features before they're officially released, consider trying the preview versions. However, be aware that these versions may contain bugs or experimental features.

In conclusion, staying updated with Visual Studio is essential for maintaining a secure, efficient, and productive development environment. Regularly applying updates, patches, and enhancements ensures that you can take full advantage of the IDE's capabilities and stay competitive in the ever-changing field of software development.

19.1 Emerging Trends in Software Development

The software development landscape is continually evolving, driven by technological advancements, changing user expectations, and emerging trends. In this section, we'll explore some of the key emerging trends in software development that are shaping the industry's future. As a developer, staying informed about these trends can help you make informed decisions, choose the right technologies, and remain competitive in the field.

1. Artificial Intelligence and Machine Learning (AI/ML)

AI and ML are transforming how software applications operate. Developers are integrating AI-driven features such as natural language processing, image recognition, and predictive analytics into their applications. This trend is expected to continue as AI and ML technologies become more accessible and powerful.

```
# Example of using an AI-powered chatbot

import chatbot_library

bot = chatbot_library.Chatbot()

response = bot.generate_response("What's the weather like today?")

print(response)
```

2. Low-Code and No-Code Development

Low-code and no-code platforms enable developers and non-developers to create applications with minimal coding effort. These platforms are ideal for rapidly prototyping and deploying applications, accelerating development cycles, and involving business stakeholders in the development process.

```
<!—Example of a low-code web app—>

<low-code-app>

<data-source type="database" source="customers"></data-source>

<list-view data-source="customers"></list-view>

</low-code-app>
```

3. Serverless Computing

Serverless computing abstracts infrastructure management, allowing developers to focus solely on writing code. With serverless platforms like AWS Lambda and Azure Functions, developers can build scalable, event-driven applications without provisioning or managing servers.

```
// Example of a serverless function
const serverlessFunction = (event, context) => {
console.log("Hello from Serverless!");
return "Function executed successfully!";
};
```

4. DevOps and Continuous Integration/Continuous Deployment (CI/CD)

DevOps practices and CI/CD pipelines are becoming standard in software development. Automation, collaboration, and continuous delivery are essential for improving software quality and accelerating time-to-market.

```
# Example of a CI/CD pipeline configuration
stages:
- build
- test
- deploy
```

5. Blockchain and Cryptocurrency

Blockchain technology is not limited to cryptocurrencies; it has applications in various industries, including supply chain management, voting systems, and more. Developers are exploring blockchain solutions and smart contracts.

```
// Example of a simple Ethereum smart contract
contract HelloWorld {
```

```
string public message = "Hello, World!";
}
```

6. Edge Computing

Edge computing brings computation closer to data sources and end-users, reducing latency and enabling real-time processing. Developers are building edge applications for IoT, augmented reality, and other latency-sensitive use cases.

```
// Example of edge computing in an IoT device
public class SensorDataProcessor {
public void processSensorData(SensorData data) {
// Perform real-time analysis
}
}
```

7. Quantum Computing

Although still in its early stages, quantum computing has the potential to revolutionize computation. Developers are exploring quantum algorithms and programming languages for future applications.

```
// Example of a quantum algorithm in Q#
operation BellTest () : Result {
using (qubits = Qubit[2]) {
H(qubits[0]);
```

```
CNOT(qubits[0], qubits[1]);
return MResetZ(qubits[0]);
}
}
```

8. Cybersecurity and Privacy

With the increasing digitization of society, cybersecurity and privacy have become paramount. Developers are focusing on secure coding practices, encryption, and compliance with data protection regulations.

```
# Example of encrypting sensitive data
import cryptography
data = "Sensitive information"
encrypted_data = cryptography.encrypt(data)
```

9. Sustainable and Green Computing

Sustainability is gaining importance in software development. Developers are considering the environmental impact of their applications, optimizing energy consumption, and adopting eco-friendly practices.

```
// Example of optimizing code for energy efficiency
function calculateEnergyEfficiency() {
// Code optimizations here
}
```

10. Remote Work and Collaboration

The shift to remote work has accelerated the adoption of collaboration tools, asynchronous communication, and remote development practices. Developers are adapting to distributed teams and flexible work arrangements.

<!—*Example of a remote team collaboration plan*—>

- Daily standup meetings via video conferencing

- Asynchronous code reviews on collaborative platforms

- Weekly progress updates in shared documents

These emerging trends in software development represent opportunities for innovation and growth. As a developer, staying informed, experimenting with new technologies, and embracing change will be essential in navigating the dynamic landscape of software development.

19.2 Future Updates and Roadmap of Visual Studio

As a software developer, keeping abreast of the latest updates and future roadmap of your integrated development environment (IDE) is crucial. Visual Studio, a widely used IDE developed by Microsoft, is continually evolving to meet the changing needs of developers. In this section, we'll delve into what you can expect in terms of future updates and the roadmap of Visual Studio.

1. Visual Studio Release Cadence

Microsoft has shifted to a more frequent release cadence for Visual Studio, with regular updates and feature releases. This approach allows developers to access new features and enhancements more quickly, improving productivity and keeping the IDE up-to-date with the latest technologies.

2. Improved Performance

Performance improvements are a recurring theme in Visual Studio updates. Microsoft is committed to making the IDE faster and more responsive. This includes optimizing code editors, solution load times, and debugging experiences to minimize interruptions during development.

```
// Example of improved code editor performance

public class PerformanceOptimizedCode

{

public void DoSomething()

{

// Optimized code here

}

}
```

3. Enhanced Collaboration Tools

Visual Studio is focusing on providing better collaboration tools for remote and distributed teams. Features like Live Share, which allow real-time collaboration on code, will continue to evolve to meet the needs of modern development teams.

```
<!—Example of setting up a Live Share session—>
```

- Share the Live Share session link with team members

- Collaborate on code in real-time, with each participant able to edit and debug

- Discuss code changes through integrated chat and audio call features

4. AI-Powered Code Assistance

AI-driven code suggestions and automated code refactoring tools will play a more significant role in Visual Studio's future. These features aim to help developers write cleaner, more efficient code with fewer errors.

```
# Example of AI-powered code suggestions

import AI_assistant

assistant = AI_assistant.CodeAssistant()

suggestions = assistant.suggest_code("Optimize this Python function")

print(suggestions)
```

5. Cross-Platform Development

Visual Studio has been expanding its support for cross-platform development, enabling developers to create applications for various platforms, including Windows, macOS, Linux, iOS, and Android. Future updates will likely include enhancements to these capabilities.

```
// Example of cross-platform development using Visual Studio

const crossPlatformApp = new CrossPlatformApp();
```

```
crossPlatformApp.buildForWindows();

crossPlatformApp.buildForMac();

crossPlatformApp.buildForAndroid();
```

6. Cloud Integration

With the growing importance of cloud computing, Visual Studio will continue to integrate with cloud services like Microsoft Azure. This includes improved cloud deployment tools and templates for building cloud-native applications.

```
# Example of deploying a web application to Azure

resources:

- type: Microsoft.Web/sites

name: mywebapp

location: West US
```

7. Focus on Accessibility and Inclusivity

Visual Studio is committed to improving accessibility and ensuring that the IDE is usable by all developers, including those with disabilities. Upcoming updates will include enhancements to keyboard navigation, screen reader support, and overall user interface accessibility.

<!—Example of improved keyboard navigation in Visual Studio—>

- Press '**Ctrl+.**' to open the quick actions menu

- Use arrow keys to navigate through suggested actions

- Press '**Enter**' to apply the selected action

8. Community Feedback and Input

Microsoft values feedback from the developer community and actively incorporates user suggestions into Visual Studio updates. Developers can provide feedback and influence the direction of the IDE by participating in user surveys, forums, and GitHub repositories.

<!—Example of providing feedback through the Visual Studio Feedback Hub—>

- Launch the Feedback Hub from Visual Studio

- Submit bug reports and feature requests

- Engage in discussions with Microsoft developers and other users

Staying informed about the future updates and roadmap of Visual Studio will help you make informed decisions about your development environment, plan for upcoming features, and leverage the latest tools to enhance your productivity as a software developer.

19.3 Visual Studio and Open Source Development

The relationship between Visual Studio and open source development has evolved significantly over the years. While Visual Studio is a Microsoft product, it has embraced open source technologies and workflows, making it a valuable tool for open source projects. In this section, we'll explore the integration of Visual Studio with open source development and how developers can benefit from this collaboration.

1. Open Source Language Support

Visual Studio supports a wide range of programming languages, including many open source languages such as Python, JavaScript, Ruby, and Go. This broad language support enables developers to work on open source projects written in their language of choice, with features like syntax highlighting, code completion, and debugging.

```
# Example of Python development in Visual Studio

def greet(name):

return f"Hello, {name}!"
```

2. Visual Studio Code (VS Code)

Visual Studio Code, often referred to as VS Code, is a free, open source code editor developed by Microsoft. It's lightweight, highly extensible, and has a vibrant extension marketplace. Many open source developers prefer VS Code for its simplicity and support for various programming languages and extensions.

<!—Example of using VS Code for web development—>

- Install VS Code extensions for HTML, CSS, and JavaScript

- Create and debug web applications with ease

- Benefit from a rich ecosystem of open source extensions

3. GitHub Integration

Microsoft's acquisition of GitHub, one of the largest platforms for hosting and collaborating on open source projects, has led to deep integration between GitHub and Visual Studio. Developers can clone, commit, and push to GitHub repositories directly from Visual Studio, making it easier to contribute to open source projects hosted on GitHub.

<!—Example of pushing changes to a GitHub repository from Visual Studio—>

- Create a new branch for your changes

- Make code modifications and commit them

- Use Visual Studio's Git tools to push your changes to GitHub

4. Open Source Extensions

Visual Studio provides a platform for developers to create and publish their own extensions, many of which are open source. These extensions enhance the functionality of the IDE and cater to specific development needs. Developers can find and contribute to open source extensions on the Visual Studio Marketplace.

<!—Example of installing an open source extension in Visual Studio—>

- Visit the Visual Studio Marketplace

- Search for an open source extension relevant to your project

- Install the extension to add new features to your IDE

5. Collaboration with Open Source Communities

Microsoft actively collaborates with open source communities and organizations. They sponsor open source projects, contribute to popular open source tools, and provide resources to support the open source ecosystem. Developers can participate in open source projects backed by Microsoft and benefit from these contributions.

<!—Example of Microsoft's collaboration with the Kubernetes open source project—>

- Microsoft is a member of the Cloud Native Computing Foundation (CNCF)

- They contribute to the development of Kubernetes, an open source container orchestration platform

- Developers can use Visual Studio to work on Kubernetes-related projects

6. Licensing and Usage

Visual Studio offers various licensing options, including a free Community edition and paid editions for professional and enterprise use. Open source developers can take advantage of the free Community edition to access most of the IDE's features while working on open source projects.

<!—Example of licensing for open source developers—>

- Open source developers can use Visual Studio Community edition for free

- Visual Studio Professional and Enterprise editions are available for commercial use

- Licensing terms may vary, so it's important to review the specific terms and conditions

The collaboration between Visual Studio and open source development has created a productive and inclusive environment for developers. Whether you're contributing to open source projects or leveraging open source technologies, Visual Studio provides a versatile and feature-rich platform for your development needs.

19.4 Integrating Emerging Technologies

The world of technology is constantly evolving, with emerging technologies shaping the future of software development. Visual Studio has been at the forefront of integrating these technologies into the development workflow, providing tools and resources to empower developers to work with cutting-edge solutions. In this section, we'll explore how Visual Studio facilitates the integration of emerging technologies.

1. Machine Learning and AI Integration

Machine learning and artificial intelligence (AI) are transforming industries, and Visual Studio has recognized their importance. Developers can leverage tools like ML.NET, a cross-platform, open source machine learning framework, to integrate machine learning capabilities into their applications. Visual Studio provides support for creating, training, and deploying machine learning models seamlessly.

```
// Example of using ML.NET in Visual Studio to create a sentiment analysis model

var context = new MLContext();

var data = context.Data.LoadFromTextFile<SentimentData>("sentiment_data.csv", separatorChar: ',');
```

```
var pipeline = context.Transforms.Text.FeaturizeText("Features", "Text")

.Append(context.BinaryClassification.Trainers.SdcaLogisticRegression())

var model = pipeline.Fit(data);
```

2. IoT Development

Internet of Things (IoT) is another rapidly growing field, and Visual Studio offers support for IoT development. Developers can use Visual Studio to build applications for IoT devices running Windows IoT Core or connect to popular IoT platforms like Azure IoT. The IDE provides templates and tools for creating IoT solutions, making it easier to prototype, develop, and deploy IoT projects.

<!—Example of IoT development using Visual Studio—>

- Develop applications for Raspberry Pi, Arduino, and other IoT devices

- Use Azure IoT Hub for device management and communication

- Visual Studio streamlines IoT development with code templates and debugging tools

3. Cloud Integration

Cloud computing has become an integral part of modern software development, and Visual Studio seamlessly integrates with various cloud platforms. Developers can connect to Azure services directly from the IDE, deploy cloud applications, and monitor resources using Azure DevOps. Visual Studio also supports cloud-native application development, enabling developers to build, test, and deploy scalable solutions.

<!—Example of cloud integration with Visual Studio—>

- Connect to Azure services within the IDE

- Develop cloud applications with Azure Functions and App Service

- Utilize Azure DevOps for continuous integration and deployment (CI/CD)

4. Containerization

Containerization technologies like Docker have gained widespread adoption, and Visual Studio offers robust support for containerized application development. Developers can create, manage, and deploy containers using Visual Studio's Docker tools. This integration allows for consistency in development and deployment environments, making it easier to build and ship containerized applications.

<!—Example of containerization with Visual Studio—>

- Create Docker containers for applications

- Debug and test containers locally

- Deploy containerized applications to container orchestration platforms like Kubernetes

5. Mixed Reality Development

Visual Studio extends its capabilities to mixed reality development, enabling developers to create applications for augmented reality (AR) and virtual reality (VR) devices. With tools like Mixed Reality Toolkit (MRTK), developers can build immersive experiences for devices like Microsoft HoloLens and Windows Mixed Reality headsets.

<!—Example of mixed reality development using Visual Studio—>

- Develop AR and VR applications with HoloLens and Windows Mixed Reality

- Utilize the Mixed Reality Toolkit for building immersive experiences

- Debug and deploy mixed reality applications from within Visual Studio

6. Quantum Computing

Quantum computing is an emerging field, and Microsoft is actively involved in quantum research. While not yet mainstream, Visual Studio is positioned to support quantum computing development as the technology matures. Developers interested in quantum computing can access resources and tools provided by Microsoft's Quantum Development Kit.

<!—Example of quantum computing development resources in Visual Studio—>

- Explore quantum computing with Microsoft's Quantum Development Kit

- Access quantum programming languages like Q# in Visual Studio

- Stay updated on quantum computing advancements and integration in Visual Studio

The integration of emerging technologies into Visual Studio empowers developers to stay at the forefront of innovation. Whether it's machine learning, IoT, cloud computing, containers, mixed reality, or quantum computing, Visual Studio provides the tools and resources needed to explore, experiment, and develop solutions in these exciting domains. As technology continues to advance, Visual Studio remains a trusted companion for developers looking to embrace new possibilities.

19.5 The Evolving Role of Developers

The landscape of software development is constantly evolving, and developers play a central role in shaping its future. As we look ahead, it's essential to understand the evolving role of developers in the context of Visual Studio and the broader technology ecosystem.

1. Full-Stack Developers

The demand for full-stack developers continues to rise. Visual Studio equips developers with the tools to work on both frontend and backend development, making it easier to transition between different parts of a project. Full-stack developers are well-versed in various technologies and can bring end-to-end solutions to the table.

<!—Full-stack development with Visual Studio—>

- Use Visual Studio for web and desktop application development

- Learn multiple programming languages, frameworks, and technologies

- Bridge the gap between frontend and backend development

2. DevOps Engineers

DevOps practices have become integral to software development. Developers are increasingly involved in the DevOps process, from writing code to deployment and monitoring. Visual Studio supports DevOps through its integration with Azure DevOps, Docker, and CI/CD pipelines.

<!—DevOps with Visual Studio—>

- Collaborate with operations teams to streamline development pipelines

- Automate testing, integration, and deployment processes

- Monitor application performance and troubleshoot issues in real-time

3. Cloud-Native Developers

As cloud adoption grows, developers are focusing on building cloud-native applications. Visual Studio simplifies cloud-native development by providing templates, tools, and integration with Azure services. Developers are expected to design applications that can scale dynamically in the cloud.

<!—Cloud-native development with Visual Studio—>

- Develop microservices and serverless applications

- Use Azure Functions and Kubernetes for container orchestration

- Optimize applications for scalability, resilience, and cost-efficiency

4. AI and Machine Learning Specialists

The integration of AI and machine learning into applications is a growing trend. Developers skilled in AI and ML can leverage Visual Studio's ML.NET and Azure Machine Learning tools to create intelligent applications. This evolving role requires an understanding of data science and model deployment.

<!—AI and ML development with Visual Studio—>

- Implement machine learning models in applications

- Use Azure Machine Learning for model training and deployment

- Collaborate with data scientists to refine and improve models

5. Security Champions

Security is a paramount concern in software development. Developers are expected to have a security-first mindset and follow best practices to protect applications and data. Visual Studio provides security tools and analysis to help developers identify and mitigate vulnerabilities.

<*!—Security in Visual Studio—*>

- Perform security code reviews and vulnerability assessments

- Implement secure coding practices and encryption

- Stay informed about the latest security threats and mitigation strategies

6. Continuous Learners

In this rapidly evolving industry, developers must be continuous learners. Visual Studio, along with online resources and communities, supports developers in staying updated with the latest technologies, best practices, and emerging trends. The role of a developer now includes a commitment to ongoing education and adaptation.

<*!—Continuous learning with Visual Studio—*>

- Participate in online developer communities and forums

- Attend conferences, webinars, and workshops

- Embrace new tools and technologies introduced in Visual Studio updates

As technology continues to advance, the role of developers will remain dynamic. Visual Studio, as a versatile and comprehensive development environment, adapts to these changes and empowers developers to excel in their evolving roles. Developers who embrace these changes and continue to learn and grow will be well-positioned to thrive in the ever-changing world of software development.

20.1 Analyzing Successful Visual Studio Projects

In the final chapter of this book, we dive into the world of real-world case studies and projects that have leveraged Visual Studio to achieve success. Analyzing successful projects provides valuable insights into how to apply the knowledge and skills gained throughout this book in practical scenarios.

Understanding the Importance of Case Studies

Case studies are real-world stories of how organizations and developers have used Visual Studio to address specific challenges, innovate, and deliver exceptional software solutions. By studying these cases, you can:

- Gain practical insights into using Visual Studio for diverse projects.
- Learn from the experiences and best practices of others.
- Discover creative solutions to common development challenges.

The Structure of a Case Study

A typical case study structure includes the following sections:

1. **Introduction**: Briefly introduce the project, its goals, and the context in which it was developed.
2. **Challenges**: Identify the challenges or problems the project aimed to solve.

3. **Solution**: Describe the solution architecture, technologies, and methodologies used.
4. **Implementation**: Dive into the technical details of how Visual Studio was employed in the project.
5. **Results**: Discuss the outcomes, benefits, and any measurable improvements achieved.
6. **Lessons Learned**: Share insights gained from the project, including what went well and what could have been done differently.
7. **Conclusion**: Summarize the key takeaways and the impact of the project.

Case Study Examples

Let's explore a few examples of case studies that you might encounter in this chapter:

E-commerce Platform Migration

Introduction: A large e-commerce company needed to migrate its legacy platform to a more scalable and modern system.

Challenges: The existing platform was outdated, and scalability issues were hindering growth.

Solution: Visual Studio was used to refactor and modernize the codebase. Azure services were leveraged for scalability.

Implementation: Detailed code examples and Visual Studio features used for refactoring.

Results: Increased website performance, improved user experience, and a significant boost in sales.

Lessons Learned: Emphasizing the importance of planning and testing before migration.

Mobile App Development for Healthcare

Introduction: A healthcare startup aimed to develop a mobile app for patient management.

Challenges: The project required compliance with strict healthcare data security regulations.

Solution: Visual Studio and Xamarin were chosen for cross-platform development, and Azure was used for secure data storage.

Implementation: Code snippets demonstrating Xamarin app development and Azure integration.

Results: Successful app launch, positive user feedback, and compliance with healthcare regulations.

Lessons Learned: Highlighting the need for rigorous security measures in healthcare apps.

IoT Solution for Agriculture

Introduction: An agriculture tech company sought to create an IoT solution for smart farming.

Challenges: Developing reliable IoT devices and integrating data analytics.

Solution: Visual Studio and Azure IoT services were employed for device development and data analysis.

Implementation: Overview of IoT device code and Azure IoT Hub configuration.

Results: Improved crop yield, reduced water usage, and data-driven farming decisions.

Lessons Learned: The importance of IoT device reliability and data accuracy.

AI-Powered Chatbot for Customer Support

Introduction: A customer support center aimed to enhance efficiency with an AI-powered chatbot.

Challenges: Training the chatbot to understand and respond to customer inquiries accurately.

Solution: Visual Studio was used for chatbot development, and Azure Cognitive Services powered the AI.

Implementation: Code snippets illustrating chatbot logic and Azure Cognitive Services integration.

Results: Reduced response times, increased customer satisfaction, and cost savings.

Lessons Learned: The iterative nature of chatbot training and continuous improvement.

In this chapter, you will delve into these case studies and more, gaining valuable insights into how Visual Studio can be a transformative tool in various domains. Each case study offers a unique perspective on using Visual Studio effectively to achieve project goals, overcome challenges, and deliver successful software solutions. By the end of this chapter, you will have a deeper understanding of the real-world impact of Visual Studio in diverse industries and scenarios.

Industry Insights and Expert Interviews

In this section, we'll explore industry insights and expert interviews that shed light on the significance of Visual Studio in the software development landscape. By hearing from experienced professionals and industry leaders, you'll gain a broader perspective on the impact and relevance of Visual Studio in various domains.

Interview with a Software Development Manager

Q: Can you share your experience with Visual Studio and how it has influenced your development projects?

A: Certainly. Visual Studio has been a cornerstone of our development process for years. Its integrated development environment (IDE) streamlines our workflow, from writing code to debugging and testing. It's a versatile tool that caters to various programming languages and platforms, which is essential for our diverse projects. Additionally, Visual Studio's collaboration features have improved our team's productivity and code quality.

Q: Are there specific features or tools in Visual Studio that have made a significant difference in your projects?

A: Debugging is where Visual Studio truly shines. The debugger is powerful and intuitive, making it easier to identify and fix issues quickly. We also rely heavily on version control integration to manage code changes effectively. Another standout feature is the extensive library of extensions available in the Visual Studio Marketplace, which allows us to tailor the IDE to our specific needs.

Q: How has Visual Studio contributed to your team's collaboration and project management?

A: We use Team Foundation Server (TFS) for version control and work item tracking. TFS enables seamless collaboration among team members, ensuring that everyone is on the same page regarding project status and tasks. The ability to create and manage work items directly within Visual Studio simplifies project management and keeps our projects organized.

Insights from a DevOps Engineer

Q: From a DevOps perspective, how does Visual Studio fit into the development and deployment pipeline?

A: Visual Studio plays a crucial role in our DevOps practices. It allows us to create automated build and release pipelines using Azure DevOps Services. This integration automates the deployment process, ensuring that our applications are consistently deployed to various environments. Additionally, Visual Studio provides excellent support for containerization, making it easier to manage and deploy microservices.

Q: How does Visual Studio help streamline the collaboration between development and operations teams?

A: Visual Studio's integration with Azure DevOps Services fosters collaboration between development and operations teams. Developers can define deployment pipelines and infrastructure as code, while operations teams can manage infrastructure provisioning and scaling. This collaboration accelerates the delivery of new features and ensures the stability of our applications.

A Conversation with a Visual Studio Extension Developer

Q: As a developer of Visual Studio extensions, what motivates you to contribute to the ecosystem?

A: The Visual Studio community is vibrant, and there's a constant demand for extensions that enhance productivity. Contributing to the ecosystem allows me to address specific needs and challenges faced by developers. It's rewarding to see how my extensions can simplify tasks, improve code quality, and save time for fellow developers.

Q: Can you share some insights into the process of creating Visual Studio extensions?

A: Developing Visual Studio extensions is well-documented, and Microsoft provides extensive resources and tools. The process involves using the Visual Studio Extensibility SDK, which offers templates and guidance for extension development. Ensuring compatibility with different Visual Studio versions and regular updates are essential to maintain a successful extension.

Q: How do you see the future of Visual Studio extensions and customization?

A: With Visual Studio's continuous evolution, the possibilities for extensions are limitless. I anticipate more integration with cloud services and AI-driven features to enhance developer productivity. As developers' needs evolve, extension developers will continue to play a crucial role in customizing the IDE to meet those needs.

In this section, you've gained insights from professionals who have harnessed the power of Visual Studio in their respective roles and projects. Their experiences highlight the adaptability and versatility of Visual Studio across different domains, from software development management to DevOps practices and extension development. These interviews emphasize the enduring relevance of Visual Studio in the ever-evolving field of software development.

Lessons from Failed Projects

In this section, we'll delve into valuable lessons learned from failed projects involving Visual Studio. While Visual Studio is a powerful tool for software development, its effectiveness largely depends on how it's utilized. Understanding the common pitfalls and challenges faced by development teams can help you avoid similar issues in your projects.

Lack of Clear Project Scope

One of the recurring themes in failed projects is a lack of clear project scope and objectives. Without a well-defined scope, development teams may find themselves constantly changing requirements, which can lead to scope creep and project delays. It's essential to have a detailed project plan that outlines the goals, features, and timelines.

```
// Example: Defining project scope in Visual Studio

public class ProjectScope

{

public string ProjectName { get; set; }

public List<string> ProjectObjectives { get; set; }

public DateTime ProjectDeadline { get; set; }
```

```
public ProjectScope(string name, List<string> objectives, DateTime deadline)

{

ProjectName = name;

ProjectObjectives = objectives;

ProjectDeadline = deadline;

}

}
```

Inadequate Testing and Quality Assurance

Failure to prioritize testing and quality assurance can lead to project failures. In some cases, teams rush through the testing phase to meet deadlines, resulting in undetected bugs and issues in the final product. Visual Studio provides robust testing tools, including unit testing frameworks and code analysis, which should be utilized effectively.

```
// Example: Writing unit tests in Visual Studio using MSTest

[TestClass]

public class MyUnitTest

{

[TestMethod]

public void TestMethod1()

{
```

```
// Arrange

int num1 = 10;

int num2 = 20;

// Act

int result = num1 + num2;

// Assert

Assert.AreEqual(30, result);

}

}
```

Poor Version Control Practices

Version control is essential for collaboration and code management, but poor version control practices can lead to disastrous outcomes. Inadequate branching and merging strategies, inconsistent commit messages, and neglecting to use version control altogether are common mistakes. Visual Studio integrates with various version control systems, so teams should adopt best practices in this regard.

```
// Example: Using Git version control in Visual Studio

// Initialize a Git repository

git init

// Add files to the repository

git add .

// Commit changes with a descriptive message
```

```
git commit -m "Added new feature"

// Create a new branch

git checkout -b new-feature

// Merge changes from a branch

git checkout main

git merge new-feature
```

Insufficient Documentation

Proper documentation is often underestimated but is crucial for project success. Lack of documentation can make it challenging for team members to understand the codebase, leading to confusion and errors. Visual Studio allows you to generate code comments and documentation, which should be consistently utilized.

```
/// <summary>

/// This class represents a customer in the system.

/// </summary>

public class Customer

{

public int CustomerId { get; set; }

public string Name { get; set; }

public string Email { get; set; }

/// <summary>

/// Calculates the total purchase amount for the customer.
```

```
/// </summary>

/// <returns>The total purchase amount.</returns>

public decimal CalculateTotalPurchaseAmount()

{

// Implementation logic here

}

}
```

Inadequate Communication and Collaboration

Communication breakdowns within development teams can have detrimental effects on project outcomes. When team members do not communicate effectively or lack collaboration tools, it can lead to misunderstandings and conflicts. Visual Studio offers collaboration features like Live Share and integration with collaboration platforms that should be utilized to foster teamwork.

In summary, understanding the challenges and lessons from failed projects involving Visual Studio is crucial for successful software development. By addressing issues related to project scope, testing, version control, documentation, and collaboration, you can enhance your project's chances of success and leverage Visual Studio to its full potential. Avoiding these pitfalls and implementing best practices will contribute to a more efficient and productive development process.

Project Showcase: From Concept to Code

In this section, we'll explore the journey of a software development project, highlighting the key stages from concept to code using

Visual Studio. A successful project goes through various phases, each crucial for its ultimate success. We'll use a hypothetical project, a task management application, to illustrate these stages.

1. Project Initiation

Every project begins with an idea or a need. In our case, the concept is a task management application that allows users to create, assign, and track tasks. The first step is to define the project's goals, objectives, and scope. Visual Studio's project templates and planning tools can help in this initial phase.

2. Planning and Design

Once the project's scope is defined, it's time to plan and design. This phase involves creating detailed project plans, defining requirements, and designing the application's user interface. Visual Studio provides various design tools, such as Windows Forms and WPF designers, to help create a visually appealing and functional UI.

```
// Example: Designing a Windows Forms UI in Visual Studio

public partial class TaskManagementForm : Form

{

public TaskManagementForm()

{

InitializeComponent();

}

private void btnCreateTask_Click(object sender, EventArgs e)

{
```

```
// Implementation logic for creating tasks

}

// Other UI event handlers and controls

}
```

3. Development

With the project plan and design in place, the development phase begins. Developers write code, implement features, and integrate functionality. Visual Studio's code editor and debugging tools play a crucial role in this phase. The development team collaborates using version control systems like Git, ensuring code is managed efficiently.

```
// Example: Implementing task creation logic in C#

public class TaskManager

{

public Task CreateTask(string title, string description, DateTime dueDate)

{

// Implementation logic to create a task

}

// Other methods for task management

}
```

4. Testing and Quality Assurance

Testing is an integral part of the development process. Visual Studio offers tools for automated testing and code analysis. Testers write test cases, conduct functional and integration tests, and identify and report issues. This phase ensures the application meets quality standards.

```
// Example: Writing unit tests in Visual Studio using MSTest

[TestClass]

public class TaskManagerTests

{

[TestMethod]

public void CreateTask_ValidInput_ReturnsTask()

{

// Arrange

TaskManager taskManager = new TaskManager();

// Act

Task task = taskManager.CreateTask("Sample Task", "Test task creation", DateTime.Now.AddDays(7));

// Assert

Assert.IsNotNull(task);

}

// Other test methods
```

}

5. Deployment and Release

Once the application is thoroughly tested and meets the project's requirements, it's ready for deployment. Visual Studio provides tools for creating installers, packaging applications, and publishing to various platforms. The deployment phase ensures that users can access and use the application.

6. Maintenance and Updates

After deployment, the project transitions into the maintenance phase. This involves ongoing support, bug fixes, and updates. Visual Studio's monitoring and diagnostics tools help in identifying and addressing issues in production.

7. Project Completion and Evaluation

Finally, the project is completed, and an evaluation is conducted. This phase assesses whether the project met its goals, stayed within scope, and achieved the desired outcomes. Lessons learned are documented for future projects.

In conclusion, Visual Studio is a versatile and powerful tool that supports the entire software development lifecycle, from project initiation to completion. By following these stages and leveraging Visual Studio's features, development teams can successfully turn concepts into fully functional applications. Each phase contributes to the overall project's success, ensuring that it meets user needs and quality standards.

Building a Comprehensive Portfolio with Visual Studio

Creating a portfolio is a crucial step for any developer looking to showcase their skills and experience. In this section, we'll explore how Visual Studio can be a valuable tool in building a comprehensive portfolio that reflects your capabilities and expertise.

1. Selecting Projects for Your Portfolio

The first step in building your portfolio is to choose the projects you want to include. These projects should demonstrate a variety of skills and technologies. Visual Studio provides project templates for web development, desktop applications, mobile apps, cloud services, and more. Consider including projects that showcase your proficiency in different domains.

2. Cleaning and Organizing Code

Before adding projects to your portfolio, ensure that your code is clean, well-organized, and follows best practices. Use Visual Studio's built-in code analysis and refactoring tools to improve code quality. This not only makes your portfolio more impressive but also reflects your commitment to writing maintainable code.

```
// Example: Using Visual Studio's code refactoring tools

public class Calculator

{

public int Add(int a, int b)

{

return a + b;
```

```
}
public int Subtract(int a, int b)
{
return a - b;
}
// Other methods
}
```

3. Creating Project Documentation

For each project in your portfolio, provide clear and concise documentation. Describe the project's purpose, your role, technologies used, and any challenges you faced. Visual Studio allows you to generate code documentation using XML comments, making it easier to create project documentation.

```
/// <summary>
/// Represents a class for performing mathematical operations.
/// </summary>
public class Calculator
{
/// <summary>
/// Adds two integers.
/// </summary>
/// <param name="a">The first integer.</param>
```

```
/// <param name="b">The second integer.</param>
/// <returns>The sum of the two integers.</returns>
public int Add(int a, int b)
{
return a + b;
}
// Other methods
}
```

4. Showcasing UI/UX Design

If your projects involve user interfaces, pay attention to the design and usability. Visual Studio provides design tools for creating visually appealing UIs. Include screenshots or interactive prototypes in your portfolio to highlight your UI/UX skills.

5. Version Control and Collaboration

Mention your experience with version control systems like Git and collaboration tools like Team Foundation Server (TFS) or GitHub. Showcase your ability to work in a team environment and your familiarity with industry-standard collaboration practices.

6. Highlighting Specializations

If you have specialized in a particular area, such as database management, cloud development, or game development, dedicate sections of your portfolio to highlight these skills. Describe how you used Visual Studio to accomplish tasks in these domains.

7. Continuous Learning and Certifications

If you have completed certifications or training related to Visual Studio or specific technologies, include them in your portfolio. Visual Studio offers integration with learning platforms, making it easy to showcase your commitment to continuous learning.

8. Hosting Your Portfolio

Once you've assembled your portfolio, consider hosting it online. Visual Studio can help you create web applications to showcase your projects. Use web hosting services or platforms like Azure to make your portfolio accessible to potential employers or clients.

Building a comprehensive portfolio with Visual Studio allows you to present your skills and experience effectively. Whether you're a student, a junior developer, or an experienced professional, your portfolio serves as a powerful tool for making a lasting impression in the competitive world of software development. Continuously update your portfolio as you work on new projects and acquire additional skills to keep it relevant and impressive.

www.ingramcontent.com/pod-product-compliance
Lightning Source LLC
LaVergne TN
LVHW090303210926
848480LV00001B/114